D1225115

THE NEW TEEN TITANS

ARCHIVES ▼ VOLUME 3

ARCHIVE ⬤ EDITIONS

DC COMICS

LEN WEIN
EDITOR-ORIGINAL SERIES

BOB JOY
EDITOR-COLLECTED EDITION

ROBBIN BROSTERMAN
SENIOR ART DIRECTOR

PAUL LEVITZ
PRESIDENT & PUBLISHER

GEORG BREWER
VP-DESIGN & DC DIRECT CREATIVE

RICHARD BRUNING
SENIOR VP-CREATIVE DIRECTOR

PATRICK CALDON
EXECUTIVE VP-FINANCE &
OPERATIONS

CHRIS CARAMALIS
VP-FINANCE

JOHN CUNNINGHAM
VP-MARKETING

TERRI CUNNINGHAM
VP-MANAGING EDITOR

DAN DIDIO
SENIOR VP-EXECUTIVE EDITOR

STEPHANIE FIERMAN
SENIOR VP-SALES & MARKETING

ALISON GILL
VP-MANUFACTURING

RICH JOHNSON
VP-BOOK TRADE SALES

HANK KANALZ
VP-GENERAL MANAGER, WILDSTORM

LILLIAN LASERSON
SENIOR VP & GENERAL COUNSEL

JIM LEE
EDITORIAL DIRECTOR-WILDSTORM

PAULA LOWITT
SENIOR VP-BUSINESS & LEGAL
AFFAIRS

DAVID MCKILLIPS
VP-ADVERTISING & CUSTOM
PUBLISHING

JOHN NEE
VP-BUSINESS DEVELOPMENT

GREGORY NOVECK
SENIOR VP-CREATIVE AFFAIRS

CHERYL RUBIN
SENIOR VP-BRAND MANAGEMENT

JEFF TROJAN
VP-BUSINESS DEVELOPMENT,
DC DIRECT

BOB WAYNE
VP-SALES

THE NEW TEEN TITANS ARCHIVES
VOLUME 3

ISBN: 1-4012-1144-5
ISBN 13: 978-1-4012-1144-8

The New Teen Titans created by Marv Wolfman and George Pérez

PUBLISHED BY DC COMICS.
COVER, FOREWORD AND COMPILATION
COPYRIGHT © 2006 DC COMICS.

ORIGINALLY PUBLISHED IN SINGLE MAGAZINE
FORM IN NEW TEEN TITANS 17-20 AND TALES
OF THE NEW TEEN TITANS 1-4. COPYRIGHT
©1982 DC COMICS. ALL RIGHTS RESERVED.

THE NEW TEEN TITANS AND ALL RELATED
CHARACTERS, THE DISTINCTIVE LIKENESSES
THEREOF AND ALL RELATED ELEMENTS ARE
TRADEMARKS OF DC COMICS. THE STORIES,
CHARACTERS AND INCIDENTS FEATURED
IN THIS PUBLICATION ARE ENTIRELY
FICTIONAL. DC COMICS DOES NOT READ
OR ACCEPT UNSOLICITED SUBMISSIONS
OF IDEAS, STORIES OR ARTWORK.

DC COMICS
1700 BROADWAY
NEW YORK, NY 10019

A WARNER BROS. ENTERTAINMENT COMPANY.

PRINTED IN HONG KONG.
FIRST PRINTING.

THE DC ARCHIVE EDITIONS

COVER ILLUSTRATION BY GEORGE PÉREZ.

COLOR RECONSTRUCTION BY DREW MOORE.

SERIES DESIGN BY ALEX JAY/STUDIO J.

PUBLICATION DESIGN BY PETER HAMBOUSSI.

TABLE OF CONTENTS

TABLE OF CONTENTS

FOREWORD

There are a lot of different versions of this story going around, but this is the way that I remember it.

After a several-year stint producing the top titles for our sterling competition across town, I was back at DC Comics, writing and/or editing a wide variety of books and having a great time doing it. Within a year after I returned to DC, Marv Wolfman had followed me back and was now writing many of the company's top titles. So, one afternoon, we were sitting around my office, trying to come up with some new project to do together, when one of us — I'm guessing Marv, probably — suggested we revive the Teen Titans.

From such acorn-sized thoughts do mighty oak-like legends grow.

Now you have to understand, I've known Marv since I was 11 years old. We grew up together. We produced fanzines together. And we pretty much became professionals together. Our first published writing work for DC was a Jerry Lewis story involving his efforts to make pizza. (Don't ask.) Our second story, which appeared just two days later, presented private detective Jonny Double to the world. And our third story, which saw print about a week after that, was an issue of the original Teen Titans comic that introduced a young Russian super-hero called Starfire. (And where have we all heard that name before?) After a couple of other slight tandem efforts together, Marv and I went our separate ways professionally, though we remained fast friends.

Okay, so now here we were, more than a decade later, and we've decided to try to revive the book that, in its own way, had pretty much given us our start. So what do we do next?

Well, first, we have to obtain the permission of then-President and Publisher Jenette Kahn. We arrange for a meeting, and then the two of us go traipsing into her office and tell her we have an idea for a new book.

"What is it?" asks Jenette, enthusiastically.

We lean forward, look Jenette straight in the eye, and reply, "We want to revive the Teen Titans."

Ever see the movie *The Producers*? You know that moment when people are performing the musical they've produced for the first time, and you pan across the audience, and they all have that slack-jawed, astonished, I-can't-believe-I'm-seeing-this expression that has come to be called the "Springtime for Hitler look"? Well, that's pretty much what Jenette looked like at that moment.

"Wh-wh-why in Heaven's name would I want you to revive the Titans?" she stammered. "I mean, we cancelled that book, even though it was still making money, because we were so embarrassed by it creatively. What possible reason would I have to let you bring it back?"

"Because," said Marv and I in unison, self-satisfied grins plastered on our faces, "We'll do it right."

And Jenette, bless her heart, stared at us and thought for a moment and finally said, "Cool. Go for it."

And that's how The New Teen Titans came to be. Now all we had to do was make good on our promise.

I don't recall if the new characters or the new artist came first, though I'm pretty sure it was Marv who suggested now-superstar artist George Pérez for the book. I've never been anything less than thrilled that George accepted the assignment, even though he himself admits he only expected it to last for a few months.

At some point, Marv and George presented to me the new cast of characters who were to be the backbone of the book. Aside from bringing back classic Titans like Robin, Kid Flash and Wonder Girl, they'd decided to make a regular out of occasional member Beast Boy, whom we were now calling the Changeling, because, frankly, we always thought Beast Boy was a silly name. Marv and George had also added new members Cyborg and an incredibly sexy alien girl who could only be named Starfire, borrowing that name we had first used all those years before. I looked over the new lineup and liked it, but

I still thought something was missing from the mix.

"I think you need some sort of mystical character in the group," I told Marv. At first, he was less than enthusiastic about the idea. We discussed it for a while as I explained my reasons (which, sadly, I can no longer remember) and Marv, ever the professional, agreed to go home and give the matter some thought. A few days later, he came storming into my office and shouted, "You were absolutely right." He and George then presented me with Raven, who became the glue that held everything together. We decided on stellar artist Romeo Tanghal to ink George's extraordinary pencils. And, with that, we were off and running.

A few months later, DC offered the world a sneak preview of the New Teen Titans in issue #26 of DC COMICS PRESENTS. The response was immediate and overwhelming. You liked us. You really liked us. The following month, THE NEW TEEN TITANS #1 hit the stands, and we never looked back.

At least, that's the way I remember it.

This particular volume of THE NEW TEEN TITANS ARCHIVES has some sentimental value for me. For one thing, it features the return of the first super-hero I ever co-created, in a story with one of my all-time favorite titles. For another, it brings back a couple of classic DC villains, plus one you've probably never heard of. But, most important, in issue #20, Your Humble Editor himself gets to put in an appearance in a little backup story that I'm still living down to this day.

For the record, for all those who've asked over the years, no, I do not actually own a stuffed bear named Fluffy. And I never really collected teddy bears. I did learn, however, that if you allow your friends to buy you two of anything, all your other friends will automatically assume that you... well, you get my point.

Seriously though, what makes this volume different from those that preceded it is the inclusion of our first Titans miniseries.

By the beginning of our second year, it was pretty obvious that the New Teen Titans was a hit. It was outselling every other DC title by... okay, let's just say it was a lot. Since companies are generally in business to make a profit, the Powers That Be soon came to us and asked what we could do to produce more Titans material. After some serious thought, we conceded that we could give up eating, sleeping, and any sort of serious social interaction, and maybe squeeze out just a few more Titans stories.

Actually, we realized that a miniseries would give us the opportunity to do something we had already been wanting to do, which was to focus attention on the new Titans characters so as to bring new readers up to speed and explore our heroes' backgrounds in greater depth than was previously possible. Marv and George were more than willing to take on the extra workload, at least for those four months, so we plowed ahead, with the blessings of the DC hierarchy.

Looking back over that miniseries now, I think Marv and George did an incredible job. But then, that's what we came to expect of them, and over all those years, they never failed to deliver.

To those of you who are reading these timeless Titans tales for the first time, I have to admit that I envy you a little bit. It's like trying for the first time what is soon to become your favorite flavor of ice cream — one bite and you're gonna be hooked.

— Len Wein
May, 2006

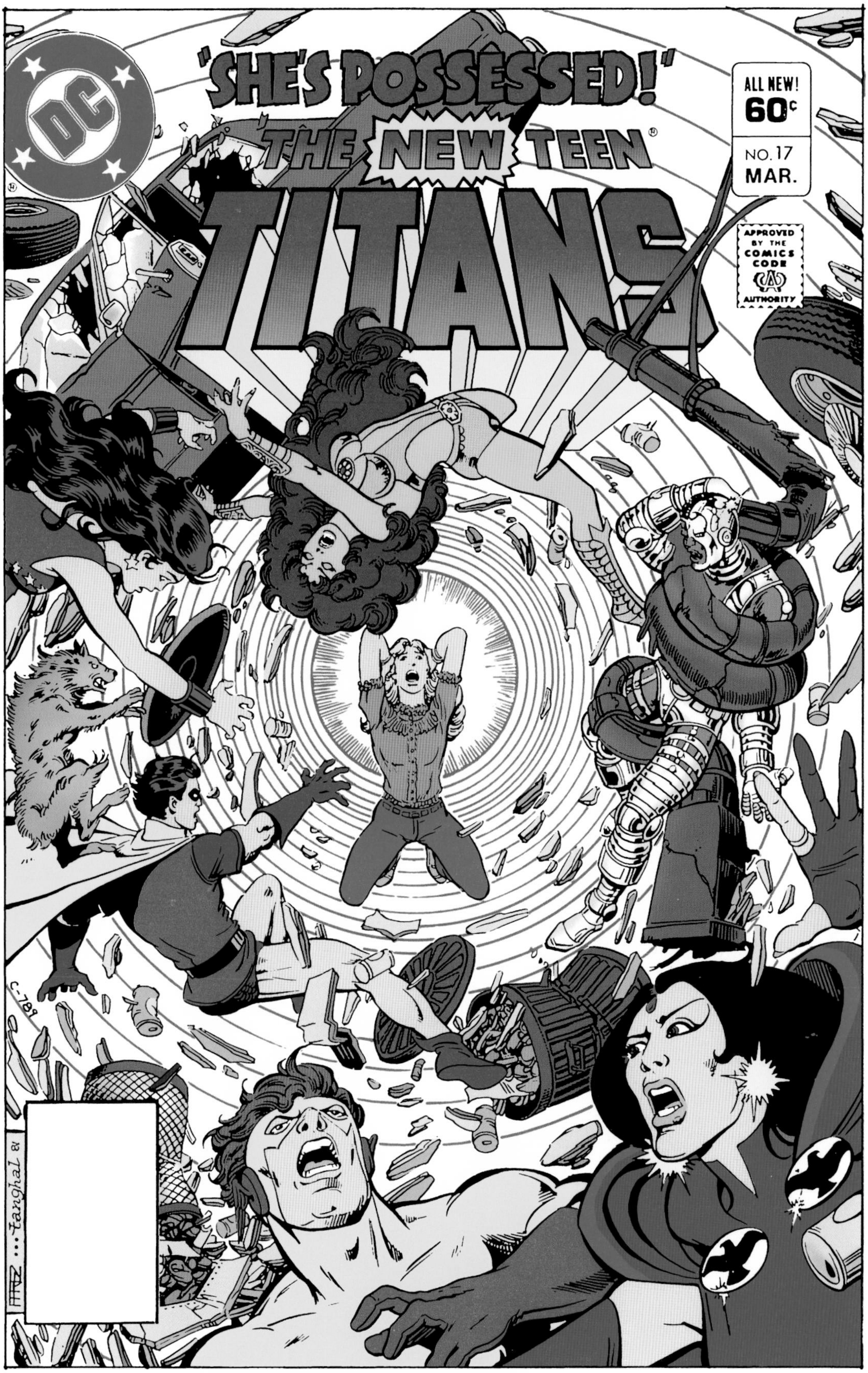
"SHE'S POSSESSED!"
THE NEW TEEN TITANS
ALL NEW! 60¢
NO. 17 MAR.
APPROVED BY THE COMICS CODE AUTHORITY
C-789

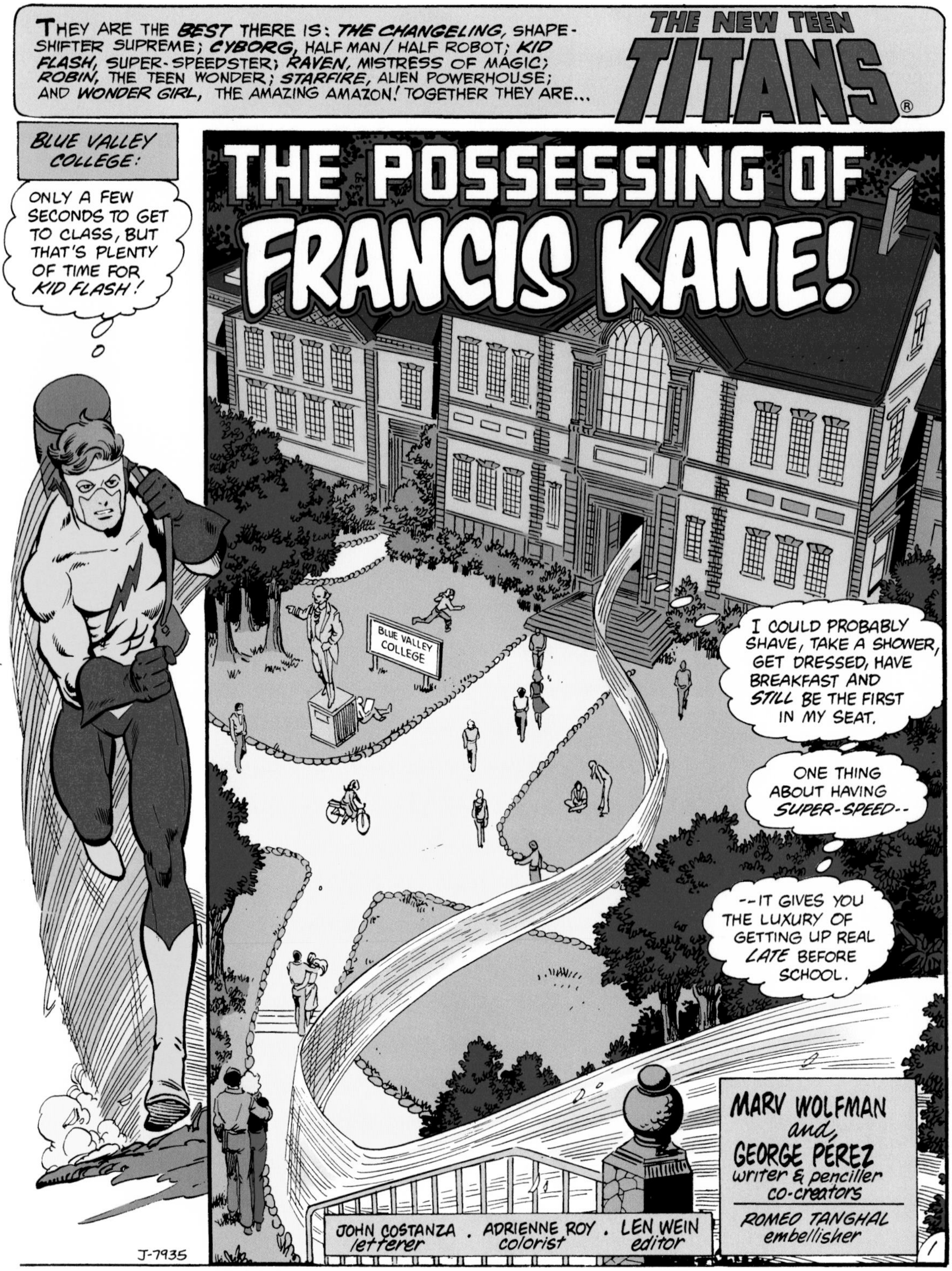

THEY ARE THE BEST THERE IS: THE CHANGELING, SHAPE-SHIFTER SUPREME; CYBORG, HALF MAN / HALF ROBOT; KID FLASH, SUPER-SPEEDSTER; RAVEN, MISTRESS OF MAGIC; ROBIN, THE TEEN WONDER; STARFIRE, ALIEN POWERHOUSE; AND WONDER GIRL, THE AMAZING AMAZON! TOGETHER THEY ARE...
THE NEW TEEN TITANS®
THE POSSESSING OF FRANCIS KANE!
BLUE VALLEY COLLEGE:
ONLY A FEW SECONDS TO GET TO CLASS, BUT THAT'S PLENTY OF TIME FOR KID FLASH!
BLUE VALLEY COLLEGE
I COULD PROBABLY SHAVE, TAKE A SHOWER, GET DRESSED, HAVE BREAKFAST AND STILL BE THE FIRST IN MY SEAT.
ONE THING ABOUT HAVING SUPER-SPEED--
--IT GIVES YOU THE LUXURY OF GETTING UP REAL LATE BEFORE SCHOOL.
MARV WOLFMAN and, GEORGE PEREZ writer & penciller co-creators
ROMEO TANGHAL embellisher
JOHN COSTANZA letterer . ADRIENNE ROY colorist . LEN WEIN editor
J-7935
1

MY COSTUME ZIPS BACK INTO MY SPECIAL *RING*, AND SUDDENLY I'M *ME* AGAIN.

I USED TO DYE MY HAIR *BROWN* WHEN I BECAME KID FLASH, BUT I WAS NEVER TOO *HAPPY* WITH THAT.

BESIDES, I HARDLY EVER *USE* MY SUPER-SPEED IN BLUE VALLEY ANYMORE--

--SO NOBODY'S LIKELY TO ASSOCIATE RED-HEADED *WALLY WEST* WITH THE FASTEST TEEN ON EARTH.

THIS IS *FRANCIS KANE*. WATCH HER, FOR HERS IS A STORY UNLIKE *ANY* YOU HAVE READ BEFORE.

AND FOR US, IT BEGINS RIGHT HERE...

FRAN? HEY, I'M REALLY GLAD TO SEE YOU'RE BACK IN SCHOOL.

ME *TOO*, WALLY. BUT I NEED SOME HELP WITH *MAKE-UP* WORK.

THEN YOU CAME TO THE RIGHT PERSON. WANNA HIT THE BOOKS AFTER CLASS AT *YOUR* PLACE?

WELL, MY *MOM*, SHE--

LET *ME* HANDLE YOUR MOM, OKAY?

WELL, OKAY. AND *THANKS*.

LET US SKIP THE FINERIES OF FRENCH HISTORY, CALCULUS AND THOSE OTHER VITAL SUBJECTS, AND...

WALLY, I DON'T THINK MY MOM'S GOING TO *LIKE* THIS.

IS SHE--

--STILL ACTING *CRAZY*? YEAH. EVER SINCE THE *ACCIDENT* SHE HASN'T BEEN *HERSELF*.

YOU KNOW, SHE'S ACTUALLY TRYING TO *CONTACT THE DEAD*. MY MOM! MRS. SUBURBAN HOUSEWIFE HERSELF!

SHE'S SURE SHE CAN SPEAK WITH MY *DAD* AND *BROTHER* AGAIN.

YOUR *WINDOW SHADES* ARE ALL DRAWN.

I'M *SCARED* FOR HER, WALLY. REALLY *SCARED*.

THAT'S *RIGHT*. NO NATURAL LIGHT ENTERS THE KANE HOUSE THESE DAYS.

2

PROMISE YOU WON'T *LAUGH,* BUT SHE'S INTO *SEANCES,* AND...

FRANCIS! COME *HERE!*

THE AIR FEELS *STRANGE* IN HERE, FRAN. LIKE IT'S CHARGED WITH *ELECTRICITY.*

MOM, I BROUGHT A *FRIEND,* WALLY...

BUT, *MOM...?*

PUT ON THE *ROBES,* FRANCIS. *NOW!*

NOW!

I FEEL THAT I'M SO *CLOSE* TO SPEAKING TO YOUR FATHER AND BROTHER. DO AS I *SAY.*

WOW! I'D EXPECT TO SEE THIS IN A *JOHN CARPENTER* MOVIE, BUT--

--PLEASE, WALLY, DON'T *SAY* ANYTHING. PLEASE--?

MOM THINKS I'M SOME SORT OF *LINK* TO MY DAD AND BROTHER.

AND THE WAY SHE IS-- WELL, I DON'T WANT TO *ANGER* HER.

I'M SORRY I *SAID* ANYTHING, FRAN. REALLY.

OH, WELL, MAYBE THIS WILL *HELP* ME IN MY *ABNORMAL PSYCHE* CLASS.

STRANGE, UNEARTHLY CHANTING BEGINS NOW. INCENSED CANDLES SEEM TO FLAME HIGHER...

WE ADMIT THAT WHAT YOU HAVE *SEEN* UNTIL NOW IS *STRANGE,* TO SAY THE LEAST...

BUT WHAT COMES *NEXT* FAIRLY LEAPS OFF THE RICHTER SCALE OF REALITY... 3

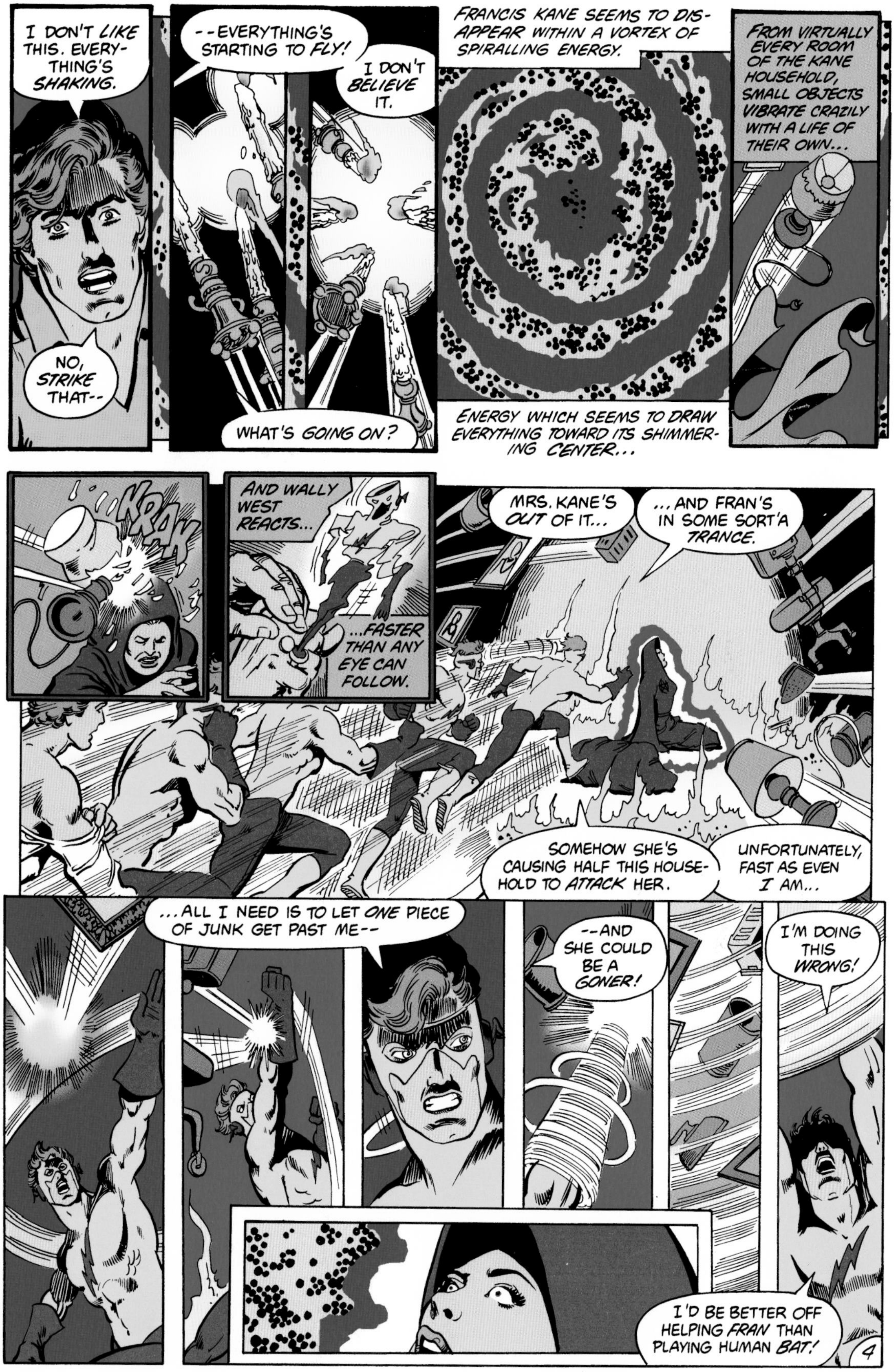
I DON'T LIKE THIS. EVERYTHING'S SHAKING.
NO, STRIKE THAT--
--EVERYTHING'S STARTING TO FLY!
I DON'T BELIEVE IT.
WHAT'S GOING ON?
FRANCIS KANE SEEMS TO DISAPPEAR WITHIN A VORTEX OF SPIRALLING ENERGY.
ENERGY WHICH SEEMS TO DRAW EVERYTHING TOWARD ITS SHIMMERING CENTER...
FROM VIRTUALLY EVERY ROOM OF THE KANE HOUSEHOLD, SMALL OBJECTS VIBRATE CRAZILY WITH A LIFE OF THEIR OWN...
KRAK
AND WALLY WEST REACTS...
...FASTER THAN ANY EYE CAN FOLLOW.
MRS. KANE'S OUT OF IT...
...AND FRAN'S IN SOME SORT'A TRANCE.
SOMEHOW SHE'S CAUSING HALF THIS HOUSEHOLD TO ATTACK HER.
UNFORTUNATELY, FAST AS EVEN I AM...
...ALL I NEED IS TO LET ONE PIECE OF JUNK GET PAST ME--
--AND SHE COULD BE A GONER!
I'M DOING THIS WRONG!
I'D BE BETTER OFF HELPING FRAN THAN PLAYING HUMAN BAT!
4

FRAN? *FRAN!?!* IT'S NO *USE!* I CAN'T GET *THROUGH* TO HER.

MAN-O-MAN. I JUST CAN'T *BELIEVE* THAT SEANCE THING HAD ANYTHING TO *DO* WITH THIS.

IT'S JUST NOT *POSSIBLE.* I'M *CERTAIN* IT'S NOT.

BUT THAT DOESN'T *STOP* WHAT'S GOING ON HERE, DOES IT?

EXPLAIN IT IF YOU CAN. SPRINGS, SECURELY NAILED TO DEEP-PILED EASY-CHAIRS, SUDDENLY TEAR LOOSE...

MADNESS SEEMS TO GROW AS PLASTER WALLS CRACK OPEN...

...AS APPLIANCES THAT REQUIRE TWO GROWN MEN TO *MOVE* THEM--

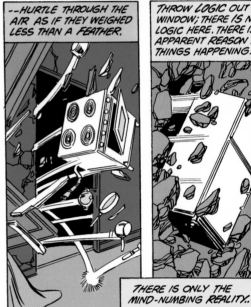

--HURTLE THROUGH THE AIR AS IF THEY WEIGHED LESS THAN A *FEATHER.*

THROW *LOGIC* OUT THE WINDOW; THERE IS NO LOGIC HERE. THERE IS NO APPARENT REASON FOR THINGS HAPPENING...

THERE IS ONLY THE MIND-NUMBING REALITY...

...THE EVER-PRESENT DANGER...

...AND THE ABSOLUTE PRESENCE OF *LUCK* THAT KID FLASH IS THERE TO MAKE CERTAIN THAT WHATEVER DAMAGE IS INFLICTED...

...IS NOT *FATAL.*

M...MOMMA...

MOMMA!

MOMMA!!

I...FEEL SO *STRANGE,* MOMMA. MY *HEAD* HURTS, AND--

MOMMA! WH-WHAT *HAPPENED?*

HUH? FRAN'S *AWAKENING,* AND EVERY-THING'S *FALLING.*

WHY DO I EXPECT TO HEAR *ROD SERLING'S* VOICE NOW?

MAYBE IT'S BECAUSE I GOTTA BE IN *THE TWILIGHT ZONE!*

WELL, EVEN IF I *AM,* I'D BETTER CHANGE BACK TO *WALLY WEST.*

I DON'T FEEL LIKE EXPLAIN-ING WHY *KID FLASH* WAS HERE.

AND SOON...

WALLY? WHAT *HAPPENED* HERE? I CAN'T REMEMBER ANYTHING!

I WISH I COULD *TELL* YOU, FRAN, BUT I DON'T *KNOW.*

I *KNOW* WHAT IT IS. I *KNOW.*

SHE SHOULD HAVE *DIED* WITH THE OTHERS, *THAT'S* WHAT.

THEY WANT HER TO *JOIN* THEM. AND THEY'RE *RIGHT.* SHE *SHOULD* HAVE DIED. SHE SHOULD HAVE *DIED!*

NO, MOMMA, PLEASE DON'T *SAY* THAT.

THE ACCIDENT WASN'T MY *FAULT.* IT WASN'T.

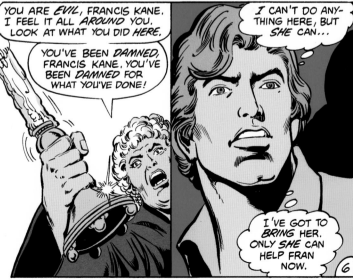

YOU ARE *EVIL,* FRANCIS KANE. I FEEL IT ALL *AROUND* YOU. LOOK AT WHAT YOU DID *HERE.*

YOU'VE BEEN *DAMNED,* FRANCIS KANE, YOU'VE BEEN *DAMNED* FOR WHAT YOU'VE DONE!

I CAN'T DO ANY-THING HERE, BUT *SHE* CAN...

I'VE GOT TO *BRING* HER. ONLY *SHE* CAN HELP FRAN NOW.

6

ONE *WEEK* PASSES, AND...

REALLY, RAVEN, THANKS FOR *COMING.* MRS. KANE WON'T LET FRAN SEE A *DOCTOR--*

--BUT MAYBE *YOU* CAN LEARN SOMETHING... ANYTHING--?

I AM GLAD TO *HELP,* WALLACE...

...THOUGH I DO NOT TREAT THE CONCEPT OF GHOSTS AND SPIRITS AS *LIGHTLY* AS YOU.

MY SOUL-SELF PROVES THE *EXISTENCE* OF SPIRITUAL FORMS.

OKAY, *OKAY.* LOOK, I'M JUST *WORRIED* ABOUT FRAN.

YOU HAVE *FEELINGS* FOR HER?

YEAH, I'VE KNOWN HER SINCE I WAS *SEVEN.* WE'VE BEEN FRIENDS, BUT THAT'S *ALL.*

YOU SHOULD KNOW ABOUT THINGS LIKE *THAT.*

BUT BEFORE THE MISTRESS OF MYSTICISM RESPONDS...

OH, WOW, WALLY. I'M GLAD YOU *GOT* HERE.

IT'S GOTTEN *WORSE.* SHE REALLY THINKS I'M AN *EVIL FORCE* AND...

WHOA THERE, FRAN, CALM DOWN. I'D LIKE YOU TO MEET *RAVEN.*

RAVEN? DIDN'T I SEE YOUR PICTURE IN *'PEOPLE'?* WITH THE *TEEN TITANS?* HOW DO YOU KNOW *WALLY?*

UHH, *I* SAW THAT ARTICLE, TOO. I CALLED HER FOR *HELP.*

WELL, I DON'T KNOW WHAT EVEN *YOU* CAN DO, RAVEN. THERE'S MY MOM ...SHE SPENDS ALL HER TIME IN *SEANCES* NOW.

THE FACTS OF MY *FATHER'S* AND *BROTHER'S* DEATHS *CONSUME* HER EVERY THOUGHT.

I SENSE TERRIBLE *PAIN* WITHIN YOUR MOTHER. AND HURT AND LONELINESS.

YOUR MOTHER IS REACHING OUT FOR ANSWERS TO *HELP* HER--

THEN...

...EACH OF *FIVE* CANDLES FLICKERS WITH *UNHOLY LIFE...*

7

AND AS THEY DO...

RAVEN, DO YOU SEE--?

I *SEE*, WALLACE. HER MIND HAS JUST BECOME A *BLANK*.

DO YOU FEEL THE *FORCE* EMANATING FROM HER? I HAVE NEVER FELT ITS LIKE *BEFORE*--

--YET, SHE IS WITHOUT *PAIN*. I SENSE NOTHING HURTING HER, NO STRUGGLING TO *EXPEL* THE FORCE.

IT IS AS IF SHE HAS BEEN INSTANTLY AND TOTALLY *POSSESSED!*

WHAT'S GOING ON WITH HER, RAVEN? WHAT'S *HAPPENING?*

WHAT IS HAPPENING, WALLY WEST...

...IS SOMETHING FAR *BEYOND YOUR POSSI-BLE COMPREHENSION.*

REALITY AS YOU KNOW IT, AS YOU HAVE COME TO ACCEPT AND *EXPECT* IT--

--IS TOTALLY AND IRREVOCABLY *RUPTURED!*

FRANCIS IS BOTH THE *CAUSE* OF THIS MADNESS AND THE *VICTIM.*

THAT IS MY *INTENTION.*

I DON'T *CARE* ABOUT THAT, RAVEN.

WHAT IS HAPPENING TO HER IS BEYOND HER *CONTROL,*

JUST *DO* SOMETHING!

IT RISES FROM RAVEN'S LITHE BODY LIKE SOME DEMON FROM ANOTHER DIMENSION. THIS IS HER *SOUL-SELF,* AS SHE CALLS IT...

...AND WHAT *IT* CAN DO IS AS UNEXPLAINABLE AS THE VERY FORCES IT SEEKS TO STOP...

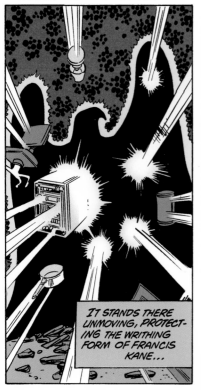

IT STANDS THERE UNMOVING, *PROTECT-ING* THE WRITHING FORM OF FRANCIS KANE...

...*EVEN* AS WALLY WEST PROTECTS THE OTHERS FROM THE RAVAGES OF MADNESS.

IT STANDS THERE, SEEMINGLY *ABSORBING* ALL THAT STRIKES IT WITHIN THE IM-POSSIBLE BLACKNESS OF ITS FORM.

I FEEL THE TREMORS *ENDING.* FRANCIS KANE *REVIVES.*

AND I NEED PROTECT HER *NO MORE* THIS DAY.

W-WALLY--? I'M *SCARED!* WHAT'S *HAPPENING* TO ME?

YOU ARE SOME-HOW THE *NEXUS,* THE CHAIN BETWEEN REALITY AND... SOMETHING *ELSE.*

WHAT THAT *IS* AND HOW YOU *BECAME* IT, I DO NOT KNOW.

I DO, WITCH-WOMAN. SHE IS *EVIL* AS I SAID... AND THE FORCES THAT POSSESS HER--

--DEMAND HER *DEATH.*

SHE SHOULD HAVE *DIED* WITH THE OTHERS... AND THIS IS HER PUNISHMENT FOR *LIVING.*

AND RAVEN SIGHS...

CHAPTER TWO: THE DEVIL WITHIN HER!

SHE'S *POSSESSED? FERGET* IT. THOSE THINGS ONLY HAPPEN IN CHEAP MOVIES.

TWO WEEKS PASS...

I FEEL SO *SORRY* FOR FRAN. I DON'T THINK THERE'S A MILLIMETER OF HER THAT HASN'T BEEN PROBED, SCRAPED, PINCHED, OR PRICKED.

I DUNNO. ANYONE WHO LOOKS LIKE *THAT* COULD SURE POSSESS *ME*.

MY DAUGHTER *DESERVES* WHAT BECOMES OF HER. SHE IS AN EVIL FORCE AND WILL *REMAIN* SO UNTIL SHE PAYS FOR WHAT WAS DONE.

FRANCIS IS NOT *EVIL*, MRS. KANE. I COULD *SENSE* THAT IF SHE WERE.

IT HURTS, *WATCHING* HER LIKE THIS. I KEEP FEELING IT'S *WRONG* TO PROBE ANYONE LIKE THAT.

EXCUSE ME...

WHAT *IS* IT, DOCTOR? HOW IS SHE?

SHE IS HIGHLY *ANEMIC.* BRAINSCAN INDICATES A HIGHER THAN NORMAL *MAGNETIC* READING IN HER BRAIN. YOU ASK HOW IS SHE AND I SAY I DON'T *KNOW.*

I'M A *DOCTOR.* I CAN GIVE YOU *FACTS.* BUT FROM WHAT YOU TELL ME-- WELL, I JUST DON'T *HAVE* FACTS.

THERE ARE THINGS WE KNOW *NOTHING* ABOUT. HOLISTIC MEDICINE, EVEN ACUPUNCTURE. THEY WORK, BUT *WHY*? WHO *KNOWS*?

10

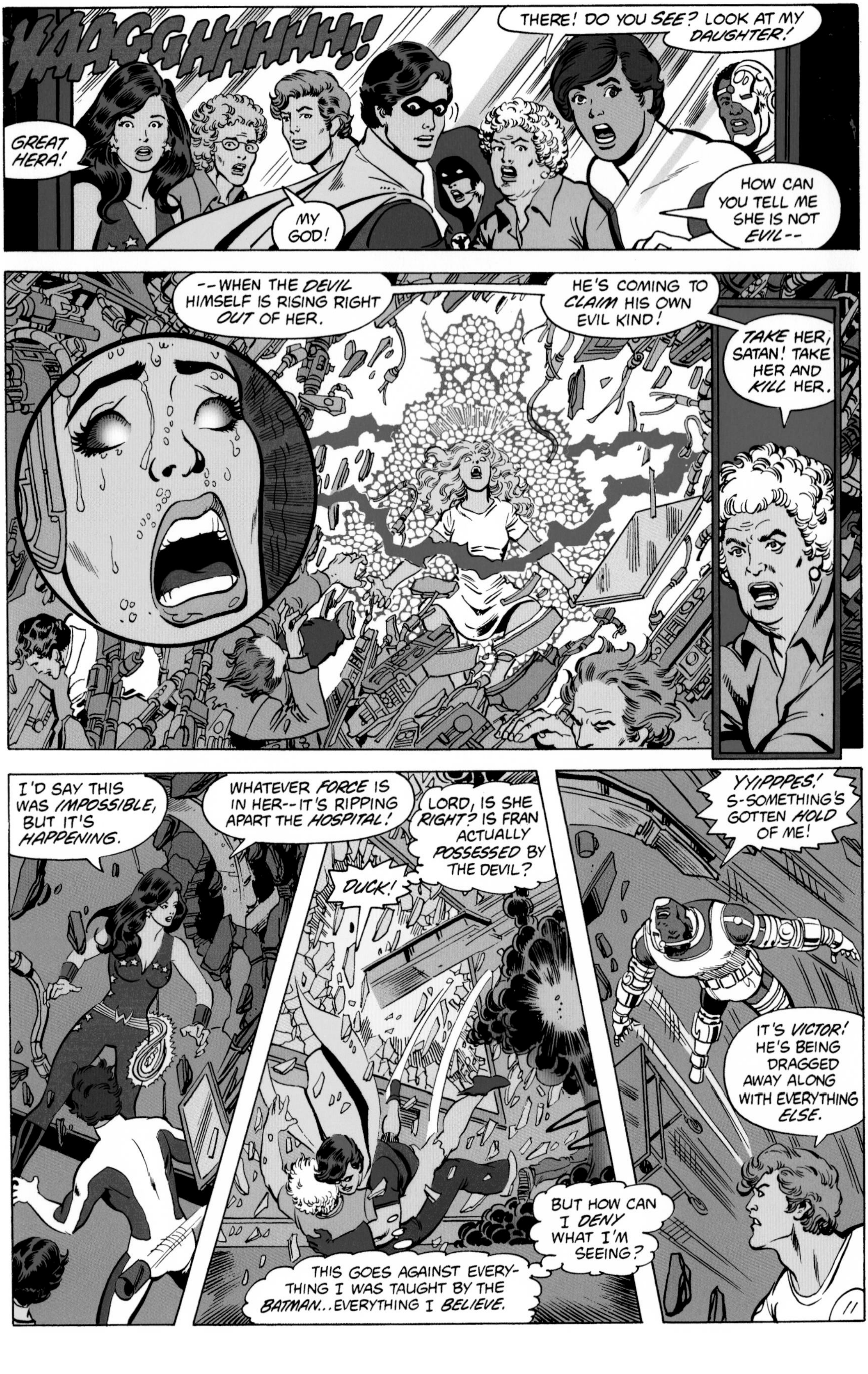

YAAGGHHHHH!!
GREAT HERA!
MY GOD!
THERE! DO YOU SEE? LOOK AT MY DAUGHTER!
HOW CAN YOU TELL ME SHE IS NOT EVIL--
--WHEN THE DEVIL HIMSELF IS RISING RIGHT OUT OF HER.
HE'S COMING TO CLAIM HIS OWN EVIL KIND!
TAKE HER, SATAN! TAKE HER AND KILL HER.
I'D SAY THIS WAS IMPOSSIBLE, BUT IT'S HAPPENING.
WHATEVER FORCE IS IN HER--IT'S RIPPING APART THE HOSPITAL!
LORD, IS SHE RIGHT? IS FRAN ACTUALLY POSSESSED BY THE DEVIL?
DUCK!
BUT HOW CAN I DENY WHAT I'M SEEING?
THIS GOES AGAINST EVERY-THING I WAS TAUGHT BY THE BATMAN... EVERYTHING I BELIEVE.
YYIPPPES! S-SOMETHING'S GOTTEN HOLD OF ME!
IT'S VICTOR! HE'S BEING DRAGGED AWAY ALONG WITH EVERYTHING ELSE.
11

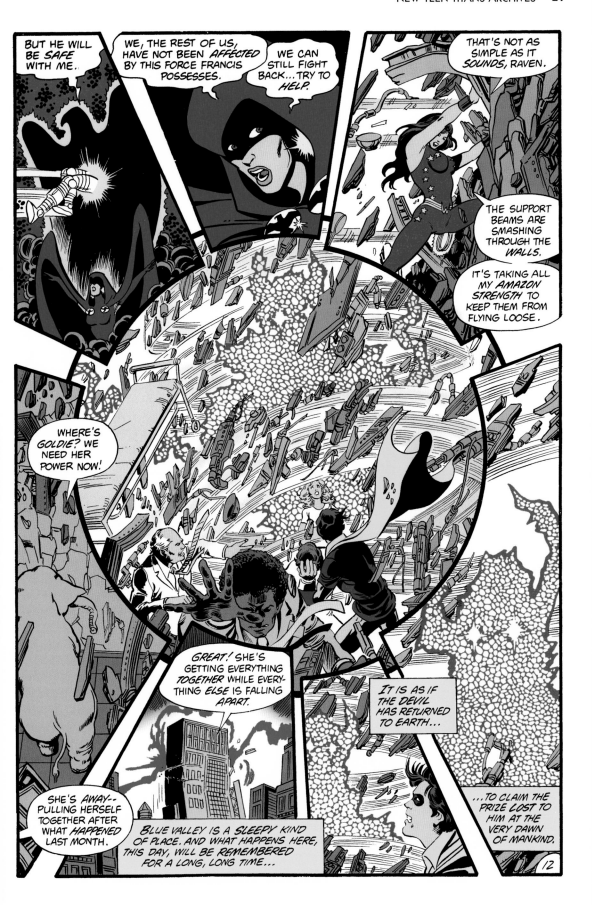

BUT HE WILL BE *SAFE* WITH ME...

WE, THE REST OF US, HAVE NOT BEEN *AFFECTED* BY THIS FORCE FRANCIS POSSESSES.

WE CAN STILL FIGHT BACK...TRY TO *HELP*.

THAT'S NOT AS SIMPLE AS IT *SOUNDS*, RAVEN.

THE SUPPORT BEAMS ARE SMASHING THROUGH THE WALLS.

IT'S TAKING ALL MY *AMAZON STRENGTH* TO KEEP THEM FROM FLYING LOOSE.

WHERE'S *GOLDIE?* WE NEED HER POWER NOW!

GREAT! SHE'S GETTING EVERYTHING *TOGETHER* WHILE EVERY- THING *ELSE* IS FALLING *APART*.

IT IS AS IF THE DEVIL HAS RETURNED TO EARTH...

SHE'S *AWAY--* PULLING HERSELF TOGETHER AFTER WHAT *HAPPENED* LAST MONTH.

BLUE VALLEY IS A *SLEEPY* KIND OF PLACE. AND WHAT HAPPENS HERE, THIS DAY, WILL BE REMEMBERED FOR A LONG, LONG TIME...

...TO CLAIM THE PRIZE *LOST* TO HIM AT THE VERY DAWN OF MANKIND.

12

BUT MADNESS IS EVERYWHERE, AND IT EXISTS IN ALL FORMS...

YOU ARE THE CAUSE OF THIS, FRANCIS.

AND, AS I BROUGHT YOU *INTO* THIS WORLD AND WISH TO SAVE THE WORLD FROM YOU--

--I CAN TAKE YOU *OUT* AGAIN!

SHE'S *STOPPED*, ROBIN.

LEAVE ME BE. DON'T YOU SEE WHAT SHE IS *DOING?*

IF THIS CITY *DIES*, IT IS BECAUSE YOU WOULDN'T LET ME *KILL* HER.

MRS. KANE! S-SOMEONE -- STOP HER!

HOLD ON, GUYS... SOMETHING *BIG* IS HAPPENING...

SKRAKK 'KKKKKK

LOOK, IT'S *OVER*. FRAN'S COMING *OUT* OF IT. EVERYTHING SEEMS TO HAVE SETTLED.

ARE YOU *ALL RIGHT*, VICTOR?

I DON'T EVER WANNA GO THROUGH THAT *AGAIN*.

BUT YOU *WILL*, AGAIN AND AGAIN AND *AGAIN*.

DON'T YOU *SEE*, THEY WANT HER BECAUSE SHE DIDN'T *DIE* WITH THEM. THEY *WANT* HER...

...SATAN WANTS HER.

BAH! THIS IS *USELESS*. I AM *DONE* WITH YOU, FRANCIS KANE. YOU ARE NO LONGER MY *DAUGHTER*.

I WASH MY HANDS OF YOU FOR NOW AND *FOREVER*.

MOMMA...NO, PLEASE DON'T GO.

MOMMA, I NEED YOU, MOMMA!

AND RAVEN CRIES...

13

CHAPTER THREE: THE SUMMONING OF--?

TWO DAYS PASS, BUT EVENTS MARCH ON. WE ARE NOW HALF A CONTINENT AWAY, IN NEW YORK AND THE FAMED TITANS' TOWER...

MOM WON'T ANSWER MY CALLS. SHE DOESN'T WANT ANYTHING TO DO WITH ME.

MAYBE SHE'S RIGHT. SHE COULD BE, YOU KNOW. MAYBE I'D BE BETTER OFF DEAD.

DON'T SAY THAT, FRANCIS. WE'LL HELP YOU. I GUARANTEE IT.

I SURE HOPE SO, WALLY, BUT I THINK IT'S TOO LATE.

"W-WALLY"--? YOU KNOW--?

VIC, ARE YOU SURE OF THIS--?

I GREW UP WITH YOU. I EVEN HAD A CRUSH ON YOU ONCE.

YOU REALLY CAN'T HIDE THINGS LIKE THIS. I CAN TELL.

19

SURE AS I *CAN* BE, SHORT-PANTS. EVERYTHIN', INCLUDIN' *ME*, THAT FRANNIE AFFECTED-- WAS *METAL*.

AND THE DOC SAID SHE HAD INCREASED *MAGNETIC WAVES* IN HER BRAIN.

MY DAD DID SOME *RESEARCH* ON MAGNETISM A FEW YEARS AGO. I'M CHECKING IT OUT.

SO WHAT ARE THOSE TECHNICIANS *DOING* TO YOU?

JUST A LITTLE SOMETHIN' I THINK WILL *HELP* US.

OKAY, VIC-- I'LL SPEAK WITH YOU *LATER*. GOOD LUCK.

UHH, KID FLASH, ROB SAYS HE'S ALMOST *READY*.

OKAY, GAR. THANKS.

WE'RE JUST DOING SOME TESTING. NOTHING *SERIOUS*.

IT WOULDN'T *MATTER*, REALLY. WALLY...?

YEAH--?

... THANK YOU. FOR *EVERYTHING*.

LISTEN, BEFORE WE BEGIN--

-- CAN YOU TELL US ABOUT THE *ACCIDENT*?

IT MIGHT *HELP*.

"*ACCIDENT? SURE.* I WAS DRIVING WITH MY BROTHER AND FATHER. WE WERE COMING HOME FROM THE MALL...

"*EVERYTHING WAS FINE.* IN FACT WE WERE EVEN TALKING ABOUT GOING ON A *CAMPING TRIP* DURING WINTER RECESS.

15

"DON'T ASK WHY WHAT HAPPENED NEXT HAPPENED. I DON'T KNOW.

"BUT SUDDENLY HALF THE CAR SEEMED TO EXPLODE.

"THEN IT SWERVED. I SWEAR IT TURNED ON ITS OWN.

"I EVEN REMEMBER FIGHTING THE WHEEL-- BUT I COULDN'T GET IT TO RESPOND.

"NOW, I'M PROBABLY CRAZY HERE, BUT EVEN BEFORE WE HIT THE GUARD RAIL--

"-- IT TWISTED AWAY FROM US. WE HADN'T HIT IT YET, BUT THE RAIL BROKE OPEN. REALLY!

"AND THE CAR JUST SEEMED TO LEAP OFF THE CLIFF AS IF IT WERE DETERMINED TO COMMIT SUICIDE.

"NOW, I MUST HAVE DREAMED THIS, BUT I REMEMBER THE CAR FALLING...

"...I EVEN REMEMBER HEARING THE EXPLOSION.

"BUT I--I SOMEHOW FLOATED AWAY... FLOATED TO SAFETY. PLEASE, DON'T LOOK AT ME THAT WAY."

IT MUST HAVE BEEN A DREAM, RIGHT? I MUST HAVE FALLEN OUT OF THE CAR BEFORE IT WENT OVER THE CLIFF.

THAT'S THE ONLY THING THAT MAKES ANY SENSE.

RIGHT?

16

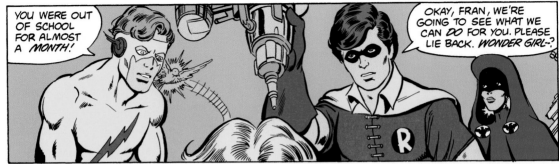

THEY WAIT IMPATIENTLY. HALF AN HOUR PASSES. THEN...

THEN *FRANCIS KANE* SCREAMS...

...AND THIS *FIFTH-FLOOR* FORMER STORAGE ROOM FAIRLY *EXPLODES!*

WE'RE BEING *BLOWN RIGHT OUT* THE *WINDOW!*

I DON'T BELIEVE HER *POWER!*

SHE'S A LIVING *ATOM-BOMB!*

MAN, WHEN I SAID HER POWER WAS *INCREASING--*

UP THERE *--LOOK!*

--I THINK I WAS UNDERSTATING THE OBVIOUS.

IT RISES FROM *TITANS' TOWER* LIKE SOME DARK, EVIL *NIGHTMARE*, SOME BLASPHEMY OF REALITY...

AND WHAT IT APPEARS TO BE FRIGHTENS EVEN THESE USUALLY UNFLAPPABLE TITANS. SUPER-VILLAINS IS ONE THING. YOU CAN *FIGHT* A THING OF SHAPE AND SUBSTANCE. BUT HOW CAN YOU BATTLE A *DEMON* THAT MUST HAVE BEEN BORN IN THE DEEPEST, FIERY PITS OF HELL? 18

I--I'M PICKING UP AN OVERWHELMING SURGE OF *HORROR*...

SOULS CLOSE BY CRYING OUT IN *FEAR*.

LOOK OVER THERE, RAVEN, AND YOU'LL *SEE* WHAT'S WRONG.

GREAT *HERA!*

THAT THING-- WHATEVER IT IS-- IS ATTACKING *MANHATTAN!*

IT *BEGINS* THEN. POWER GROWS WITH TERRIBLE FEROCITY.

NOTHING SEEMS ABLE TO *ESCAPE* THIS DEMONIC, UN- QUENCHABLE THIRST FOR THINGS *METAL.*

IT *FEEDS*, GROWING EVEN *STRONGER*. AND STRONGER, IT CRIES OUT FOR *MORE* TO FEED UPON, MORE TO SATE ITS RAVENOUS APPETITE...

PRAY FOR THIS CITY, FOR NOW IT STANDS ON THE PATH TO *MADNESS*...

IT'S STARTING TO LOOK LIKE FRAN'S MOM MAY'VE BEEN *RIGHT.*

GUYS, I DON'T *LIKE* THIS. I DON'T LIKE IT *AT ALL!*

19

THE DEMON, IF THAT IS WHAT IT TRULY IS, WILL SOON HOLD SWAY OVER ALL MANHATTAN INSTEAD OF ONE SMALL TRACT OF LAND...

THEN ITS VORACIOUS HUNGER WILL LEAD IT TO QUEENS AND BROOKLYN, TO THE BRONX AND STATEN ISLAND...

NEW JERSEY WILL FOLLOW, THEN CONNECTICUT, AND THEN--

THEN EVEN THE WORLD MAY NOT BE ENOUGH TO SATISFY ITS HUNGER.

STREET LAMPS, CARS, EVEN BUSES-- ALL HEADING THIS WAY.

HOW DO YOU *STOP* SOME-THING LIKE THAT? *HOW?*

I STILL DON'T KNOW IF THAT THING IS A *DEMON*--BUT MAYBE THERE'S A WAY TO *SHORT-CIRCUIT* IT--?

NO.

TO STOP ITS GROWTH WE MUST REACH *FRANCIS.*

COME-- WHILE MY SOUL-SELF ACTS AS OUR *SHIELD.*

BUT I FEAR TIME IS ON THAT CREATURE'S SIDE.

20

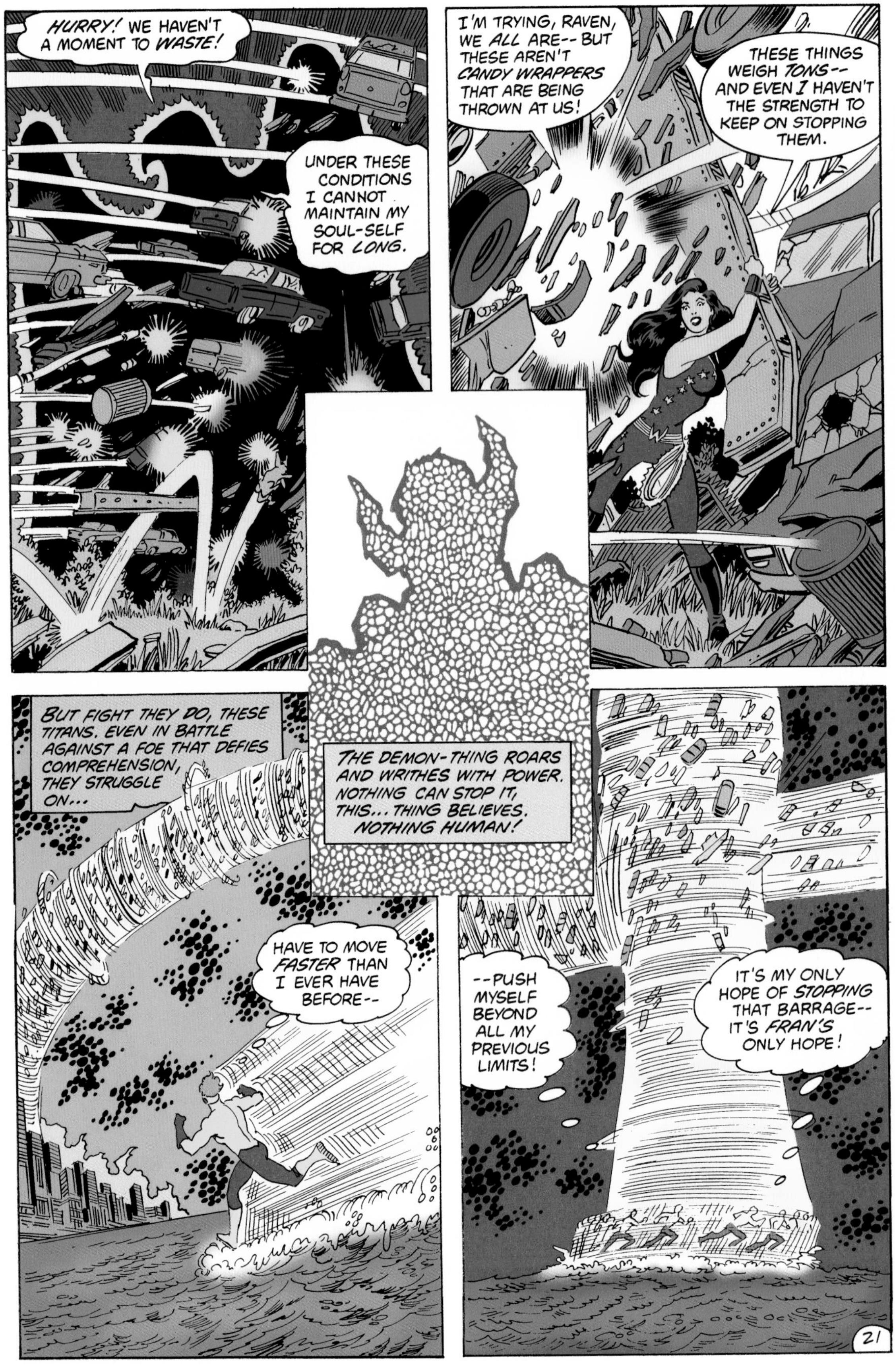
HURRY! WE HAVEN'T A MOMENT TO WASTE!
UNDER THESE CONDITIONS I CANNOT MAINTAIN MY SOUL-SELF FOR LONG.
I'M TRYING, RAVEN, WE ALL ARE-- BUT THESE AREN'T CANDY WRAPPERS THAT ARE BEING THROWN AT US!
THESE THINGS WEIGH TONS-- AND EVEN I HAVEN'T THE STRENGTH TO KEEP ON STOPPING THEM.
THE DEMON-THING ROARS AND WRITHES WITH POWER. NOTHING CAN STOP IT, THIS... THING BELIEVES. NOTHING HUMAN!
BUT FIGHT THEY DO, THESE TITANS. EVEN IN BATTLE AGAINST A FOE THAT DEFIES COMPREHENSION, THEY STRUGGLE ON...
HAVE TO MOVE FASTER THAN I EVER HAVE BEFORE--
--PUSH MYSELF BEYOND ALL MY PREVIOUS LIMITS!
IT'S MY ONLY HOPE OF STOPPING THAT BARRAGE-- IT'S FRAN'S ONLY HOPE!
21

FOR EACH TITAN, IT IS THE SAME... REACH YOUR LIMITS, PUSH BEYOND... NO MATTER THE RISK TO YOU... NO MATTER THE TERRIBLE DANGER...

IT'S *KILLING* ME, TRYING TO KEEP THIS MASSIVE *BULK* TOGETHER...

BUT... IT HAD BETTER WORK ...IT HAD *BETTER*...

...WON'T BE ABLE TO *SHAPE-CHANGE* AGAIN FOR *DAYS*...

ROBIN, PULL *RAVEN* THROUGH -- *HURRY!*

THE ONSLAUGHT IS GETTING *WORSE!* I-I DON'T KNOW HOW MUCH *LONGER* I CAN HOLD OUT!

IF RAVEN'S *SOUL-SELF* WAS STILL WITHIN HER, THERE WOULD BE *NO PROBLEM* FOR THE EMPATH TO TRANSPORT HERSELF TO FRANCIS KANE'S SIDE...

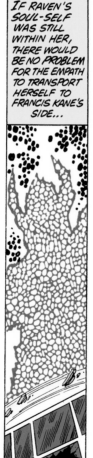

BUT NOW SHE CAN MERELY FOLLOW *ROBIN* AND PRAY THEY REACH THE GIRL'S SIDE *IN TIME*...

WE'RE *HERE*-- BUT WHAT CAN YOU *DO?*

YOU COULDN'T ROUSE HER FROM HER TRANCE THE *LAST* TIME!

I *KNOW*, ROBIN... WHATEVER IT IS THAT HAS *POSSESSED* HER WILL NOT RELINQUISH ITS HELLISH GRIP.

BUT FRANCIS IS THE *KEY* TO THAT DEMON. SOMEHOW SHE MUST BE *REACHED*.

SOMEHOW WE MUST BREAK *THROUGH* THAT... THAT *THING'S* HOLD!

22

MAN, NOW I KNOW WHAT AN *ELEPHANT* FEELS LIKE WHEN ATTACKED BY *GNATS!*

STILL, I CAN'T KEEP THIS UP *MUCH LONGER!*

THE PAIN OF KEEPING THIS FORM IS TERRIBLE, I NEED A BREAK... NEED SOME TIME TO--

OH, NO... OH, NUTS...

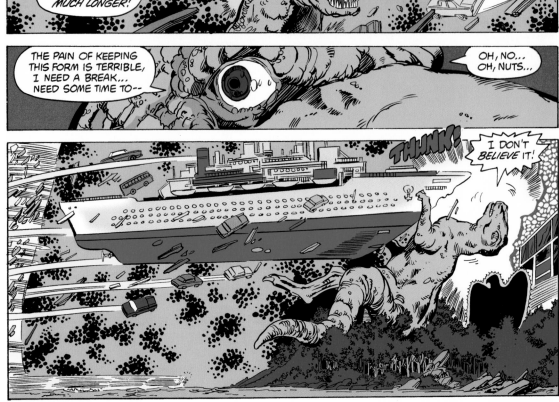

THUNK!

I DON'T *BELIEVE* IT!

I HAD TO COME BACK. HOW *IS* SHE?

I DO NOT *UNDERSTAND* THIS, WALLACE.

I REACH *INTO* HER, BUT I CANNOT SEEM TO *HELP.*

YOU'VE GOT TO KEEP *TRYING,* RAVEN. I THINK YOU'RE RIGHT THAT SHE'S THE *VITAL LINK* HERE.

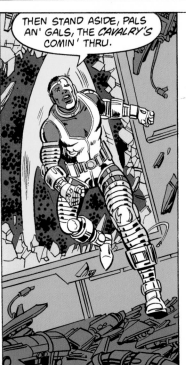

THEN STAND ASIDE, PALS AN' GALS, THE *CAVALRY'S* COMIN' THRU.

VIC? *HURRY,* MAN. WE'RE DEAD CENTER IN A *BATTLE ZONE!*

23

YOU'RE TELLIN' *ME?* I JUST WADED THROUGH "*GODZILLA ON MONSTER ISLAND*" BACK THERE.

HEY, HOLD ON, FRANNIE-- ME AN' *S.T.A.R.* WORKED UP A GIZMO JUST FOR *YOU.*

EVERYONE'S GOT *MAGNETIC WAVES* IN THEIR *BRAIN!* SEEMS LIKE FRANNIE HERE SOMEHOW GOT HERS *BOOSTED.*

WE SET UP AN *ANTI-MAGNETIC REVERSER* AN' BUILT IT RIGHT INTO *ME.*

WITH LUCK, THIS BABY SHOULD DO THE *TRICK!*

FRANCIS KANE SCREAMS AS NEGATIVE POLARITY SIZZLES THROUGH HER BRAIN...

SHE WRITHES LIKE SOME PAINED, THRASHING ANIMAL AS THE DEMON-THING THAT HAS POSSESSED HER...

IT IS GONE... *GONE!* I SENSE NO SIGN OF IT ANYWHERE.

YOU *OKAY,* VIC?

MAN, I FEEL LIKE THEY PULLED OUT EVERY TOOTH IN MY MOUTH-- WITH *PLIERS!*

OH, GOD, WALLY... IT IS *OVER,* I CAN TELL.

OVER? NOT QUITE. PERHAPS THE TOUGHEST WORK IS STILL AHEAD...

YECCH! THIS PLACE IS A *MESS!* MAYBE WE OUGHTA HOLD A *GARAGE SALE.*

STILL, THERE IS A *BRIGHT* SIDE TO ALL THIS.

...ALSO SCREAMS AN INHUMAN, PLAINTIVE WAIL...

...THEN SOMEHOW EXPLODES IN ONE SINGLE, CORUSCATING INSTANT OF TERROR.

YEAH, YOU'RE LETTING *ME* DO ALL THE WORK.

NAH, NOT *THAT,* WONDY--

24

I JUST FOUND US A NIFTY *SOUVENIR* OF THIS CASE.

I THINK IT SUMS UP *EVERYTHING,* DON'T YOU?

HELP KEEP OUR CITY CLEAN PLEASE *DON'T LITTER*

AND WONDER GIRL'S HEARTY LAUGH FEELS *GOOD...*

EPILOGUE - I

ANOTHER DAY PASSES, AND...

THE DOCTORS SAY THE EXTRA MAGNETIC WAVES IN MY BRAIN ARE *GONE.* IT'S REALLY *OVER.*

WHAT ABOUT YOUR *MOM,* FRAN? HAVE YOU *TOLD* HER?

YEAH, WALLY, I *TOLD* HER.

AND SHE *STILL* DOESN'T WANT TO *KNOW* ME.

SHE STILL THINKS I'M SOME DREADFUL *EVIL THING* WHO SHOULD HAVE *DIED* ALONG WITH MY FATHER AND BROTHER.

BUT, YOU KNOW, I'M SO GLAD I *DIDN'T.*

WALLY, THANK YOU. THANK YOU FOR *EVERYTHING.*

I--I THINK I'M *FALLING IN LOVE* WITH YOU ALL OVER AGAIN.

WHAT ARE YOU GOING TO DO *NOW,* FRAN? WHERE ARE YOU *GOING?*

I DON'T KNOW, WALLY. BUT I'LL *SURVIVE.*

I'M *ALIVE!* I'M ALIVE AND I'LL DO JUST *FINE.*

I--I THINK YOU *WILL,* FRAN...

I'M *SURE* YOU WILL.

EPILOGUE 2 :

FOR THE TITANS, THE STORY IS OVER. YET FOR US, IT CONTINUES FOR JUST A MOMENT MORE, IN ANOTHER DIMENSION INHABITED BY ONLY ONE LIVING SOUL...

I-I WAS SO VERY CLOSE TO *SUCCESS.* I HAD FOUND THAT GIRL--

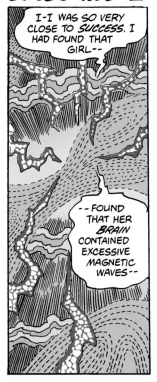

--FOUND THAT HER *BRAIN* CONTAINED EXCESSIVE MAGNETIC WAVES--

--WAVES I COULD *CONTROL* TO BRING ME OUT OF THIS DIMENSION *GREEN LANTERN* BANISHED ME TO.

BUT, BECAUSE OF THOSE *TITANS,* I'VE *FAILED-- FAILED!*

BLAST THEM ALL. I AM *DOCTOR POLARIS -- THE MASTER OF MAGNETISM--*

--THE MOST *POWERFUL* BEING WHO HAS EVER LIVED...

...DOCTOR POLARIS... STILL SCATTERED THROUGH THIS MAGNETIC DIMENSION...

...DOCTOR POLARIS ...*DEFEATED* YET AGAIN...

ARGHHH! I WAS SO CLOSE... SO VERY CLOSE TO *ESCAPING...*

BUT I WILL... SOME DAY I *WILL...* SOME DAY I WILL...

BUT THAT IS A STORY FOR ANOTHER DAY...

IN ISSUE #18 OF THE TEEN TITANS, MARV WOLFMAN & LEN WEIN INTRODUCED A RUSSIAN SUPER-HERO NAMED STARFIRE! IN ISSUE #18 OF THE NEW TITANS--STARFIRE RETURNS!

A PRETTY GIRL IS LIKE A-- MALADI!

THE NEW TEEN TITANS

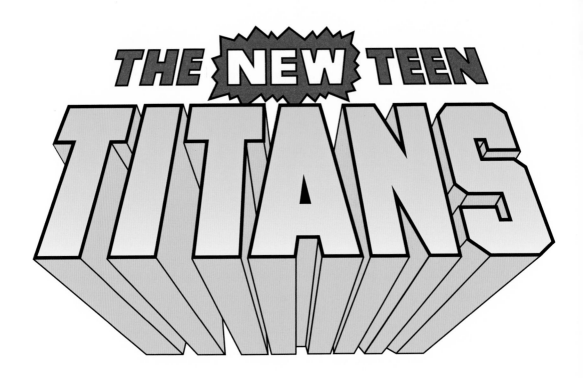

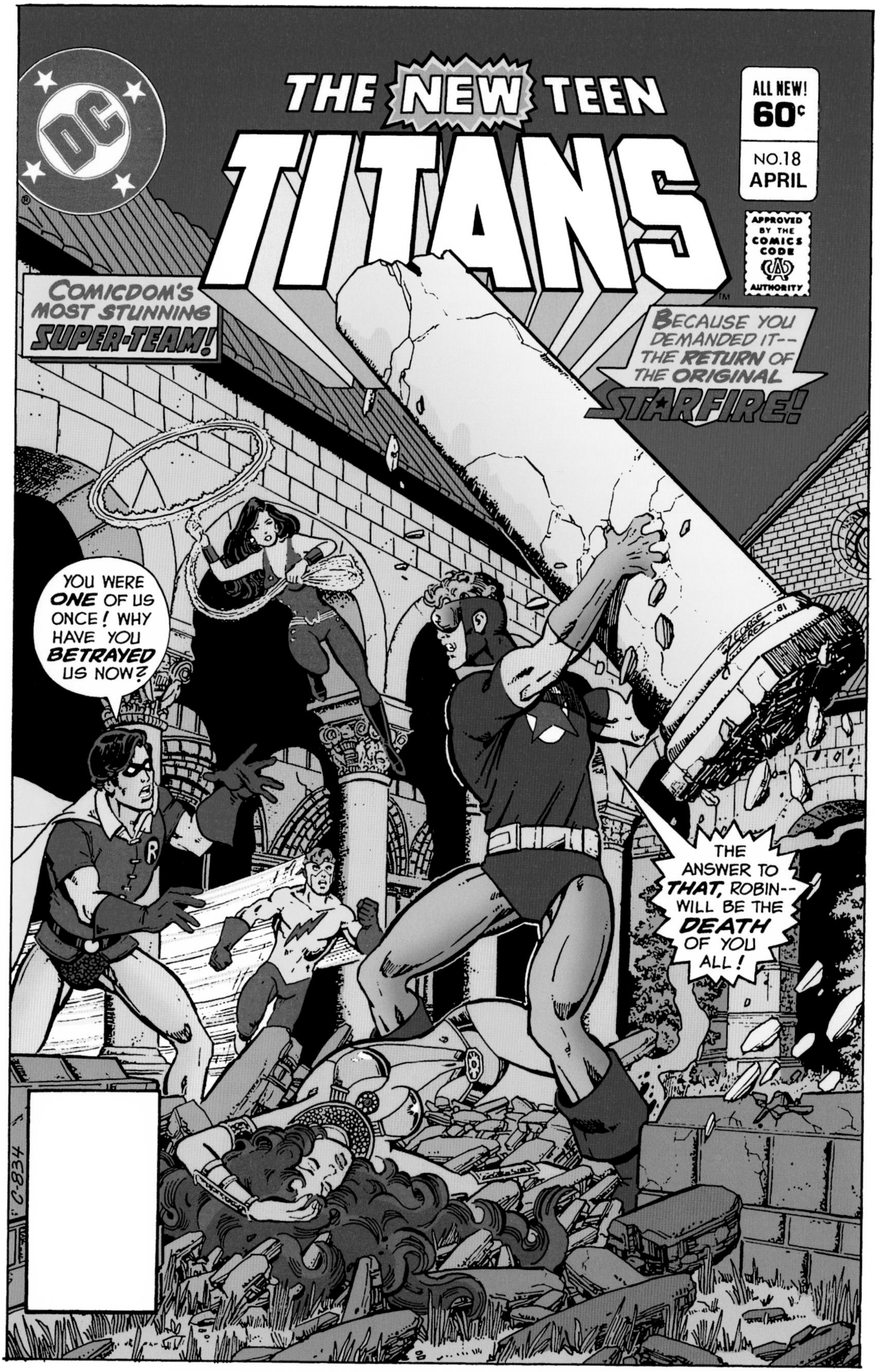
THE NEW TEEN
TITANS
ALL NEW! 60¢
NO.18 APRIL
APPROVED BY THE COMICS CODE AUTHORITY
COMICDOM'S MOST STUNNING SUPER-TEAM!
BECAUSE YOU DEMANDED IT-- THE RETURN OF THE ORIGINAL STARFIRE!
YOU WERE ONE OF US ONCE! WHY HAVE YOU BETRAYED US NOW?
THE ANSWER TO THAT, ROBIN-- WILL BE THE DEATH OF YOU ALL!

THEY ARE THE *BEST* THERE IS: *THE CHANGELING*, SHAPE-SHIFTER SUPREME; *CYBORG*, HALF MAN / HALF ROBOT; *KID FLASH*, SUPER-SPEEDSTER; *RAVEN*, MISTRESS OF MAGIC; *ROBIN*, THE TEEN WONDER; *STARFIRE*, ALIEN POWERHOUSE; AND *WONDER GIRL*, THE AMAZING AMAZON! TOGETHER THEY ARE...

MARV WOLFMAN & GEORGE PÉREZ .
writer-co-creators-artist

ROMEO TANGHAL .
embellisher

COSTANZA .
letterer

ADRIENNE ROY . LEN WEIN
colorist   editor

WHAT DO A COMET PLUNGING INTO THE WASTELANDS OF SIBERIA...

...A VIOLENT REVOLUTION IN EL SALVADOR--

--AND A YOUNG RUSSIAN *BRIDE*-TO-BE ALL HAVE IN COMMON?

THE AMAZING ANSWER IS REVEALED IN...

A PRETTY GIRL IS LIKE A-- MALADI!

SORROW KNOWS NO BOUNDARIES; TRAGEDY NO MAN-MADE BORDERS. AND DEATH SLICES SADLY THROUGH THE HUMAN FABRIC REGARDLESS OF WHERE IT MAY BE...

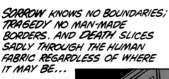

CASE IN POINT: AN ALMOST FORGOTTEN CUBBYHOLE BURIED DEEP IN THE SOVIET UNION...

BUREAU OF SCIENTIFIC RECORDS

PLEASE, DO NOT TELL ME THIS. HE CANNOT BE DEAD.

NO, NOT MY TOMAS. NOT MY DARLING SON.

YES, YES, I AM ALL RIGHT. BUT PLEASE, TELL ME AGAIN... ARE YOU CERTAIN AN AMERICAN DID THIS?

IT IS ALWAYS AMERICANS.

"I HATE THEM, ALL OF THEM. DURING THE WAR MY BROTHER PAVEL WAS KILLED WHILE SHARING A FOXHOLE WITH AN AMERICAN...

"...WHO WAS ASLEEP INSTEAD OF ON GUARD DUTY.

"AND MY DARLING SONYA, KILLED WHILE I SERVED IN HANOI...

"...WHEN AN AMERICAN PLANE DROPPED ITS FILTHY BOMBS ON OUR HOTEL."

AMERICANS! ALWAYS AMERICANS BRING DEATH TO THE LOVED ONES OF MAREK SLAVIK.

BUT NEVER AGAIN!

AH, YES, HERE IT IS AS I REMEMBERED... FORGOTTEN SINCE THE DARK DAYS OF THE COLD WAR.

I FILED THIS HERE. I EVEN BOXED AWAY THE COMPLETED PROTOTYPE.

PAVEL, SONYA, NOW TOMAS-- THE AMERICANS WILL PAY AT LAST FOR WHAT THEY DID TO YOU...

CLASSIFIED PROJECT #RL40-39-

TERMINATED 1957

OH, SHALL THEY PAY.

2

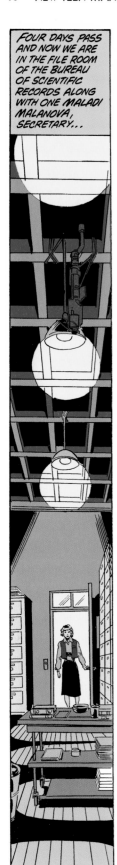

FOUR DAYS PASS AND NOW WE ARE IN THE FILE ROOM OF THE BUREAU OF SCIENTIFIC RECORDS ALONG WITH ONE *MALADI MALANOVA,* SECRETARY...

MALADI HAS BEEN SENT HERE BY A GRIEF-STRICKEN *MAREK SLAVIK* TO FETCH SOME UNIMPORTANT *PAPERS.*

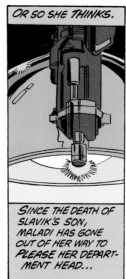

OR SO SHE *THINKS.*

SINCE THE DEATH OF *SLAVIK'S* SON, *MALADI* HAS GONE OUT OF HER WAY TO *PLEASE* HER DEPARTMENT HEAD...

...THOUGH THIS NIGHT SHE WOULD HAVE PRE-FERRED TO DINE WITH HER *FIANCÉ*...

...RATHER THAN BRING EXPECTANT GLEE TO THE DARK FORCES OF *DEATH* HIMSELF.

THIS IS WHAT YOU WANTED?

YES, YES, MALADI. NOW, I HAVE ARRANGED FOR YOU TO *DELIVER* THIS TO OUR OPERATIVE IN NEW YORK.

DELIVER? WILL IT TAKE *LONG?*

YOU KNOW I AM TO BE *MARRIED* NEXT MONTH.

I WILL BE BACK *IN TIME,* NO?

YOU WILL NOT HAVE TO *WORRY,* MY DEAR MALADI...

...SADLY, NOT EVER AGAIN.

3

ANOTHER WEEK PASSES BEFORE WE MAKE OUR WAY TO THE DARKENED DOCKS OF NEW YORK'S WEST SIDE...

ABOUT *TIME* YOU SHOWED UP. I'M DOWN TO MY LAST *CIGARETTE.*

AND I SEE YOU'RE STILL AS *WARM* AND *CHARMING* AS EVER.

WONDER GIRL, THIS IS *KING FARADAY* OF THE *F.B.I.* HE MAKES "*DIRTY HARRY*" LOOK LIKE *PRINCE CHARMING.*

'WONDER GIRL'? LISTEN, KID, I WANTED *YOU*, NOT YOUR *PROM DATE.*

YOUR FRIEND HAS ALL THE CHARM OF A *TERMINAL DISEASE.*

YEAH, AND I'M *CUTE*, TOO.

NOW LOOK AT THIS *PHOTO*, KID-- IT EXPLAINS WHY I *CALLED* YOU.

YOU *REMEMBER* THIS JOE, OR MAYBE I SHOULD SAY '*IVAN*'? HIS NAME IS *LEONID KOVAR*, ONLY YOU REMEMBER HIM AS--

STARFIRE? HE'S THE RUSSIAN SUPER-HERO WE MET A FEW YEARS BACK.

RIGHT, BRIGHT-EYES, AND ONE OF OUR CONTACTS IN THE *KREMLIN* TELLS US HE'S ON HIS WAY HERE...IN *SECRET.*

SO WE FIGURED YOU SUPER-TYPES, *KNOWING* KOVAR, COULD FOLLOW HIM AND TELL US WHAT HE'S *UP TO.*

4

I *REMEMBER* STARFIRE...

...WE MET IN *SWEDEN* WHEN WE ALL FOUGHT AN INTERNATIONAL JEWEL THIEF NAMED *ANDRE LE BLANC.*

TROUBLE IS, WE WERE STILL TOO *INEXPERIENCED* TO USE OUR POWERS *WISELY,* AND LE BLANC KEPT *DEFEATING* US.

"BUT WE *WON* IN THE END, OF COURSE."

THIS STARFIRE NEVER *USED* HIS POWERS, ALTHOUGH HE SAID HE *HAD* SOME...

"...GOT THEM FROM A SUPPOSED *METEOR* THAT FELL IN *SIBERIA* BACK IN *1908.*

"*ONLY* WHEN HE AND HIS FATHER FOUND THE CRASH SITE, THEY DISCOVERED IT HAD *NOT* BEEN A *METEOR* BUT A *DEMOLISHED ROCKET SHIP.*

"KOVAR SAID HE SNEAKED INTO THE SHIP AT NIGHT, FIDDLED AROUND WITH THE CONTROLS...

"...THEN SOMEHOW A BOLT OF *POWER* SURGED THROUGH HIS BODY.

"SOMEHOW IT *INCREASED* HIS *SPEED,* HIS *STAMINA,* HIS *STRENGTH* AND *AGILITY.*

"HE BECAME *RUSSIA'S* FIRST REAL *SUPER-HERO!*"

STARFIRE WENT BACK TO HIS OWN COUNTRY, BUT WE ALL DEPARTED *FRIENDS...*

...THOUGH WHO *KNOWS?* A LOT CAN *HAPPEN* IN A FEW YEARS...

5

...SO YOU SEE WHAT THE TROUBLE IS. MAYBE KOVAR'S *STILL* A FRIEND. BUT HE COULD BE AN *ENEMY.*

HE WAS CALLED *STARFIRE?* JUST LIKE *ME?*

"STARFIRE" WAS A ROUGH TRANSLATION OF HIS *RUSSIAN* NAME.

AND WHEN WE SAW YOUR *STARBOLT* POWERS...WELL, WE FIGURED THE NAME WOULD FIT *YOU* AS WELL.

BESIDES, WE DIDN'T THINK KOVAR WOULD *MIND.*

I NEVER *TRUSTED* HIM, DICK. YOU CAN'T TRUST *ANY* OF HIS PEOPLE.

LOOK WHAT THEY DID IN *AFGHANISTAN* AND *ANGOLA.*

NEVERTHELESS, WALLY, WE HAVE A *JOB* TO DO.

AND AN *IMPORTANT* ONE. FARADAY'S CONTACTS MENTIONED SOMETHING ABOUT A *PLAGUE-CARRIER.*

AND WE DON'T KNOW *HOW* KOVAR FITS INTO THAT...

...OR *WHY* THE RUSSIANS DIDN'T *INFORM* OUR GOVERN-MENT HE WAS COMING.

GREAT, SO NOW WE'RE *SPIES.* LISSEN, KORY, I GOT AN *IDEA.* WHY DON'T *WE* SPLIT AND HAVE SOME *FUN?*

PLEASE, GARFIELD-- *DON'T.*

THAT SORT OF TALK...IT STILL *BOTHERS* ME.

OH, KORY, I'M SORRY. I *FOR-GOT* WHAT HAPPENED TO YOUR FRIEND *FRANKLIN...* IT STILL *HURTS?*

IT *DOES.*

A MONTH'S GONE BY SINCE FRANKLIN DIED AND SHE'S STILL SO GLUM... SO *SAD.*

OH, I WISH I COULD *DO* SOMETHING FOR YOU, KORY. I ONLY WISH I COULD *HELP.*

6

THREE DAYS AGO AT J.F.K. INTERNATIONAL AIRPORT, NEW YORK...

A YOUNG RUSSIAN GIRL MOVES QUICKLY THROUGH CUSTOMS...

CONTACT!

OUTSIDE, MOE SHREIVNITZ, A NEW YORK CABBIE, TAKES THE YOUNG GIRL'S LUGGAGE...

EASTERN NATIONAL

TAXI STAND

CONTACT!

FIFTY-THREE MINUTES LATER, DOORMAN "CAP'N" JACK McCARTHY HELPS THE YOUNG RUSSIAN INTO THE HOTEL FOUNTAINE...

CONTACT!

ONE WEEK PASSES AND WE RETURN TO J.F.K. AIRPORT...

...WHERE ANOTHER RUSSIAN TRAVELLER IMPATIENTLY WAITS FOR HIS LUGGAGE TO BE PROCESSED THROUGH CUSTOMS.

EXCUSE ME. ARE YOU ALL RIGHT?

N...NO... DON'T FEEL TOO GOOD...

...FEEL LIKE... I'M GOING TO...DIE.

OH, MY GOD! SOMEONE-- CALL FOR AN AMBULANCE!

IS HE DEAD?

I--I DON'T KNOW, I'VE NEVER SEEN ANYTHING LIKE THIS.

HE WOULD HAVE BEEN THE FIRST.

I HAVE ARRIVED IN TIME.

SO INTENT IS LEONID KOVAR THAT HE FAILS TO SEE A SMALL GREEN FLY FLUTTERING NEARBY.

7

DID WE SAY GREEN FLY...?

INDEED, GREEN AS IN...

CHANGELING! HAS KOVAR *ARRIVED* YET?

BETTER *BELIEVE* IT, ROBBIE.

LISSEN, ONE OF THE CUSTOMS AGENTS *KEELED OVER* WHEN KOVAR SHOWED UP.

AND FARADAY SAID SOMETHING ABOUT A *PLAGUE-CARRIER.*

WE FOUND OUR *CARRIER,* ROBIN.

C'MON, WALLY, THAT JUST DOESN'T *SOUND* LIKE THE KOVAR WE MET.

I GUESS WE'LL JUST HAVE TO *SEE* ABOUT THAT, WONDER GIRL.

MEANWHILE, WE *FOLLOW* KOVAR.

HIS CAB'S FOLLOWING THE AMBULANCE THAT TOOK AWAY THAT CUSTOMS AGENT.

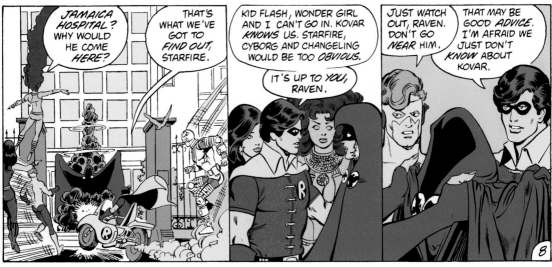

JAMAICA HOSPITAL? WHY WOULD HE COME *HERE?*

THAT'S WHAT WE'VE GOT TO *FIND OUT,* STARFIRE.

KID FLASH, WONDER GIRL AND I CAN'T GO IN. KOVAR *KNOWS* US. STARFIRE, CYBORG AND CHANGELING WOULD BE TOO *OBVIOUS.*

IT'S UP TO *YOU,* RAVEN.

JUST WATCH OUT, RAVEN. DON'T GO *NEAR* HIM.

THAT MAY BE GOOD *ADVICE.* I'M AFRAID WE JUST DON'T *KNOW* ABOUT KOVAR.

8

I DO NOT *LIKE* THIS PLACE. I SENSE SO MUCH *PAIN*, SO MANY TORTURED MINDS.

THIS IS NOT A *SAFE* PLACE FOR AN *EMPATH* TO TREAD.

PLEASE, THE MAN WHO WAS JUST BROUGHT IN HERE, TELL ME HOW HE *IS*.

IT'S HARD TO SAY. I'VE NEVER SEEN RADIATION-CREATED *CELL-DETERIORA-TION* LIKE THIS BEFORE...

...BUT IF WE CAN'T FIND A *CURE* WITHIN 96 HOURS, HE'LL BE *DONE FOR*.

RADIATION POISONING? I MUST TELL *RICHARD*.

UHH, EXCUSE ME, MISS. DO YOU NEED ANY *HELP*?

NO. I HAVE WHAT I *CAME* HERE FOR.

GOOD-BYE.

OH, MY.

OH, MY.

TWO DAYS PASS...

BORING! BORRRRING!

I'M GETTING *SICK* OF TAILING THAT JERK.

MORE THAN ONE HUNDRED PEOPLE HAVE COME DOWN WITH THAT SAME RADIATION POISONING, BUT KOVAR WASN'T NEAR *ANY* OF THEM.

I DON'T *UNDERSTAND* THIS, WONDER GIRL.

AND KOVAR SEEMS TO BE *SEARCHING* FOR SOMETHING. BUT *WHAT* IS IT? OR *WHO* IS IT?

9

STILL, I THINK WE'RE *RIGHT* IN NOT PICKING HIM UP. I DON'T THINK HE'S *CONNECTED* WITH THIS RADIATION PLAGUE.

I *DO!* LET'S GO DOWN THERE AND MAKE HIM *TELL* US.

HE'S THE ONE WHO'S GOT THE *ANSWERS* WE WANT.

SHE IS REGISTERED HERE. *AT LAST.*

THIS SHOULD ALL BE OVER *SOON* NOW.

WHAT *FLOOR,* MAC?

609, PLEASE. SIXTH FLOOR.

WAIT!

THERE SHE IS!

OPERATOR, DO NOT *CLOSE* THIS DOOR.

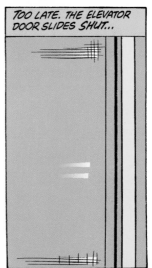

TOO LATE. THE ELEVATOR DOOR SLIDES SHUT...

...THOUGH APPARENTLY THAT MEANS *LITTLE* TO THE RUSSIAN SUPER-HERO NAMED STAR-FIRE.

SKRASHH

10

WE WAIT FOR HIM... *EH?* LOOK, DOWN THERE. DO YOU SEE THAT *WOMAN?*

SHE LOOKS *ILL.*

ILL? SHE LOOKS LIKE SHE'S ON A FIRST NAME BASIS WITH *DEATH.*

SHE CAN BARELY *STAND.*

SOMEHOW I SENSE SHE HAS SOMETHING TO *DO* WITH THIS.

WELL, SHE'S TAKEN OFF IN A *CAB.* LOOKS LIKE YOUR HUNCH WAS *WRONG,* RAVEN.

BUT...

I TAKE IT BACK. THERE'S OUR FRIENDLY *"RED"* HERRING *NOW.* HE'S AFTER THAT POOR *GIRL.*

BTAM!

BUT HE WON'T GET *NEAR* HER.

HOLD IT, *BOTH* OF YOU!

BELIEVE IT, STARRY.

DO NOT *WORRY,* ROBIN. I WILL MERELY *STUN* HIM.

WHAT?

I AM BEING *ATTACKED?* BUT BY *WHOM?*

DON'T TELL ME YOU'VE *FORGOTTEN* YOUR OLD FIGHTING PARTNERS ALREADY?

OR IS YOUR *MEMORY* AS POOR AS YOUR COUNTRY'S *HONOR?*

SWAK!

KID FLASH?!?

11

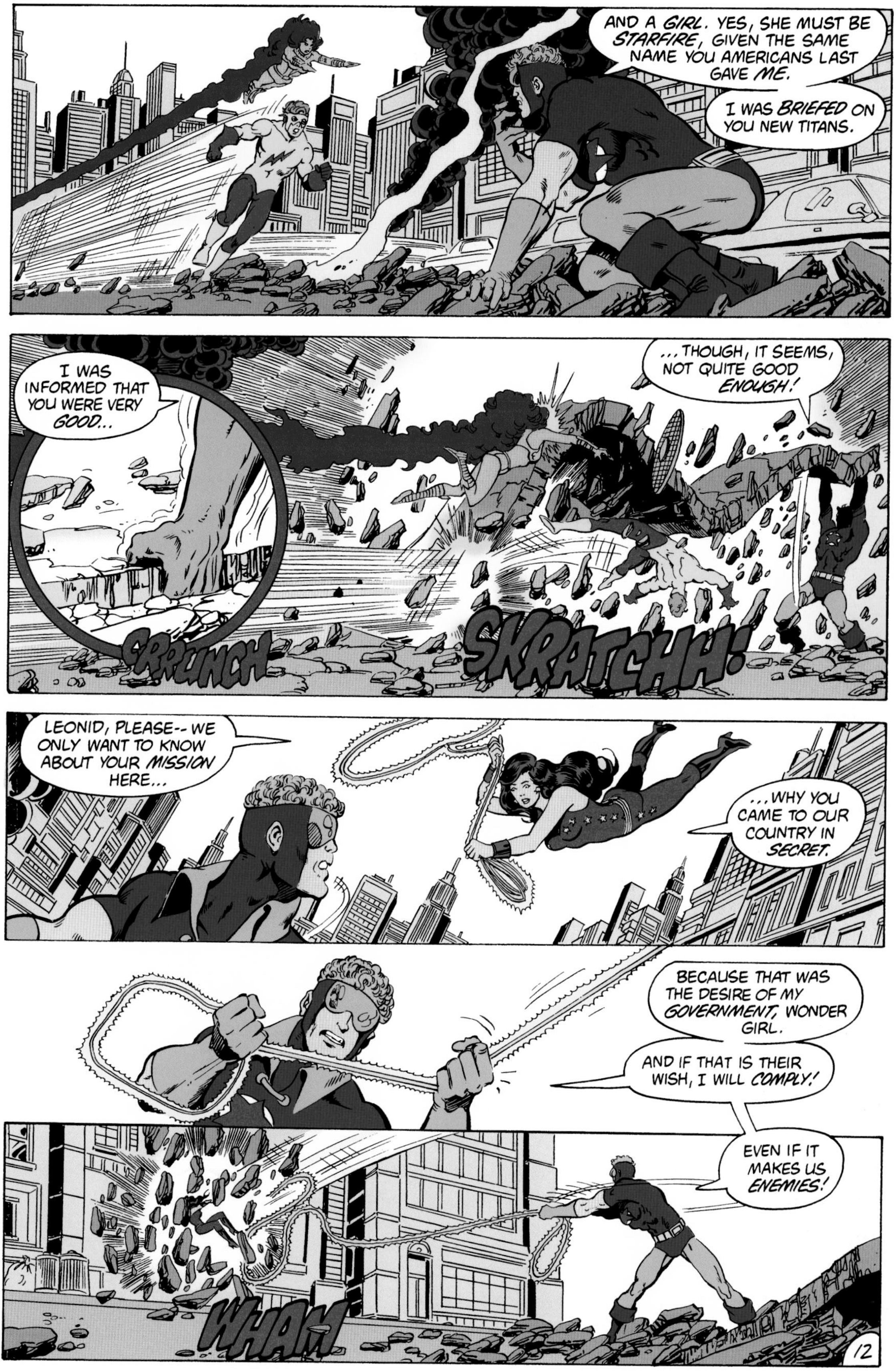
AND A GIRL. YES, SHE MUST BE STARFIRE, GIVEN THE SAME NAME YOU AMERICANS LAST GAVE ME.
I WAS BRIEFED ON YOU NEW TITANS.
I WAS INFORMED THAT YOU WERE VERY GOOD...
...THOUGH, IT SEEMS, NOT QUITE GOOD ENOUGH!
CRRUNCH
SKRATCHH!
LEONID, PLEASE--WE ONLY WANT TO KNOW ABOUT YOUR MISSION HERE...
...WHY YOU CAME TO OUR COUNTRY IN SECRET.
BECAUSE THAT WAS THE DESIRE OF MY GOVERNMENT, WONDER GIRL.
AND IF THAT IS THEIR WISH, I WILL COMPLY!
EVEN IF IT MAKES US ENEMIES!
WHAM
12

KOVAR BRACES HIMSELF, WAITING FOR THE ATTACK HE KNOWS MUST COME. BUT WHEN IT ARRIVES, IT COMES IN A FORM HE HAS NOT EXPECTED...

SKREEE

SOUND! I-IT'S DEAFENING ME!

BE GLAD I DIDN'T *UP* IT A COUPLE 'A NOTCHES, PALLY-- 'CAUSE THAT WOULD 'A BLOWN OUT YER *EARDRUMS!*

NOW, YA READY TO TALK THIS OVER?

NO!

MEBBE, BLUE-EYES, BUT WHEN WE *OUT-NUMBER* YOU SEVEN TO ONE-- WELL, CIRCUMSTANCES SORTA *CHANGE.*

A TALKING *OCTOPUS?* YOU MUST BE THE *CHANGELING!*

I HAVE *TOLD* YOU! I HAVE A MISSION TO PERFORM IN *SECRET!*

UNDER THESE SAME CIRCUMSTANCES, I WOULD NOT EXPECT *YOU* TO TALK!

LEONID, DON'T YOU SEE HOW *FRUITLESS* THIS IS? WE DON'T WANT TO *HURT* YOU.

WE KNOW ABOUT THE *PLAGUE!* WE JUST DON'T KNOW WHAT YOUR *INVOLVEMENT* IS.

PLEASE *LEVEL* WITH US!

I *CANNOT!*

STILL, LEONID KOVAR, IF YOUR MISSION IS TO FURTHER *SPREAD* THIS PLAGUE, WE CANNOT ALLOW IT TO *CONTINUE.*

OOOPS!

IF THIS WAS UP TO *ME,* I WOULD.

BUT MY GOVERNMENT ORDERED MY *SILENCE.* I WILL DO AS THEY DEMAND!

SO, FOR NOW, YOU WILL SIMPLY *REST...*

13

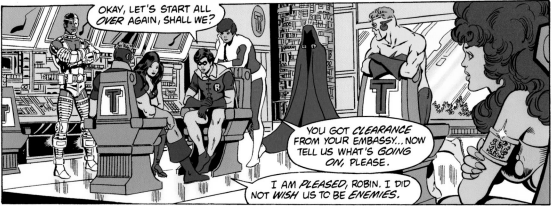

OKAY, LET'S START ALL *OVER* AGAIN, SHALL WE?

YOU GOT *CLEARANCE* FROM YOUR EMBASSY... NOW TELL US WHAT'S *GOING ON*, PLEASE.

I AM *PLEASED*, ROBIN. I DID NOT *WISH* US TO BE *ENEMIES*.

SURE YOU DON'T! JUST LIKE YOUR GOVERNMENT DOESN'T WANT TO INTIMIDATE *POLAND*, EH?

I AM NOT HERE TO *FIGHT* WITH YOU, KID FLASH.

AND I AM *SURPRISED* THAT YOU WOULD JUDGE *ONE MAN* BY THE ACTIONS OF HIS *GOVERNMENT*.

C'MON, HE'S THEIR *AGENT*. HE'S TOLD US *THAT* MUCH.

DID YOU NOT SAY *YOU* UNDER-TOOK THE MISSION OF FOLLOW-ING ME FOR *YOUR* GOVERNMENT?

DO YOU *CONDONE* ALL YOUR GOVERNMENT'S IMPERIALISTIC POLICIES?

LET'S CUT THIS OUT, SHALL WE? WHAT ABOUT THE *GIRL*?

BECAUSE HIS *SON* WAS KILLED BY AN AMERICAN IN *EL SALVADOR*, A MINOR OFFICIAL IN MY GOVERNMENT DECIDED ON A COURSE OF *PERSONAL VENGEANCE*.

HE *IRRADIATED* A WOMAN WITH A DEADLY BACILLUS AND SENT HER HERE TO NEW YORK ON A PHONY MISSION.

SHE IS *UNAWARE* THAT SHE SPREADS THIS RADIATION-INDUCED PLAGUE TO ANYONE SHE *TOUCHES*-- EVEN THOUGH WITH EVERY PASSING HOUR SHE BRINGS HERSELF CLOSER TO *DEATH*.

14

MALADI MALANOVA CANNOT BE *SAVED*, BUT HER *VICTIMS* CAN...

...A *SIMPLE* ENOUGH PROCEDURE IF THE VICTIM HAS SUFFERED THIS PLAGUE FOR LESS THAN *FOURTEEN DAYS.*

I WAS SENT TO YOUR COUNTRY IN SECRET NOT ONLY TO *STOP* THE GIRL, BUT ALSO TO PREVENT *PANIC.*

WE WERE AFRAID YOUR PEOPLE WOULD NOT *BELIEVE* THIS WAS MERELY THE DOING OF ONE GRIEF-STRICKEN *MADMAN.*

AND YOU EXPECT US TO *BELIEVE* IT? C'MON, MAYBE YOUR MASTERS PULLED THE WOOL OVER *YOUR* EYES, BUT WE'RE NOT *FOOLED.*

I WILL NOT HEAR THIS *ANY* LONGER, KID FLASH!

SWAK

AND I WAS A *FOOL* TO WASTE THIS MUCH *TIME* WITH YOU.

I KNOW WHERE MALADI'S SUPPOSED *MEETING* IS TO TAKE PLACE TOMORROW--

--AND THOUGH I HAVE NOT BEEN ABLE TO *STOP* HER BEFORE NOW...

...I WILL NOT FAIL *AGAIN.*

HE'S GETTING AWAY!

FOLLOW HIM, CHANGELING.

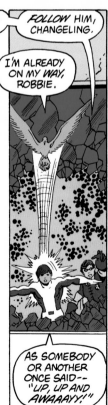

I'M ALREADY ON MY *WAY,* ROBBIE.

AS SOMEBODY OR ANOTHER ONCE SAID-- "*UP, UP AND AWAAAYY!*"

15

MEANWHILE, ACROSS TOWN, IN THE OFFICE OF ONE DOCTOR STANISLAV KRYSZEWSKI.

UNBELIEVABLE, SIMPLY *UNBELIEVABLE.*

STANISLAV KRYSZEWSKI

I HAVE NOT SEEN *RADIATION DISEASE* SUCH AS THIS SINCE *HIROSHIMA.*

SEVERE *CONTAMINATION...* SHE CANNOT *LIVE.*

AND SHE DOESN'T *REALIZE* THAT YET, DOCTOR. SHE JUST ASKED ME HOW TO GET TO THE *CLOISTERS.*

SHE CAN BARELY *STAND,* BUT SHE WANTS TO GO TO A *MUSEUM...?*

HAVE HER *COME IN,* MADELINE, WILL YOU?

DOCTOR, PLEASE TELL ME WHAT IS *HAPPENING* TO ME?

I FEEL SO *WEAK,* SO TERRIBLY *SICK.*

AND I AM SO *AFRAID...* I DO NOT *UNDERSTAND.*

WITH GOOD *REASON,* MALADI. PLEASE, DO *SIT DOWN.*

YOU MUST GO TO THE *HOSPITAL* WHERE--

NO, NO HOSPITAL. I *CANNOT...*

I...HAVE SOMETHING TO *DO...*

...THEN... I HAVE TO BE *MARRIED...*

NO...I CANNOT GO TO ANY *HOSPITAL...*

MADELINE, PLEASE HURRY-- CALL THE *POLICE.* SHE MUST BE *STOPPED.*

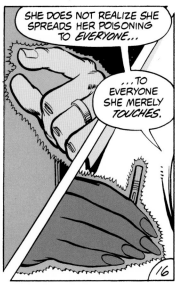

SHE DOES NOT REALIZE SHE SPREADS HER POISONING TO *EVERYONE...*

...TO EVERYONE SHE MERELY *TOUCHES.*

16

BUT, AT THAT SELFSAME MOMENT, ACROSS THE EAST RIVER...

NOTHING UP *HERE*...

...SO *WHAMMO!* ANOTHER PATENTED GAR LOGAN *SHAPE-CHANGE,* AND...

...*STILL* NOTHING! *BLAST!* I WAS REALLY HOPING I COULD BRING BACK KOVAR *MYSELF*--

--I HAVEN'T DONE ANYTHING WORTH *SPIT* SINCE WE ALL RETURNED FROM *ZANDIA.*

I DON'T WANT THE OTHERS TO THINK THAT ALL I DO IS GET IN THE *WAY.*

YOU *SPOT* ANY-THING, GAR?

ZILCH! KOVAR'S FLOWN THE COOP.

AND *YOU* ALL THOUGHT HE WAS PLAYING *STRAIGHT.*

WHY ARE YOU SO *DOWN* ON HIM, WALLY? I'VE NEVER HEARD YOU *SPEAK* LIKE THIS.

MAYBE BECAUSE I KNEW OUR *POLITICS* WERE ALWAYS *DIFFERENT.*

LOOK, I DON'T PUT YOU DOWN FOR BEING *LIBERALS.* WHY ATTACK ME FOR BEING A MID-WESTERN *CONSERVA-TIVE?*

FORGET *POLITICS!* ALL *I* CARE ABOUT IS FINDING THE *GIRL.*

LISTEN, SHE WAS *WEAK...* SHE JUST MIGHT GO TO A DOCTOR OR CLINIC...

...SO WE START CALLING EVERY *MEDICAL FACILITY* IN NEW YORK.

ON A *WEDNES-DAY?* EVERY DOCTOR IN TOWN'S OUT PLAYING *GOLF!*

MORE THAN AN *HOUR* PASSES BY FRUITLESSLY, UNTIL...

I HAVE *FOUND* HER, ROBIN. A DOCTOR KRYSZEWSKI...

OF COURSE SHE'D PICK A DOCTOR WITH A *RUSSIAN* NAME.

TELL HIM WE'RE ON OUR *WAY.*

17

A DAY PASSES. ABOVE A HILLTOP IN *FORT TRYON PARK* STANDS A MAGNIFICENT RE-CREATION FROM THE MIDDLE AGES. OPENED IN 1938, *THE CLOISTERS* IS MORE THAN A MUSEUM. IT IS A LIVING LINK TO A LIFESTYLE THAT DIED ALMOST EIGHT CENTURIES AGO...

FROM ITS STONE PORTALS TO ITS HANGING UNICORN TAPESTRIES, THE CLOISTERS PROVES THAT IMMORTALITY OF SORTS DOES INDEED EXIST...

...A CONCEPT THAT THIS DYING GIRL WOULD FIND A *GRIM JEST* INDEED.

MALADI...

YOU? OH, MY GOD!

PLEASE...DO NOT *LOOK* AT ME LIKE THIS.

I WAS SENT HERE TO *FIND* YOU.

YOU WERE *LIED* TO, YOU KNOW. WE *HAVE* NO AGENTS HERE.

I--I DID NOT WANT TO *THINK* THAT; BUT I *KNEW* IT...

WHY DID HE *DO* IT?

MISPLACED *HATRED?* IT IS HARD TO *TELL.*

BUT *FORGET* SLAVIK. I CARE ABOUT *YOU!*

MALADI!

W-WHY DID THEY SEND *YOU*...YOU OF *ALL* PEOPLE?

YOUR *TOUCH* SPREADS PAIN AND *DEATH*, MALADI.

I WAS SENT HERE TO SEE THAT YOU *DIE!*

18

NO WAY!

I KNEW IT, KOVAR! I JUST KNEW IT!

YOU'RE A SOULLESS KILLER, JUST LIKE YOUR GOVERNMENT!

WHOOOM

IT APPEARS KID FLASH IS CORRECT. YOUR MISSION HERE IS TO KILL.

CANNOT YOU SEE THAT I HAVE TO?

EVERY MAN, WOMAN AND CHILD SHE TOUCHES COULD DIE.

NO, YOU DON'T UNDERSTAND. NONE OF YOU POSSIBLY CAN.

CKREEEE

I WILL HAVE TO HANDLE THIS MY OWN WAY!

SPLAM

FORGET IT! YOU AIN'T KILLIN' NO ONE!

'SPECIALLY NOT SOME POOR, INNOCENT GIRL!

HOLY HANNAH! YOUR PUNCH BLASTED HIM CLEAN THROUGH THE WALL!

WELL, WHEREVER HE GOES, I GO!

THIS TIME THAT COMMIE'S NOT GETTING AWAY!

LEONID KOVAR CRASHES THROUGH THE GREAT STONE WALL OF THE GOTHIC CHAPEL...

19

...WHILE, IN THE CUXA CLOISTER OUTSIDE...

ROBIN, SHE IS *DYING* AND IN GREAT *PAIN*.

CAN YOUR *EMPATHIC POWERS* HELP HER, RAVEN?

I--I DO NOT *KNOW.* I WILL *DO* ALL I CAN.

PLEASE *TRY.* THIS IS *IMPORTANT.*

I ALWAYS DO MY BEST. I CAN DO NOTHING *LESS.*

HER PAIN WILL BECOME *MY* PAIN...

...BUT THERE'S NEVER ANYONE WHO CAN SOOTHE *YOUR* SUFFERING, IS THERE, RAVEN?

NO ONE YOU FEEL *COMFORTABLE* ENOUGH WITH TO TELL *YOUR* TROUBLES TO.

AGAIN? WHY DO YOU PERSIST IN *HOUNDING* ME?

SHE HAS TO *DIE.* SHOW HER THE *MERCY* SHE DESERVES.

MERCY? MY GOD! DID YOU PEOPLE SHOW *MERCY* IN HUNGARY OR CZECHOSLOVAKIA, IN AFGHANISTAN OR POLAND?

DON'T BE A LOUSY *HYPOCRITE.* YOUR COUNTRY GIVES YOU *ORDERS,* AND YOU'RE JUST DYING TO *OBEY* THEM...

...NO MATTER *WHO* HAS TO SUFFER.

YOU REALLY BELIEVE THIS IS A MATTER OF *POLITICS,* DON'T YOU?

THAT GIRL IS IN *PAIN.* IT TEARS ME APART EVEN *THINKING* ABOUT THAT.

KRAK!

SHE WILL DIE *ANYWAY!* LET HER DIE *MY* WAY...

...NOT BY SOME SLOW, INSINUATING *TORTURE!*

SLAMM

WE CAN'T LET YOU *KILL* HER, STARFIRE. WE *CAN'T.*

20

A GOLDEN LASSO. *WONDER GIRL'S* TOOL IN TRADE.

SURELY *YOU* ABOVE ALL THE OTHERS MUST *UNDERSTAND* ME. I ALWAYS SENSED *UNDERSTANDING* IN YOU.

PLEASE *FREE* ME. LET ME DO WHAT IS *BEST* FOR MALADI!

...JUST AS I KNOW *YOU* DON'T.

I *CAN'T*, LEONID. I KNOW *I* DON'T HAVE THE RIGHT TO MAKE DECISIONS OF LIFE AND DEATH...

BUT I *MUST.*

AND I CANNOT ALLOW YOU TO *STOP* ME.

WHILE...

BE CALM, YOUNG ONE. FEEL MY ENERGIES MERGE WITH YOUR OWN...

FEEL *MY* LIFE BECOME *YOUR* LIFE...

...BUT THE PAIN... IT *HURTS*... HURTS SO VERY MUCH...

LET ME *DIE*... IT HURTS TOO MUCH TO *LIVE*...

NO! DON'T *SAY* THAT, GIRL!

YOU *CANNOT* DIE! I WILL NOT *FORSAKE* YOU!

BUT HER PAIN... IS TOO GREAT FOR ME TO *BEAR* MUCH LONGER...

21

LEONID KOVAR RACES THROUGH THE HERB GARDEN OF THE BONNEFONT CLOISTER, AND FOR THE FIRST TIME SINCE THIS MISSION BEGAN, HE IS AFRAID...

HE IS GOOD; HE KNOWS THAT. BUT HIS FOES ARE OVERWHELMING...

...AND THEY SEEM TO BE EVERYWHERE AT ONCE...

SKRREEEE

WHAT? YOU MOVED OUT OF THE PATH OF MY STARBOLT?

BUT *NOBODY* IS THAT FAST!

OBVIOUSLY, STARFIRE, *I* AM!

SKRREEEE

THOUGH SLOWER THAN YOUR *KID FLASH*, I AM STILL FASTER THAN YOU...

FASTER, AND IF MY BRIEFING WAS CORRECT, *STRONGER!*

THERE ARE POINTS OF *PRESSURE* ALONG YOUR BODY...

POINTS I CAN *MANIPULATE* TO RENDER YOU *UNCONSCIOUS!*

THERE! I DO NOT MEAN TO *HURT* YOU, GIRL, BUT THIS WILL KEEP YOU OUT OF MY HAIR UNTIL MY MISSION IS *DONE*.

WRONG! THAT MAY HAVE WORKED ON ANYONE *ELSE*, BUT NOT *ME!*

I MAY *RESEMBLE* AN EARTHLING IN MOST WAYS, BUT NOT *ALL!*

TO ME, THOSE PRESSURE POINTS WERE LITTLE MORE THAN A GENTLE MASSAGE.

ZKRAM

WHOOMP!

22

LOOK, PALLY, WE DON'T REALLY *HATE* YA. IN FACT, LEMME GIVE YOU A GREAT BIG *HUG.*

UNNHH! YOU ARE *STRONG* IN THIS BEAR FORM, CHANGELING--

--BUT YOU ARE NOT *UNDEFEATABLE!*

BESIDES, YOU SEEK MERELY TO *RESTRAIN* ME. YOU DO NOT USE YOUR *FULL STRENGTH...*

...WHILE *I* CAN USE MINE!

SLAMM!

YOU'RE *RIGHT.* WE'RE *NOT* USING ALL OUR POWER. ALL WE WANT IS FOR YOU TO LISTEN TO *REASON.*

BUT, IF WE HAVE TO *STOP* YOU TO DO THAT, WE'RE *READY.*

SKAK!

YOU CAN *STOP* ME, BUT THAT IS *ALL RIGHT...*

...ALL I NEED IS A FEW *SECONDS* WITH MALADI...

...AND I DO MEAN TO *HAVE* THEM.

AND, BUDDY-BOY, WE MEAN TA MAKE SURE YOU *DON'T!*

ZZZZ AAKKK!

BURNT OUT MY *FINGER-LASER* DOING THAT, BUT I THINK GREEN-SLEEVES HERE IS OUT FOR THE *COUNT.*

ONLY QUESTION IS, CAN WE *KEEP* HIM THAT WAY?

WE *HAVE* TO, ROBIN.

23

YOU TELL *HIM* THAT!

LOOK!

HE'S GETTING *UP?* AFTER ALL *THAT?*

I WILL NOT ALLOW MYSELF TO BE *STOPPED.*

WHERE *IS* SHE? WHERE IS *MALADI?*

HERE SHE IS, BIG-SHOT... YER REALLY GONNA USE ALL YER BIG BAD *POWERS* ON THIS POOR GIRL?

C'MON, MISTER, LET'S SEE HOW *BRAVE* YOU ARE. WHEN YER DONE WITH *HER*, WHY NOT ATTACK AN *OLD-AGE HOME?*

I AM *SORRY.* HER ILLNESS IS BEYOND MY MEAGER POWERS TO *CURE.*

THERE IS NOTHING I CAN DO FOR HER.

BUT THERE IS SOMETHING I CAN DO.

I CAN *END* HER PAIN.

WHAT?

HAVEN'T YOU HEARD *ANYTHING* WE'VE SAID? YOU CAN'T *DO* THAT HERE.

WE'LL *FIGHT* YOU TO THE LAST TITAN, BUT WE WON'T LET YOU *KILL* HER.

WE'LL BRING HER TO THE *HOSPITAL.* THE DRUGS THEY USE WILL *EASE* HER PAIN.

ARE YOU DOING THIS *OUR* WAY, LEONID? OR DO WE *FIGHT?*

YOU ARE *WRONG* ABOUT THIS, BUT I CAN NO LONGER *FIGHT* YOU. WE WILL TAKE HER TO YOUR *HOSPITAL.*

24

FOR LEONID KOVAR EACH MOMENT OF THE PASSING WEEK IS INTERMINABLE... ENDLESS...

I AM SORRY...

...THERE WAS NOTHING MORE WE COULD DO.

BUT SHE UNDERSTOOD AT THE END. SHE ASKED IF ALL THOSE SHE INFECTED WERE CURED.

SHE SEEMED RELIEVED WHEN I TOLD HER THEY WERE.

SHE WAS A VERY BRAVE GIRL.

AND YOU WOULD HAVE KILLED HER LIKE SOME LAME HORSE. MY GOD, KOVAR, YOU'RE A DAMNED COLD FISH.

I WOULD NOT EXPECT YOU TO UNDERSTAND. BUT I VOLUNTEERED FOR THIS MISSION TO SPARE HER THE PAINS OF A SLOW, TORTUROUS DEATH.

VOLUNTEERED? GOOD GOD! WHAT FOR, KOVAR? TO GET SOME BLASTED MEDALS WHEN YOU GOT HOME?

NO. I VOLUNTEERED BECAUSE I LOVED HER.

MALADI AND I WERE ENGAGED.

AND TODAY... TODAY WAS THE DAY WE WERE TO BE MARRIED.

25

NEXT ISSUE: THE RETURN OF DOCTOR LIGHT IN THE WILDEST TITANS TALE OF ALL! GUEST-STARRING THE AMAZING WINGED WONDER--

HAWKMAN ®

PLEASE BE HERE WITH US.

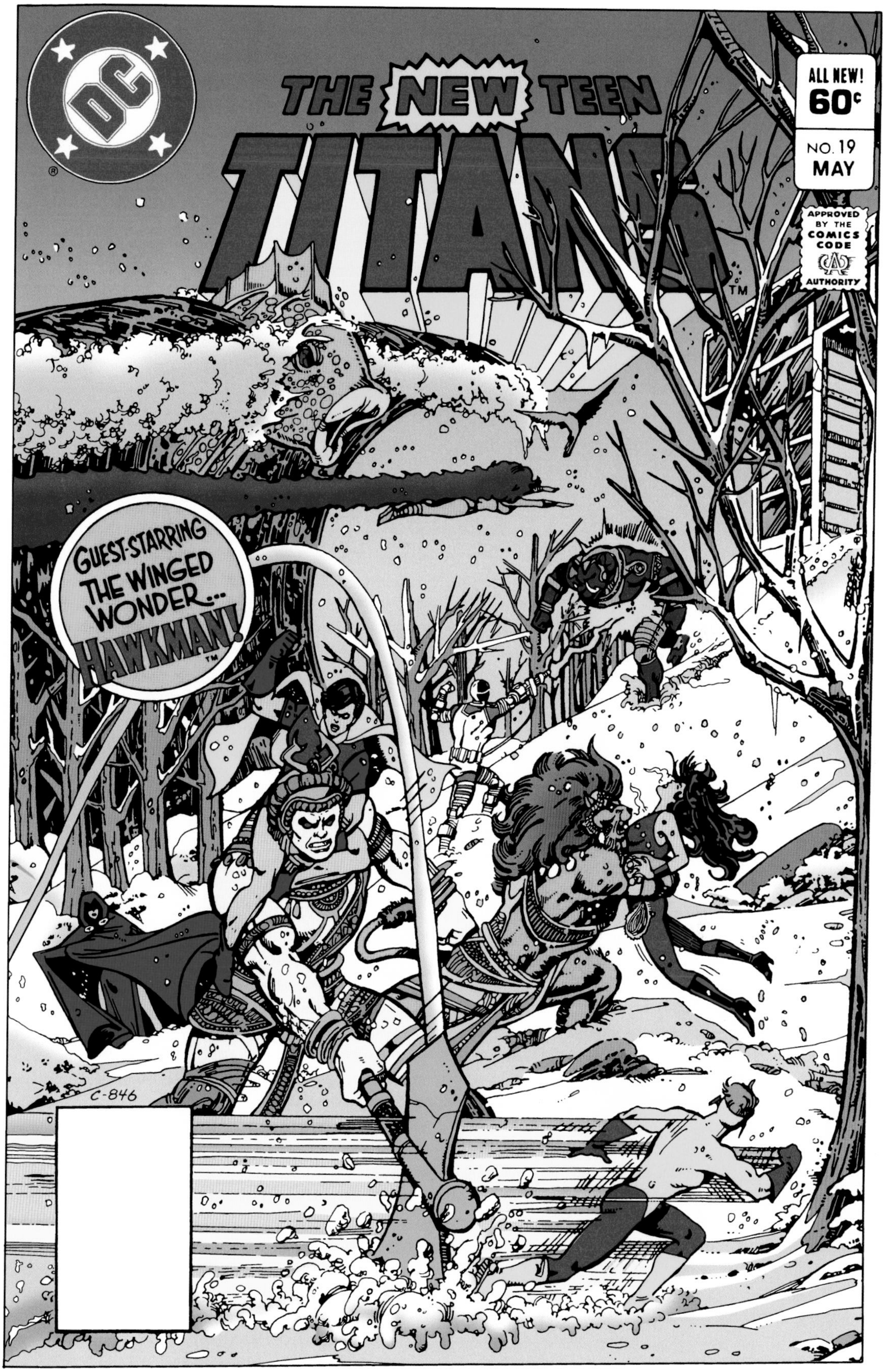
THE NEW TEEN
TITANS
ALL NEW! 60¢
NO. 19
MAY
APPROVED BY THE COMICS CODE AUTHORITY
GUEST-STARRING
THE WINGED
WONDER...
HAWKMAN!
C-846

THEY ARE THE *BEST* THERE IS: *THE CHANGELING,* SHAPE-SHIFTER SUPREME; *CYBORG,* HALF MAN / HALF ROBOT; *KID FLASH,* SUPER-SPEEDSTER; *RAVEN,* MISTRESS OF MAGIC; *ROBIN,* THE TEEN WONDER; *STARFIRE,* ALIEN POWERHOUSE; AND *WONDER GIRL,* THE AMAZING AMAZON! TOGETHER THEY ARE...

THE NEW TEEN TITANS.

CENTRAL PARK...

IT'S BEEN TWO MONTHS SINCE I'VE SPOKEN TO SARAH, AN' I STILL CAN'T BRING MYSELF TO GO DOWN THERE AN' *TALK.*

BEEN FEELIN' SO BLASTED *GUILTY* EVER SINCE THE TERMINATOR *KIDNAPPED* HER.

MAN, I HAVE NO RIGHT LETTIN' SOMEONE SO *INNOCENT* GET HURT JUST 'CAUSE SHE *KNOWS ME!*

MARV WOLFMAN · GEORGE PÉREZ
writer · co-creators · penciller
ROMEO TANGHAL
embellisher
JOHN COSTANZA
letterer
ADRIENNE ROY
colorist
LEN WEIN
editor

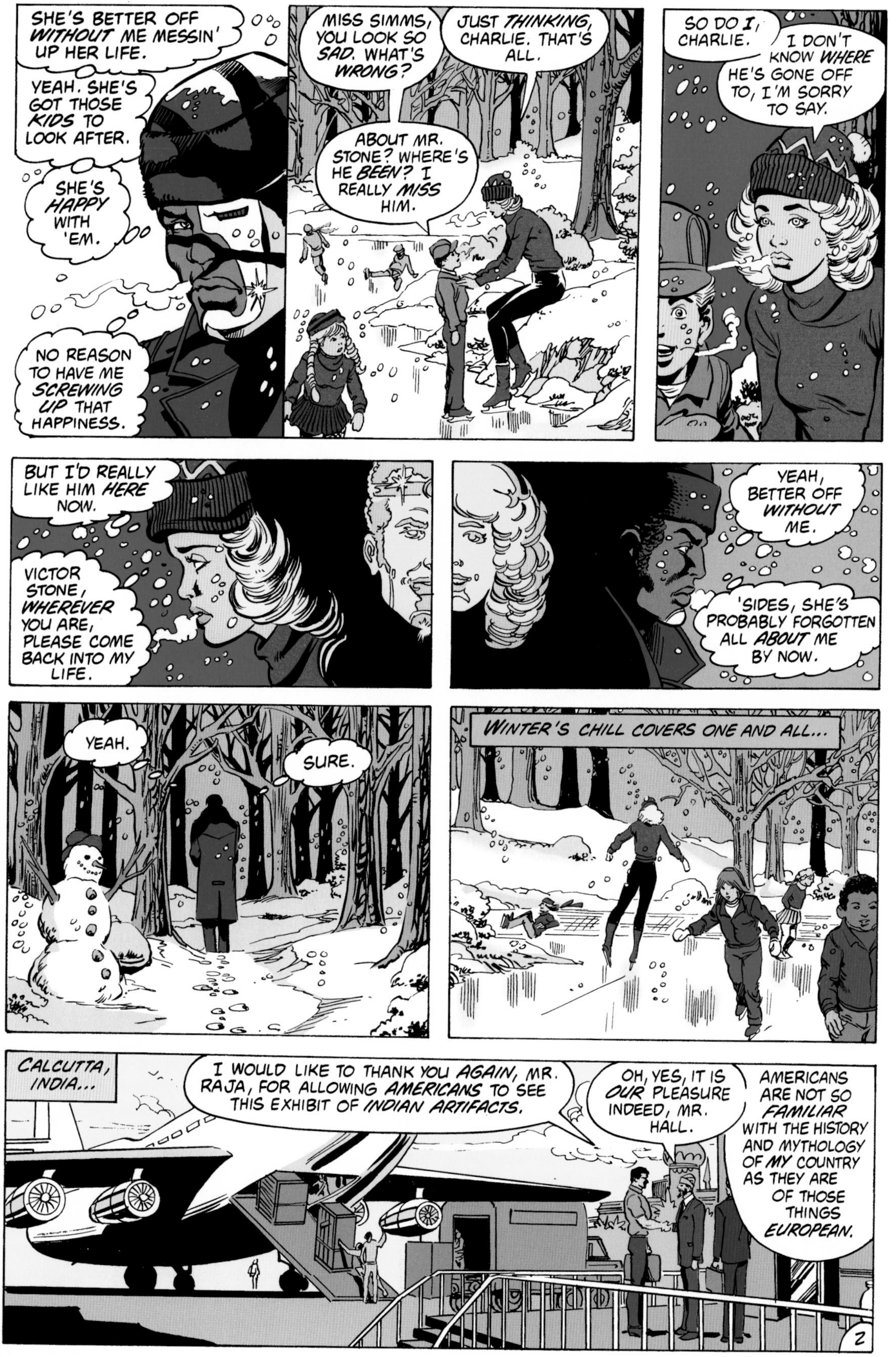
SHE'S BETTER OFF WITHOUT ME MESSIN' UP HER LIFE.
YEAH. SHE'S GOT THOSE KIDS TO LOOK AFTER.
SHE'S HAPPY WITH 'EM.
NO REASON TO HAVE ME SCREWING UP THAT HAPPINESS.
MISS SIMMS, YOU LOOK SO SAD. WHAT'S WRONG?
JUST THINKING, CHARLIE. THAT'S ALL.
ABOUT MR. STONE? WHERE'S HE BEEN? I REALLY MISS HIM.
SO DO I, CHARLIE.
I DON'T KNOW WHERE HE'S GONE OFF TO, I'M SORRY TO SAY.
BUT I'D REALLY LIKE HIM HERE NOW.
VICTOR STONE, WHEREVER YOU ARE, PLEASE COME BACK INTO MY LIFE.
YEAH, BETTER OFF WITHOUT ME.
'SIDES, SHE'S PROBABLY FORGOTTEN ALL ABOUT ME BY NOW.
YEAH.
SURE.
WINTER'S CHILL COVERS ONE AND ALL...
CALCUTTA, INDIA...
I WOULD LIKE TO THANK YOU AGAIN, MR. RAJA, FOR ALLOWING AMERICANS TO SEE THIS EXHIBIT OF INDIAN ARTIFACTS.
OH, YES, IT IS OUR PLEASURE INDEED, MR. HALL.
AMERICANS ARE NOT SO FAMILIAR WITH THE HISTORY AND MYTHOLOGY OF MY COUNTRY AS THEY ARE OF THOSE THINGS EUROPEAN.
2

OH, BUT I THINK THEY *WILL* BE WHEN WE'RE *DONE.* THE SHOW BEGINS IN NEW YORK, THEN MOVES TO CHICAGO, MIDWAY CITY, LOS ANGELES AND FINALLY WASHINGTON, D.C.

I BELIEVE MY PEOPLE WILL COME TO APPRECIATE THE *RICHNESS* OF YOUR COUNTRY.

CARTER HALL, CURATOR FOR THE MIDWAY CITY MUSEUM, TIREDLY SLUMPS INTO HIS CUSHIONED SEAT.

THE WORK HERE HAS BEEN LONG AND SOMETIMES FRUSTRATING, BUT HE HAS BEEN SUCCESSFUL...

...IN BOTH SETTING UP THIS NEW TRAVELLING EXHIBITION, AND IN TRYING TO FORGET THAT HIS WIFE SHIERA HAS SEEMINGLY ABANDONED HIM.

NEW YORK STATE CORRECTIONAL PRISON...

ONLY THE MEANEST, TOUGHEST, MOST SAVAGE CRIMINALS ARE SENT HERE.

SUPPOSEDLY THESE MEN WILL BE RELEASED IN TEN TO TWENTY YEARS WHEN THEY WILL NO LONGER SEEK A LIFE OF CRIME.

AND, IF YOU BELIEVE THAT, WE HAVE THIS BRIDGE IN BROOKLYN WE'RE JUST DYING TO SELL YOU!

HEY! YOU HEAR THAT *THE RIDDLER* STOLE FIVE MILLION BUCKS FROM RIGHT UNDER THE BATMAN'S NOSE?

THE RIDDLER?

THE RIDDLER?

THAT *DOES* IT! I'VE *HAD* IT!

THAT NO-TALENT, NO-POWERED CRETIN *SUCCEEDS...*

...WHILE *I,* WHOSE POWER IS SECOND ONLY TO *GREEN LANTERN'S,* HAVE *FAILED* IN MY EVERY CRIMINAL ATTEMPT!

WELL, NOW *DOCTOR LIGHT* IS *REALLY* MAD!

3

ALL MY LIFE I'VE *FAILED* AT EVERYTHING I'VE EVER *TRIED.*

NOBODY KNOWS WHAT UTTER *HUMILIATION* REALLY IS UNTIL SOMEONE WITH *MY* TALENT--

-- IS BESTED BY *THE ATOM,* NO LESS. LORD, THAT TOOK ME *MONTHS* TO LIVE DOWN.

BUT *NO MORE.* I WON'T ALLOW A MANIACAL *SIMPLETON* WHOSE RIDDLES EVEN "JOE MILLER" WOULD REJECT BEAT OUT *DOCTOR LIGHT!*

SUDDENLY, I HAVE A REASON TO *LIVE* AGAIN. A REASON TO SEEK OUT *SUCCESS.*

EH? *LIGHT?* WHAT IN BLAZES ARE YOU *DOING?*

GET *DOWN* FROM THERE, LIGHT!

CERTAINLY, MY GOOD FUZZ.

BY THE WAY, HAVE YOU PEOPLE PAID YOUR *ELECTRIC BILL* LATELY?

BECAUSE, SUDDENLY, *THIS* LIGHT IS *OUT!*

TA TA.

HUNH? WHERE'D HE GO? WHERE'D LIGHT *GO?*

OHH, THEY'RE GOING TO HAVE MY *HIDE.* FIRST THE *MIRROR MASTER* ESCAPES ME, NOW *THIS.*

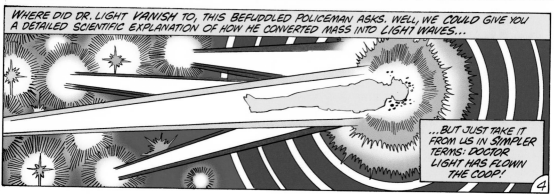

WHERE DID DR. LIGHT *VANISH* TO, THIS BEFUDDLED POLICEMAN ASKS. WELL, WE *COULD* GIVE YOU A DETAILED SCIENTIFIC EXPLANATION OF HOW HE CONVERTED MASS INTO *LIGHT* WAVES...

...BUT JUST TAKE IT FROM US IN *SIMPLER* TERMS: DOCTOR LIGHT HAS FLOWN THE *COOP!*

4

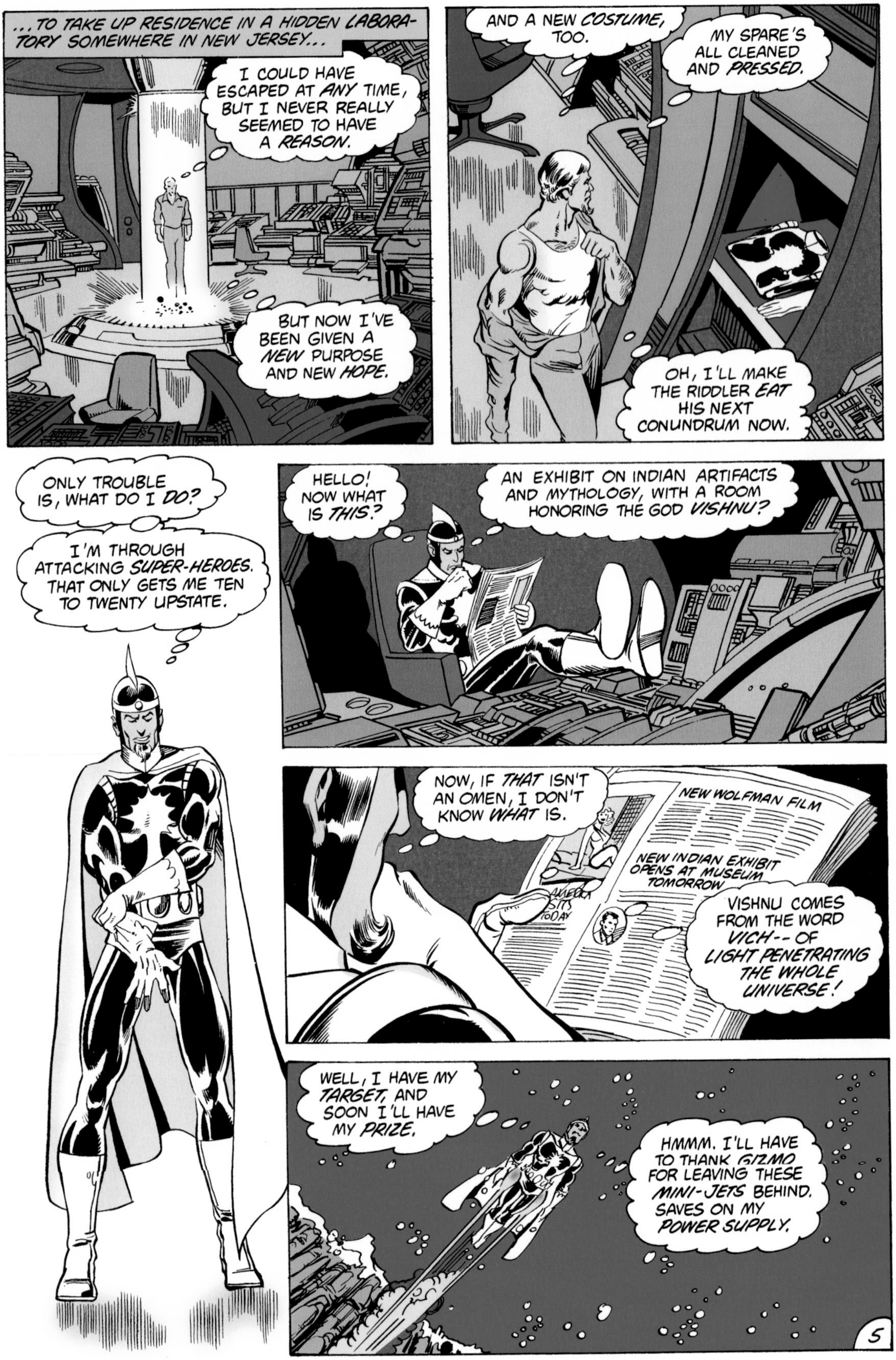
...TO TAKE UP RESIDENCE IN A HIDDEN LABORATORY SOMEWHERE IN NEW JERSEY...
I COULD HAVE ESCAPED AT ANY TIME, BUT I NEVER REALLY SEEMED TO HAVE A REASON.
BUT NOW I'VE BEEN GIVEN A NEW PURPOSE AND NEW HOPE.
AND A NEW COSTUME, TOO.
MY SPARE'S ALL CLEANED AND PRESSED.
OH, I'LL MAKE THE RIDDLER EAT HIS NEXT CONUNDRUM NOW.
ONLY TROUBLE IS, WHAT DO I DO?
I'M THROUGH ATTACKING SUPER-HEROES. THAT ONLY GETS ME TEN TO TWENTY UPSTATE.
HELLO! NOW WHAT IS THIS?
AN EXHIBIT ON INDIAN ARTIFACTS AND MYTHOLOGY, WITH A ROOM HONORING THE GOD VISHNU?
NOW, IF THAT ISN'T AN OMEN, I DON'T KNOW WHAT IS.
NEW WOLFMAN FILM
NEW INDIAN EXHIBIT OPENS AT MUSEUM TOMORROW
VISHNU COMES FROM THE WORD VICH-- OF LIGHT PENETRATING THE WHOLE UNIVERSE!
WELL, I HAVE MY TARGET, AND SOON I'LL HAVE MY PRIZE.
HMMM. I'LL HAVE TO THANK GIZMO FOR LEAVING THESE MINI-JETS BEHIND. SAVES ON MY POWER SUPPLY.
5

AND MEANWHILE, AT THE FAMED NEW YORK MUSEUM...

YOU'VE DONE A MONUMENTAL *JOB*, CARTER. YOU SHOULD BE QUITE *PROUD* OF THIS!

WELL, I'VE CERTAINLY WORKED MY *TAIL* OFF, WILLIS.

I JUST HOPE IT DRAWS A GOOD *CROWD*.

ESPECIALLY FOR *THIS*. IT'S QUITE AN *ENIGMA*, UNLIKE ANYTHING *ELSE* I'VE EVER SEEN.

THE STATUE IS OF *VISHNU* AND HIS *TEN AVATARS*--

--SUPPOSEDLY THE VARIOUS *FORMS* VISHNU TOOK ON HIS COMINGS TO EARTH.

BUT THOSE *CRYSTALS* HE'S HOLDING...

PERFECT CRYSTALS, WILLIS-- BEYOND THE *MANUFACTURING CAP-ABILITIES* OF THE TIME THIS STATUE WAS MADE.

WILLIS DARROW'S HAND REACHES TO *TOUCH* THE STRANGE STATUE, BUT...

YAHH! MAN, THAT GAVE ME A *SHOCK*. YOU HAVE THIS STATUE *WIRED*, CARTER?

NO. WE'RE USING *HEAT SENSORS* FOR SECURITY. IT HAS PROBABLY STORED UP *STATIC ELECTRIC-ITY*...

...BUT I'LL CHECK IT OUT AGAIN BEFORE WE OPEN.

YES, CARTER, I FEEL THIS WILL BE QUITE A *FEATHER* IN YOUR ALREADY-CROWDED BONNET.

A SIMPLY *REMARKABLE* EXHIBIT. 6

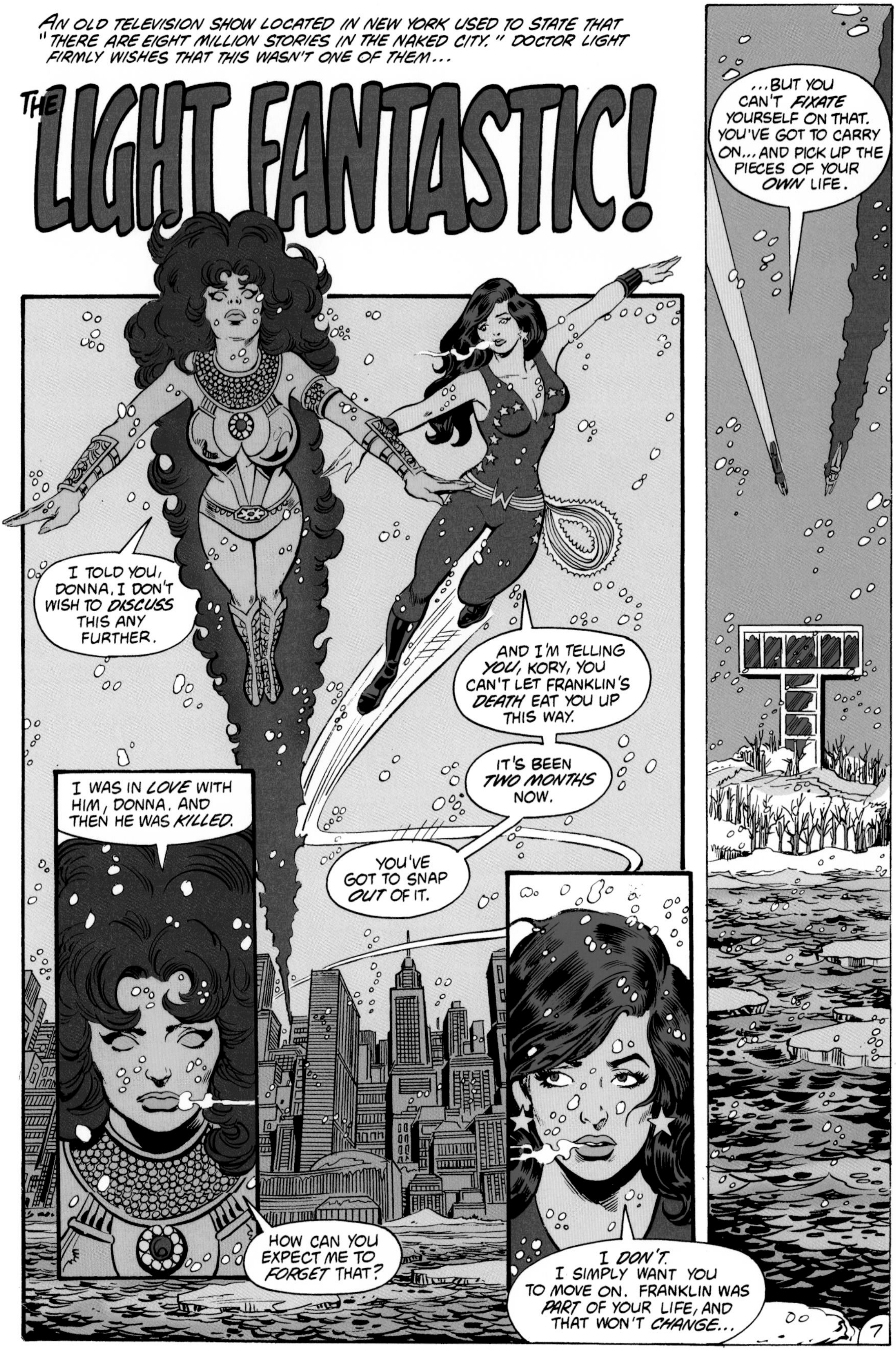
AN OLD TELEVISION SHOW LOCATED IN NEW YORK USED TO STATE THAT "THERE ARE EIGHT MILLION STORIES IN THE NAKED CITY." DOCTOR LIGHT FIRMLY WISHES THAT THIS WASN'T ONE OF THEM...
THE LIGHT FANTASTIC!
I TOLD YOU, DONNA. I DON'T WISH TO DISCUSS THIS ANY FURTHER.
AND I'M TELLING YOU, KORY. YOU CAN'T LET FRANKLIN'S DEATH EAT YOU UP THIS WAY.
IT'S BEEN TWO MONTHS NOW.
YOU'VE GOT TO SNAP OUT OF IT.
I WAS IN LOVE WITH HIM, DONNA. AND THEN HE WAS KILLED.
HOW CAN YOU EXPECT ME TO FORGET THAT?
I DON'T. I SIMPLY WANT YOU TO MOVE ON. FRANKLIN WAS PART OF YOUR LIFE, AND THAT WON'T CHANGE...
...BUT YOU CAN'T FIXATE YOURSELF ON THAT. YOU'VE GOT TO CARRY ON... AND PICK UP THE PIECES OF YOUR OWN LIFE.
7

BUT I TRULY *LOVED* HIM. I WANTED TO *MARRY* HIM, AND THEN...THEN... *X'HAL!* I REALLY WANTED TO *DESTROY* HIS KILLER, DONNA.

I CAN *UNDERSTAND* THAT, KORY. BUT IF YOU DON'T *DWELL* ON IT, THAT WILL *PASS.*

YOU'VE GOT TO LET YOURSELF *REACH OUT* AGAIN... ALLOW YOUR- SELF TO *LAUGH* WHEN THERE'S SOMETHING TO LAUGH ABOUT.

AND THERE WILL *BE* THOSE THINGS, KORY. ABSURD LITTLE *SILLY* THINGS.

I WANTED TO SO *BADLY.* I'M SORRY, DONNA, BUT CAN'T YOU SEE THAT I JUST DON'T FEEL *HAPPY* ANY LONGER?

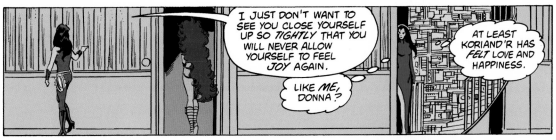

I JUST DON'T WANT TO SEE YOU CLOSE YOURSELF UP SO *TIGHTLY* THAT YOU WILL NEVER ALLOW YOURSELF TO FEEL *JOY* AGAIN.

LIKE *ME,* DONNA?

AT LEAST KORIAND'R HAS *FELT* LOVE AND HAPPINESS.

STARFIRE HAS *KNOWN* WHAT IT IS LIKE TO CARE AND BE CARED FOR.

SHE HAS EXPERIENCED ALL THOSE EMOTIONS WHICH HAVE BEEN *DENIED* ME.

I *HATE* THE TEMPLE AZARATH FOR WHAT THEY DID TO ME.

INSISTING ON *PERFECTION...* REFUSING TO CONDONE *EMOTION...*

RICHARD?

RAVEN, HI, WHAT'S UP? HOW *ARE* YOU?

UHH. ROBIN... EVERYTHING IS *FINE* WITH ME.

REALLY, RAVEN? YOU DON'T *LOOK* FINE.

AND IT DOESN'T TAKE THE WORLD'S GREATEST *DETECTIVE* TO FIGURE OUT THAT YOU'RE *BOTHERED.*

ROBIN, I WOULD PREFER NOT TO *DISCUSS* THIS.

I WOULD RATHER BE *ALONE* NOW.

8

OH, NO YOU *DON'T.* DON'T SLINK OFF AGAIN, RAVEN.

I'VE BEEN *WATCHING* YOU LATELY. PLEASE, TELL ME WHAT'S *WRONG.*

I'M YOUR *FRIEND.*

FRIEND.?

YES, RICHARD, YOU *ARE* A FRIEND. AND THAT IS WHY I WILL *SPARE* YOU MY PROBLEMS.

REST *WELL,* FRIEND... REST...

UHHHHH

YOU WILL *AWAKEN* ONLY AFTER I AM...

GONE! SHE DID IT *AGAIN.* SHE SLIPPED AWAY.

BLAST IT. ALL I WANTED TO *DO* WAS--

...HELP MYSELF TO THOSE INVALUABLE *VISHNU STATUES,* THEY'RE GOLD, PLATINUM, SILVER... SET WITH PRECIOUS STONES.

THE RIDDLER STOLE *FIVE MILLION.* DOCTOR LIGHT WILL STEAL *FIVE TIMES* THAT.

BTAMMM

AND NOW--LIGHT COMES IN MANY FORMS--INCLUDING ONE REFERRED TO AS *LIGHT AMPLIFICATION THROUGH STIMULATED EMISSION OF RADIATION--* OR *LASER* FOR SHORT.

EXPLOSION?

THAT CAME FROM THE WING WITH THE *INDIAN EXHIBIT.*

CARTER HALL

CARTER HALL RACES THROUGH THE MUSEUM...

9

UNTIL...

OF ALL THE UNEXPECTED...

DOCTOR LIGHT--?

NO TIME TO CALL THE *POLICE.* BESIDES, THEY'D BE *HELPLESS* AGAINST HIS POWER.

FORTUNATELY, I'M *NOT!*

AH, THIS IS A *SNAP.* I DOWN ONE STUPID GUARD AND THESE TREASURES ARE *MINE* FOR THE PICKING.

YES, INDEED. I'VE BEEN MAKING A *MISTAKE* ALL THIS TIME IN TRYING TO CHALLENGE *SUPER-HEROES.*

I SHOULD HAVE BEEN CONTENT WITH MERELY BEING A *THIEF!*

YOU SHOULD HAVE BEEN CONTENT REMAINING *BEHIND BARS,* LIGHT.

WHAT...?

BECAUSE THAT WOULD HAVE SAVED ME THE TROUBLE OF *RE-TURNING* YOU THERE.

OH, NO... NO!

HAWKMAN?!? WHY HIM? WHY *HIM?*

10

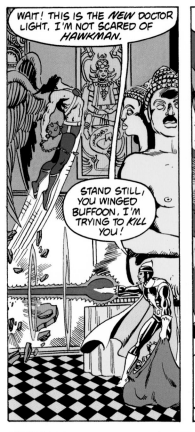

WAIT! THIS IS THE *NEW* DOCTOR LIGHT, I'M NOT SCARED OF *HAWKMAN.*

STAND STILL, YOU WINGED BUFFOON, I'M TRYING TO *KILL* YOU!

YOU'RE *ALWAYS* TRYING, LIGHT--

--FORTUNATELY, YOU NEVER *SUCCEED!*

OH, MY FEATHERED FRIEND, THAT WAS *BEFORE.* THIS TIME I *SHALL* SUCCEED.

A HIGHLY CONCENTRATED DOSE OF *STAR-LIGHT* SHOULD PLUCK YOUR FEATHERS.'

AND WITH *YOU* DEAD, I CAN GO ON WITH MY *TREASURE* HUNT.

BUT, AS USUAL, DR. LIGHT'S PLANS GO ASTRAY...

...AS HIS BEAMS FILTER THROUGH CENTURIES-OLD CRYSTAL--

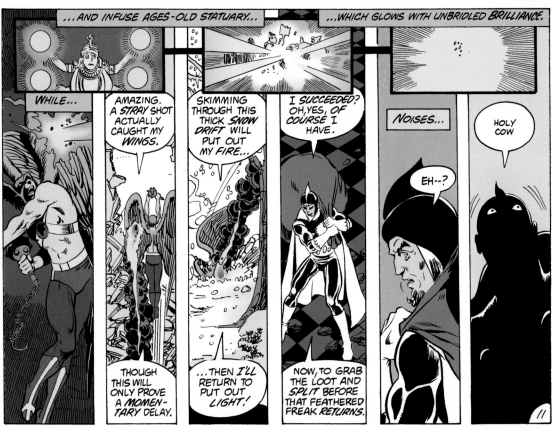

...AND INFUSE AGES-OLD STATUARY...

...WHICH GLOWS WITH UNBRIDLED BRILLIANCE.

WHILE...

AMAZING. A *STRAY* SHOT ACTUALLY CAUGHT MY *WINGS.*

THOUGH THIS WILL ONLY PROVE A *MOMEN-TARY* DELAY.

SKIMMING THROUGH THIS THICK *SNOW DRIFT* WILL PUT OUT MY *FIRE...*

...THEN I'LL RETURN TO PUT OUT *LIGHT!*

I *SUCCEEDED?* OH, YES, OF *COURSE* I HAVE.

NOW, TO GRAB THE LOOT AND *SPLIT* BEFORE THAT FEATHERED FREAK *RETURNS.*

NOISES...

EH--?

HOLY COW

11

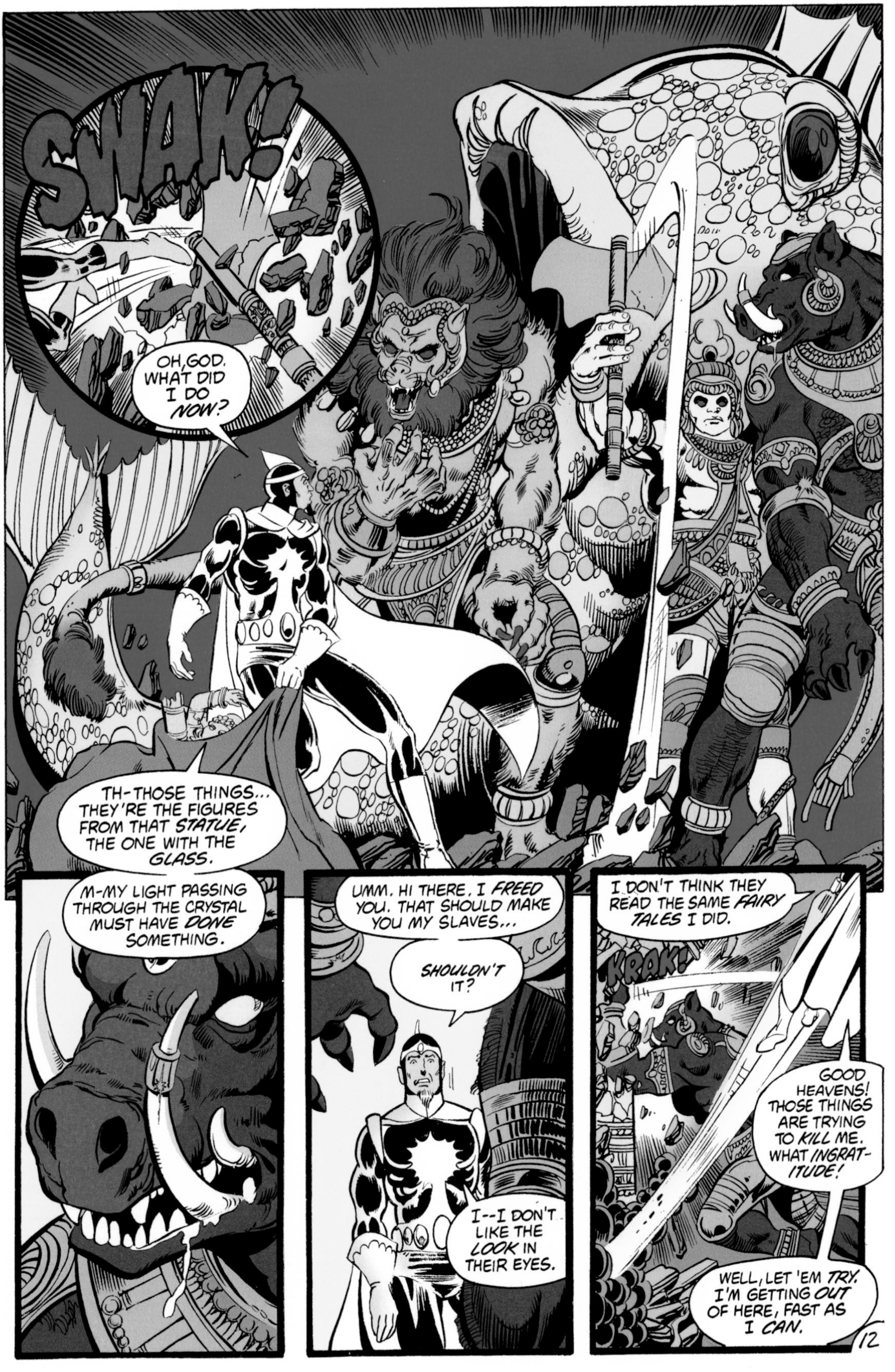
SWAK!
OH, GOD. WHAT DID I DO NOW?
TH-THOSE THINGS... THEY'RE THE FIGURES FROM THAT STATUE, THE ONE WITH THE GLASS.
M-MY LIGHT PASSING THROUGH THE CRYSTAL MUST HAVE DONE SOMETHING.
UMM. HI THERE. I FREED YOU. THAT SHOULD MAKE YOU MY SLAVES...
SHOULDN'T IT?
I--I DON'T LIKE THE LOOK IN THEIR EYES.
I DON'T THINK THEY READ THE SAME FAIRY TALES I DID.
KRAK!
GOOD HEAVENS! THOSE THINGS ARE TRYING TO KILL ME. WHAT INGRATITUDE!
WELL, LET 'EM TRY. I'M GETTING OUT OF HERE, FAST AS I CAN.
12

I GUESS THEY WERE CLOSER TO THE LEGENDS OF *KING TUT*--REACHING OUT TO *KILL* THOSE WHO UNCOVERED HIS TOMB.

WELL, UNLIKE LORD CARNARVAN'S ILL-FATED EXPEDITION, I'VE GOT CERTAIN SPECIAL *POWERS!*

THEY CAN'T HURT DOCTOR LI--

TH-THEY'RE *FOLLOWING* ME!

WHAT DO I DO *NOW?*

HAWKMAN *STILL* HASN'T COME BACK, AND I DOUBT HE COULD *STOP* THOSE THINGS EVEN IF HE DID!

BESIDES, A *LIGHT BULB* SUDDENLY WENT ON IN MY HEAD. I'VE GOT A *BRAINSTORM.*

I'LL BET THE *TITANS* COULD STOP THEM, AND IF *THEY* FAIL... SO WHAT DO *I* CARE IF *THEY'RE* KILLED, TOO?

HMMM. MAYBE I CAN LEAD THOSE CREATURES ON TO DESTROY THE *J.L.A.* AS WELL.

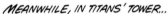

MEANWHILE, IN TITANS' TOWER...

YOU REALLY SHOULD'A *SEEN* HER, VIC. SHE WAS THIS MOUSY-LOOKING *LIBRARIAN*...

THEN SHE LET DOWN HER *HAIR*, TOOK OFF HER *GLASSES*...

AND SHE WAS *STILL* A MOUSY-LOOKING LIBRARIAN?

YEAH. SO I DATED HER *SISTER.* WOTTA *DISH.*

UH, OH, LOGAN... SOMETHING COMIN' THIS WAY, AND *FAST.*

I'M ALERTIN' THE *OTHERS.*

CYBORG'S STEEL-COVERED FINGER SWEEPS ACROSS THE COMPUTER CONTROL BOARD WITH THE EASE OF A PRACTICED PROFESSIONAL...

ALERT

13

AND, IN ROOMS ALL ACROSS TITANS' TOWER...

INTRUDER ALARM? OUR ENEMIES NEVER GIVE US A MOMENT'S *PEACE.*

ROBIN!

OH, AND I WAS HAVING SUCH A *GOOD* DREAM FOR A CHANGE.

WHY MUST I BE DISTURBED *NOW?*

STARFIRE!

MY MEDITATION IS BROKEN *AGAIN!*

ONCE MORE *VIOLENCE* DISTURBS MY INNER PEACE.

RAVEN!

OH, WELL...ONE CHAPTER TO GO.

I'LL FIND OUT WHO *KILLED* THE BUTLER SOME OTHER TIME.

WONDER GIRL!

THANK GOODNESS CLASS WAS JUST *OVER.* ONLY TOOK THREE SECONDS TO CROSS *TWO THOUSAND MILES.*

KID FLASH!

BTRAMM!

WHEW! I *MADE* IT. I'M *IN.*

BUT WHERE ARE THE *TITANS?*

IF THEY'RE OUT SAVING THE WORLD, I'M *DONE* FOR.

WE'RE *HERE,* CREEP, AN' YOU'RE *STILL* DONE FER!

SWAK

WAIT A SECOND! I'M NOT HERE TO *FIGHT* YOU!

BLAMMM

RIGHT! YOU ALWAYS GO SMASHIN' DOWN *WALLS* WHEN YOU COME VISITIN'. RIGHT?

14

LIGHT? YOU JERK! YOU COULDN'T DEFEAT US WITH YOUR *FEARSOME FIVE*... WHY ATTACK US *ALONE?*

I DIDN'T. I *DIDN'T*, I *SWEAR* I DIDN'T.

I CAME HERE FOR *HELP*. PLEASE, *LISTEN TO ME.*

FORGET IT, LIGHT, YOU'D SELL OUT YOUR OWN *MOTHER* FOR A *NICKEL.*

NO I *WOULDN'T*. NOT FOR A *NICKEL*. PLEASE, THEY'RE *AFTER* ME.

WELL, WHOEVER *'THEY'* ARE, THEY PROBABLY HAVE A GOOD *REASON!*

NO, *NO*-- JUST LOOK *OUTSIDE*. YOU'LL SEE WHAT I *MEAN.*

I DO NOT SENSE ANY *LIES*, ROBIN. HE IS GENUINELY *TERRIFIED.*

WELL, FROM THE *J.L.A.* RECORDS WE'VE GONE OVER, LIGHT'S ALWAYS RUNNING *SCARED.*

STILL, IT DOESN'T HURT TO *CHECK*, CHANGELING...?

YEAH, YEAH, I *KNOW*. DO A *RECON JOB*, RIGHT?

YOU NEVER SEND *WONDY*. NEVER SEND *STARFIRE*. ALWAYS THE *CHANGELING.*

I HATE THIS!

HURRY, GAR!

WHY DON'T WE RECRUIT SOME GOOFY *FOURTEEN-YEAR-OLD* TO DO THIS SORTA STUFF?

BAH!

GRUMBLING, THE CHANGELING *LEAVES*--

--ONLY TO *RETURN* A MOMENT LATER, WHEN...

UH... GUYS, YOU THINK I CAN *TRANSFER* MY MEMBER-SHIP TO *"THE LEGION OF SUPER-HEROES"*-- *FAST?*

YOU'RE NOT *GETTIN' ME* TO TACKLE WHAT'S OUT THERE...

15

...'CAUSE IT'S UGLY ENOUGH TO MAKE *KING KONG* LOOK LIKE A MEMBER OF *"THE ZOO CREW"!*

LIGHT! YOU SAID THESE THINGS *ATTACKED* YOU IN THE *MUSEUM?* ARE THEY FROM THE *VISHNU* COLLECTION?

UH, YEAH...

YOU *KNOW* WHAT THOSE THINGS ARE, ROBIN?

I *RECOGNIZED* THEM... THEY'RE FORMS OF *VISHNU-VARAHA,* THE WILD BULL... *NARASIMHA,* THE MAN-LION... *PARASURAMA,* OR *RAMA-WITH-THE-AXE...*

...AND *MATSYA,* THE FISH, WHOSE STORY BEARS AN AMAZING SIMILARITY TO THE LEGENDS OF NOAH.

WHATEVER THEY ARE, I DON'T *LIKE* 'EM.

COME ON, LIGHT-- WHAT DID YOU *DO* TO THEM?

N-NOTHING, *REALLY* I DIDN'T.

THEY JUST WANT TO *KILL* ME.

THEY'RE *REMARKABLY GOOD JUDGES* OF *CHARACTER.*

ONLY THEY'RE NOT VERY *PARTICULAR* ABOUT WHO ALSO GETS KILLED ALONG *WITH* YOU.

KRASH!

I'M NOT *WAITING* HERE ANY LONGER, ROBIN.

THOSE THINGS HAVE GOT TO BE *STOPPED.*

16

PLEASE, DON'T LET THEM GET *NEAR* ME. THEY'LL *KILL* ME.

YOU SHOULD HAVE CONSIDERED THIS *BEFORE* YOU SET THEM FREE, LIGHT.

LISTEN TO ME, TITANS. YOU'RE *HEROES*... YOU'RE SUPPOSED TO *SAVE* PEOPLE LIKE ME.

WILL SOMEONE PUT A *CORK* IN HIM? I'M TRYING TO *CONCENTRATE*.

HE WILL BE *CALM*, ROBIN-- THOUGH YOU *MAY REGRET* THIS LATER.

HE'D BE MORE OF A *HINDRANCE* THAN A HELP, RAVEN.

HIS POWERS COULD PROVE *USEFUL* IN STOPPING THOSE GODS.

NOW, EVERYONE *OUTSIDE*. WE'VE GOT TO PROVIDE *COVER* FOR STARFIRE.

IT SEEMS, HOWEVER, THAT THE ALIEN PRINCESS FROM TAMARAN IS QUITE CAPABLE OF HANDLING HERSELF...

IT TAKES ALL MY POWER TO EVEN *BUDGE* THESE THINGS.

AND EVEN THEN, THEY DON'T SEEM TO BE *HURT* ANY.

I THINK I'D BE MORE *WORRIED* IF THESE WEREN'T JUST *ANIMATED STATUES* OF INDIAN GODS...

THEY CAN'T POSSIBLY MOVE AS *QUICKLY* AS--

FLASH-- *MOVE* IT!

OUR LION-FRIEND HERE WAS READY TO PUT THE *BITE* ON YOU.

SMAK!

17

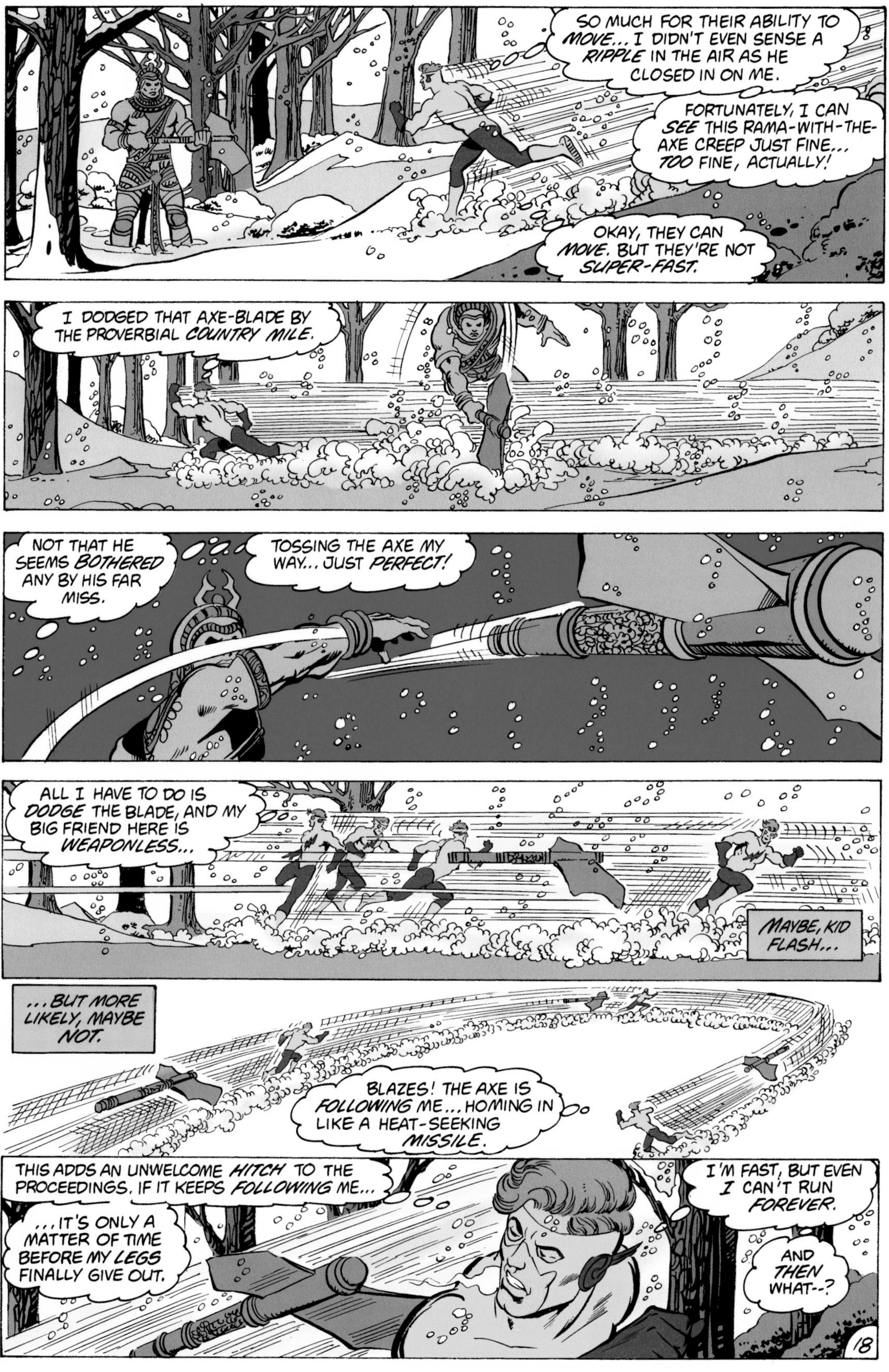
SO MUCH FOR THEIR ABILITY TO MOVE... I DIDN'T EVEN SENSE A RIPPLE IN THE AIR AS HE CLOSED IN ON ME.
FORTUNATELY, I CAN SEE THIS RAMA-WITH-THE-AXE CREEP JUST FINE... TOO FINE, ACTUALLY!
OKAY, THEY CAN MOVE. BUT THEY'RE NOT SUPER-FAST.
I DODGED THAT AXE-BLADE BY THE PROVERBIAL COUNTRY MILE.
NOT THAT HE SEEMS BOTHERED ANY BY HIS FAR MISS.
TOSSING THE AXE MY WAY... JUST PERFECT!
ALL I HAVE TO DO IS DODGE THE BLADE, AND MY BIG FRIEND HERE IS WEAPONLESS...
MAYBE, KID FLASH...
...BUT MORE LIKELY, MAYBE NOT.
BLAZES! THE AXE IS FOLLOWING ME... HOMING IN LIKE A HEAT-SEEKING MISSILE.
THIS ADDS AN UNWELCOME HITCH TO THE PROCEEDINGS. IF IT KEEPS FOLLOWING ME...
...IT'S ONLY A MATTER OF TIME BEFORE MY LEGS FINALLY GIVE OUT.
I'M FAST, BUT EVEN I CAN'T RUN FOREVER.
AND THEN WHAT--?
18

X'HAL! THIS MAN-BOAR WON'T STAY DOWN.

MY STARBOLTS MERELY SERVE TO MAKE IT MADDER THAN BEFORE.

HOLD ON, GOLDIE, WHILE I LOOSEN A LITTLE SCREW...

...AN' GIVE YOU A HELPIN' HAND!

HA! ROY ROGERS DOESN'T HAVE ANYTHING ON 'HOPALONG' CYBORG HERE.

GOT 'IM ON MY FIRST TOSS.

ONLY QUESTION NOW IS-- WHAT DO I DO WITH 'IM?

UH-OH, DONNA NEEDS MY HELP.

HEY, GOLDIE-- WHAT DO I NEED? CHOPPED LIVER?

GOT ME TOO TIGHT TO SQUEEZE FREE, BUT THAT'S ALL RIGHT.

JUST HAVING SOME TROUBLE SHIFTING MY WEIGHT...

...TO ACHIEVE ENOUGH LEVERAGE FOR MY LEGS TO KICK MY WAY FREE.

BUT, BEFORE THE AMAZON WARRIOR CAN ACT...

SKREEEEEE

DID IT, STARFIRE ...AND BEAUTIFULLY, TOO.

YOU STUNG HIM JUST ENOUGH TO MAKE HIM LOOSEN HIS GRIP.

NOW, TOGETHER, PERHAPS WE CAN LAY HIM OUT COLD!

SPLAMM

19

THIS IS GETTING *RIDICULOUS.*

I'M GETTING EXHAUSTED, BUT THAT AXE IS *GAINING* SPEED WITH EVERY PASSING SECOND.

WALLACE, LEAD HIM *THIS* WAY.

I CAN *ENVELOP* THAT WEAPON WITHIN THE FOLDS OF MY *SOUL-SELF.*

THEN SHE'S *YOUR* BABY, RAVEN...

...AND *THANKS.*

BUT...

NO! I CANNOT *DO* IT!

PAIN...TERRIBLE *PAIN* SHOOTING THROUGH ME...

...HAVE TO *LET GO*...LET THE AXE *LEAVE* ME BEFORE IT TEARS ME APART.

THE AXE RETURNED TO HIS *HAND.*

HOW DO I STOP HIM BEFORE HE THROWS IT *AGAIN?*

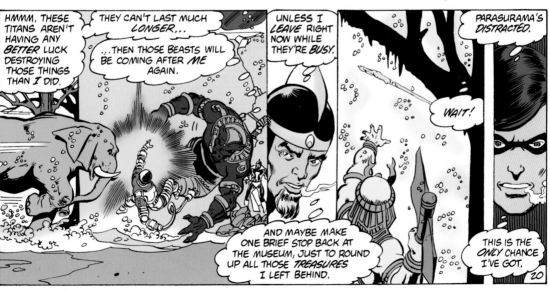

HMMM, THESE TITANS AREN'T HAVING ANY *BETTER* LUCK DESTROYING THOSE THINGS THAN *I* DID.

THEY CAN'T LAST MUCH *LONGER*...

...THEN THOSE BEASTS WILL BE COMING AFTER *ME* AGAIN.

UNLESS I *LEAVE* RIGHT NOW WHILE THEY'RE *BUSY.*

PARASURAMA'S *DISTRACTED.*

WAIT!

THIS IS THE *ONLY* CHANCE I'VE GOT.

AND MAYBE MAKE ONE BRIEF STOP BACK AT THE MUSEUM, JUST TO ROUND UP ALL THOSE *TREASURES* I LEFT BEHIND.

20

IF I CAN JUST *SLOW HIM DOWN* UNTIL THE OTHERS COME...

UNHH. GRABBING HIM IS LIKE GRABBING SLICK *STONE.* TOO HARD TO GET A GOOD HAND-HOLD.

ROBIN, *WATCH OUT!* HE'S GONNA...

HE'S ALREADY *DONE* IT, KID FLASH, BUT DON'T *WORRY...*

I'M AN *ACROBAT.* I'VE TAKEN *WORSE* FALLS THAN THIS.

OH, NO...*NO!* I FORGOT ALL ABOUT MATSYA...EH?

HAWKMAN?

SORRY FOR THE *DELAY.* IT TOOK *LONGER* TO PUT OUT MY WING-FIRE THAN I HAD EXPECTED.

KID FLASH, I NEED YOU OVER *HERE...* YOU'RE THE ONLY ONE WHO CAN *HELP* US NOW.

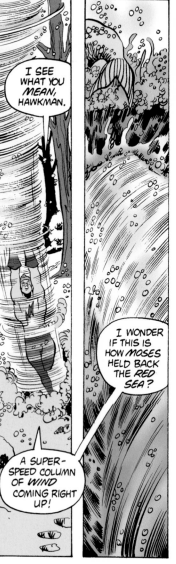

I SEE WHAT YOU *MEAN,* HAWKMAN.

I WONDER IF THIS IS HOW *MOSES* HELD BACK THE *RED SEA?*

A SUPER-SPEED COLUMN OF *WIND* COMING RIGHT UP!

ROBIN, WHERE'S *DOCTOR LIGHT?* THOSE THINGS WERE *AFTER* HIM.

LIGHT? HE TOOK OFF, BUT I DON'T KNOW *WHERE TO.*

SOMETHING TELLS ME *I* DO.

TITANS! CEASE WHAT YOU'RE DOING...

WE'RE *MOVING OUT!*

AS FOR WHERE LIGHT HAS ABSCONDED TO...

AH, THIS IS THE LIFE. THE *TITANS* ARE OUT THERE, FIGHTING AND DYING FOR *YOURS TRULY...*

21

...WHILE I'M TAKING MY SWEET TIME IN ADDING MILLIONS TO MY BANKROLL.
SORRY, LIGHT-- BUT YOU'RE DEPOSITING YOUR MONEY RIGHT BACK IN AGAIN.
ROBIN?
THUNK!
HMM. THAT MEANS MY GIANT-SIZED SPARRING PARTNERS ARE EITHER DEFEATED OR WILL BE COMING AFTER ME AGAIN.
AND THAT MEANS I HAVEN'T TIME TO WASTE ON-- WHAT? YOU AVOIDED MY LIGHT BLASTS?
C'MON, LIGHT, WHEN ARE YOU EVER GOING TO REALIZE YOU'RE A LOSER?
GIVE UP THE FIGHT AND HELP US STOP THOSE LIVING STATUES.
GIVE UP MY TREASURE TOO? NO WAY, KID.
BESIDES, WITH MY TERRIBLE POWER...
...YOU SHOULD BE A HECKUVA LOT BETTER THAN YOU ARE!
THOOM
IT'S OVER, LIGHT... SERIOUSLY OVER FOR YOU!
NOW HELP US, OR I SWEAR WE'LL LEAVE YOU TO THOSE STATUES.
AND YOU KNOW WHAT THEY'LL DO TO YOU.
YOU WOULDN'T DARE.
I WOULDN'T, WOULD I? WE'LL JUST SEE ABOUT THAT--
--SO MAKE UP YOUR MIND... REAL FAST.
HAWKMAN?
22

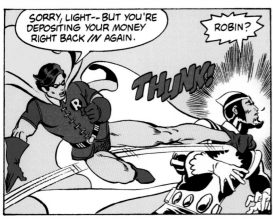

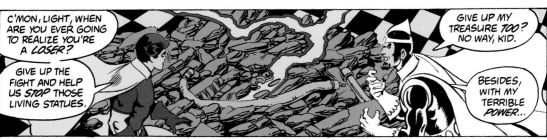

THEY'RE RIGHT *BEHIND* US, ROBIN. AND THESE ARE THE *LENSES* LIGHT USED TO BRING THEM TO LIFE.

IF WE CAN PERHAPS SEND *ANOTHER* BEAM...

HE FOCUSED SOME SORT OF *BEAM* THROUGH THEM...

YOU *HEARD* HIM, LIGHT. ARE YOU *COOPERATING*?

I--I CAN'T.

SO *HELP* ME, LIGHT...

I'M TELLING YOU, I *CAN'T*. WHEN YOU *PUNCHED* ME, YOU BROKE THE *POWER CIRCUITRY* IN MY COSTUME.

THEN THERE'S NO OTHER *HOPE*. WE *NEED* HIS POWER.

WE HAVE OUR *OWN* POWER, HAWKMAN.

WE DON'T NEED *CRYSTALS*.

HATE TO BREAK UP THE FUN, GUYS... BUT WE'VE GOT FOUR MEAN-LOOKING *VISITORS* JUST OUTSIDE.

IF YOU DON'T *WANT* 'EM...

...DO SOMETHING, REAL *QUICK*.

TOO LATE.

HURRY UP, LIGHT-- WHAT KIND OF *ENERGY* DID YOU USE?

CAN WE JURY-RIG A *SUBSTITUTE*?

I--I USED *SOLAR POWER*, SIMPLE *SUN-RAYS*.

BINGO!

STARFIRE--?

ALL RIGHT, ROBIN. I'VE *GOT* THEM.

AND I KNOW WHAT TO *DO*... BUT I STILL THINK WE DON'T *NEED* THESE CRYSTALS. 23

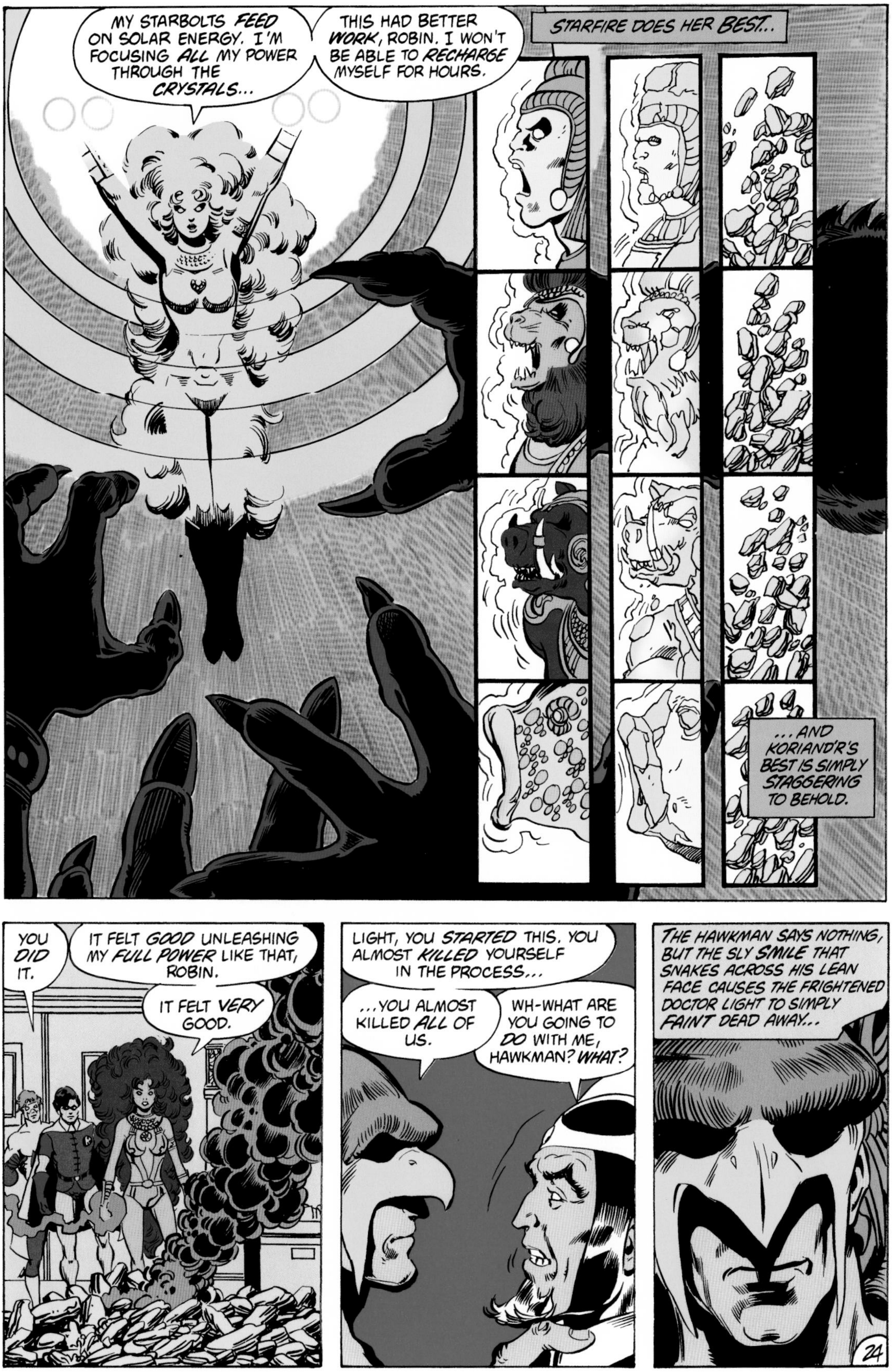
MY STARBOLTS FEED ON SOLAR ENERGY. I'M FOCUSING ALL MY POWER THROUGH THE CRYSTALS...
THIS HAD BETTER WORK, ROBIN. I WON'T BE ABLE TO RECHARGE MYSELF FOR HOURS.
STARFIRE DOES HER BEST...
...AND KORIAND'R'S BEST IS SIMPLY STAGGERING TO BEHOLD.
YOU DID IT.
IT FELT GOOD UNLEASHING MY FULL POWER LIKE THAT, ROBIN.
IT FELT VERY GOOD.
LIGHT, YOU STARTED THIS. YOU ALMOST KILLED YOURSELF IN THE PROCESS...
...YOU ALMOST KILLED ALL OF US.
WH-WHAT ARE YOU GOING TO DO WITH ME, HAWKMAN? WHAT?
THE HAWKMAN SAYS NOTHING, BUT THE SLY SMILE THAT SNAKES ACROSS HIS LEAN FACE CAUSES THE FRIGHTENED DOCTOR LIGHT TO SIMPLY FAINT DEAD AWAY...
24

EPILOGUE ONE

NEW YORK STATE CORRECTIONAL PRISON...

FOLLOWING AN ALREADY TOO FAMILIAR ROUTINE, DOCTOR LIGHT IS QUICKLY BOOKED AND PROCESSED...

WELCOME *BACK,* LIGHT.

GRUMBLE.

BY THE WAY, LIGHT, DID YOU HEAR THE LATEST ABOUT *THE RIDDLER?*

I DON'T WANT TO *HEAR* ABOUT THAT CRETIN AGAIN. DO YOU *UNDERSTAND* THAT?

I *HATE* HIS NAME! I *HATE* HIM!

THEN YOU'LL JUST *LOVE* THIS, LIGHT.

THE BATMAN *CAPTURED* HIM LAST NIGHT.

HE'S BACK SERVING *TEN-TO-TWENTY* IN GOTHAM STATE PEN.

THE RIDDLER WAS *CAUGHT?*

HE'S SERVING *TIME?*

MAYBE THIS WASN'T SUCH A *BAD* DAY AFTER ALL.

EPILOGUE TWO

THE APARTMENT OF TERRY LONG...

BING BONG

DONNA?

IS THAT *YOU,* HONEY?

MAN, AM I GLAD *YOU* SHOWED UP TONIGHT. I WAS--

OH--?

TERRY LONG? I AM REALLY SORRY TO *BOTHER* YOU, TERRY...

...BUT MY NAME'S *SARAH SIMMS*...

...AND I REALLY NEED YOUR *HELP.*

25

NEXT ISSUE: TWO TITANIC TITANS TALES! *Dear Mom & Dad...* PLUS A SECOND IMPOSSIBLE SAGA!

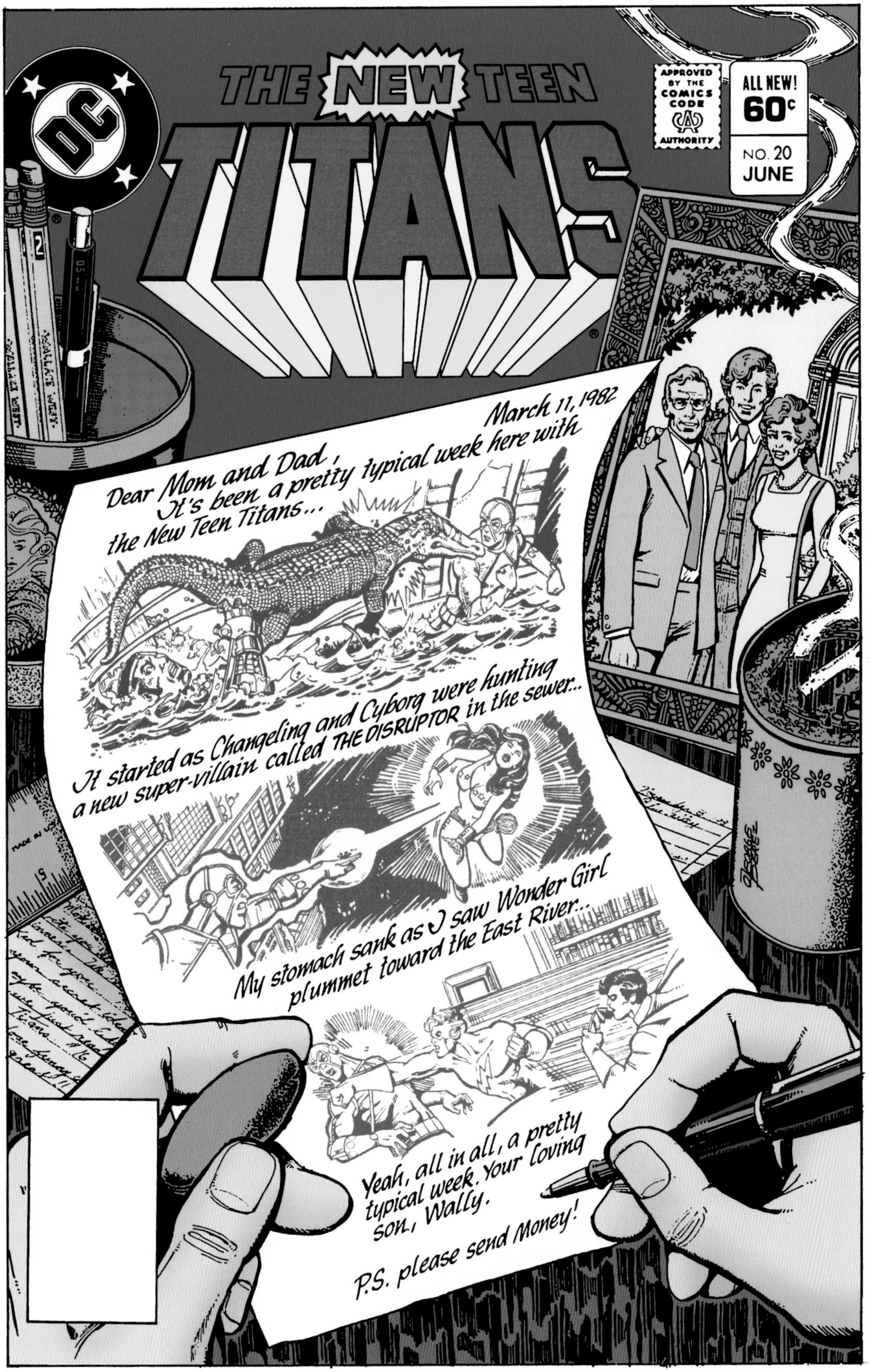
THE NEW TEEN TITANS
APPROVED BY THE COMICS CODE AUTHORITY
ALL NEW! 60¢
NO. 20 JUNE
March 11, 1982
Dear Mom and Dad,
It's been a pretty typical week here with the New Teen Titans...
It started as Changeling and Cyborg were hunting a new super-villain called THE DISRUPTOR in the sewer...
My stomach sank as I saw Wonder Girl plummet toward the East River...
Yeah, all in all, a pretty typical week. Your loving son, Wally.
P.S. please send Money!

THEY ARE THE *BEST* THERE IS: *THE CHANGELING,* SHAPE-SHIFTER SUPREME; *CYBORG,* HALF MAN / HALF ROBOT; *KID FLASH,* SUPER-SPEEDSTER; *RAVEN,* MISTRESS OF MAGIC; *ROBIN,* THE TEEN WONDER; *STARFIRE,* ALIEN POWERHOUSE; AND *WONDER GIRL,* THE AMAZING AMAZON! TOGETHER THEY ARE...

THE NEW TEEN TITANS

TITANS' TOWER, NEW YORK CITY...

SO MANY THINGS ARE *CHANGING,* AREN'T THEY?

BUT CHANGE ALWAYS SEEMS TO *UPSET* ME JUST A LITTLE.

I GUESS WHEN IT COMES RIGHT *DOWN* TO IT, I'M RATHER *STAID* IN MY WAYS...

NOT NEARLY AS SPONTANEOUS OR WILD AS THE *OTHER* TITANS. WELL, *SOMEONE'S* GOT TO BE NORMAL--

--THOUGH WHY DOES 'NORMAL' SOUND LIKE A *DISEASE* WHEN I SAY IT?

"GOOD HEAVENS, MAN --HE'S GOT TERMINAL *NORMALCY!*" "YOU SEE HIM, MANFRED? H-HE'S *NORMAL!*"

BUT IF NORMAL MEANS GENERALLY *LIKING* THINGS, OR BEING *HAPPY,* OR HAVING *PARENTS* I LOVE AND CAN TURN TO--

WELL, I *LIKE* BEING NORMAL.

MOM AND DAD, YOU RAISED LITTLE WALLY RATHER *WELL,* DIDN'T YOU? HMMM...

MAYBE IT'S TIME I LET YOU KNOW HOW I *FEEL.*

Dear Mom and Dad

MARV WOLFMAN & GEORGE PÉREZ
WRITER-- CO-CREATORS-- ARTIST
ROMEO TANGHAL *EMBELLISHER*
BEN ODA *LETTERER*
ADRIENNE ROY *COLORIST*
LEN WEIN *EDITOR*

I'VE NEVER TOLD YOU TOO MUCH ABOUT MY LIFE AS *KID FLASH*. MAYBE IT WAS MY WAY OF KEEPING YOU FROM *WORRYING*.

BUT THINGS HAVE *HAPPENED* LATELY THAT I WANT YOU TO *KNOW* ABOUT.

IT DIDN'T BEGIN WITH *ME*, HOWEVER. IT STARTED AS TWO *OTHER* TITANS, *CYBORG* AND *CHANGELING*, WERE HUNTING A NEW SUPER-VILLAIN CALLED *THE DISRUPTOR* DEEP IN THE SEWERS BELOW NEW YORK...

HEY, MY SOUND AMPLIFIER'S PICKIN' UP SOME *SLOSHIN'* COMIN' FROM THAT TUNNEL!

YAHOOO! WE FINALLY GOT THAT CREEP *CAUGHT*, RUSTPOT.

"CYBORG'S A STRANGE CHARACTER. HE'S TOUGH, STREET-BORN, AND SOMETIMES HE CAN BE REALLY MEAN. I JUST CAN'T FIGURE OUT HOW HE BECAME FRIENDS WITH THE CHANGELING...

"...WHO'S OUR *YOUNGEST* TITAN, AND IF YOU WANT MY OPINION, MOM AND DAD -- SOMETIMES THE MOST *OVERBEARING*. I DON'T THINK I'VE EVER SEEN HIM *SERIOUS*."

GOTTA TELL YA, GLITTERS, I DON'T *UNDERSTAND* THIS DISRUPTOR JERK...

...HE KEEPS POPPIN' UP, TRYIN' TO *KILL* US...

...AND THEN *TAKES OFF* AGAIN, RIGHT? YEAH, I *KNOW* IT, KID.

YEAH, YEAH, CHROME-DOME, I *GOT* IT, YOU THINK I'M *STUPID*, HUH?

DON'T WORRY IT, CYBIE -- MY BAT'S RADAR WILL *HOME-IN* ON OUR WOULD-BE *ASSASSIN*.

LISSEN, THE TUNNELS *MEET* UP AHEAD, SO I'M SAYIN' WE *SPLIT UP*. GOT IT, SALAD-HEAD?

"THE CHANGELING'S A *SHAPE-SHIFTER*. SO HE TOOK THE FORM OF A *BAT* AND SWOOPED THROUGH THOSE FOUL-SMELLING TUNNELS..."

AH HA, *FOUND* HIM RIGHT OFF. FACE IT, YOU'RE *SOLID GOLD*!

NO WONDER THE GIRLS ALL *LOVE* YA!

②

"OH, I FORGOT TO TELL YOU.... THE CHANGELING'S GOT A *NON-STOP* EGO AND A *MOUTH* TO MATCH."

"LET ME TELL YOU ABOUT THE DISRUPTOR. HE WAS YOUNG, BUT, MAN WAS HE DANGEROUS. HE HAD THE POWER TO DISRUPT THE NORMAL FLOW OF THINGS... WE LEARNED HOW HE GOT THOSE POWERS, BUT THAT CAME LATER..."

WELL, WELL, IF IT ISN'T THE *BIG BAD WOLF* HIMSELF.

WHY DON'T WE PLAY *'LITTLE RED RIDING HOOD,'* AND I'LL BE THE *WOODSMAN,* EH?

CHANGELING? I'VE BEEN *LOOKING* FOR YOU.

NO, NO, RED'S SUPPOSED TO SAY "WHAT BIG *EYES* YOU HAVE!"

I'M NOT *PLAYING GAMES* WITH YOU, CHANGELING...

AW, I KNOW, YOU *JUST DON'T LIKE* YOUR *ROLE.* TELL YA WHAT, 'RUPTY, *I'LL* BE THE BIG BAD WOLF...

AND NOW YOU SAY, 'MY, WHAT BIG *TEETH* YOU HAVE, GRAN'MA.'

OOPS, I'M NOT A *WOLF,* AM I? I'M A TYPICAL NEW YORK CITY SEWER *ALLIGATOR...*

...OR AM I A *CROCODILE?* I NEVER GET THEM RIGHT-- ARRGHH!

RROWW!

I HAVEN'T THE TIME FOR *GAMES,* CHANGELING.

I DON'T *LIKE* THIS AS IT IS, AND I CERTAINLY DON'T WANT TO *PROLONG* THINGS!

I'VE BEEN CHANGED *BACK?* HOW DID YOU *DO* THAT?

I MERELY *DISRUPTED* YOUR POWER, CHANGELING--

--AS EASILY AS I CAN DISRUPT THE FLOW OF *BLOOD* IN YOUR VEINS!

"MOM, DAD, YOU KNOW SUPER-HEROING CAN BE DANGEROUS. IT CAN ALSO BE DEADLY..."

"...AS I'M SURE THE CHANGELING MUST HAVE THOUGHT JUST THEN."

LORD, THAT WAS THE *CHANGELING!*

NEVER HEARD 'IM *SCREAM OUT* LIKE THAT BEFORE.

INTERNAL *COMPUTER* PLACES HIM ABOUT SIXTY YARDS STRAIGHT AHEAD...

...THE INFRA-RED LENS LETS ME *SEE* IN THIS GOD-FORSAKEN CESSPOOL.

JUST DON'T BE *HURT,* PAL... FOR GOD'S SAKE, DON'T BE *HURT.*

"I WROTE BEFORE THAT CYBORG COULD BE MEAN... BUT THERE'S ANOTHER SIDE TO HIM... A TENDER, CARING SIDE...

"CYBORG'S STILL AN *ENIGMA* TO ME. HE HAS THIS *EDGE* TO HIM I CAN'T YET UNDERSTAND. ANYWAY, HE'S A *GOOD* MAN.

...AS WILL *YOU.*

I'VE BEEN GIVEN A *JOB* TO DO...

"BUT AT THAT POINT, HE WAS ALSO AN *ANGRY* ONE."

YOU! BLAST YOU, MAN, WHAT HAVE YOU *DONE* TO HIM?

IF HE'S *DEAD,* DISRUPTOR, NOTHIN' ON EARTH'LL STOP ME FROM *RIPPIN'* YOU *APART.*

OH, HE'S NOT YET *DECEASED,* CYBORG, BUT HE *WILL* BE...

...AND IT'S ONE I HAVE TO SEE THROUGH TO THE *END.*

HOLD IT, MAN! WHAT IN BLAZES ARE YOU *DOIN'*--?

MY *LEGS* WON'T MOVE... I CAN'T CONTROL MY CYBORG PARTS.*

*CYBORG STANDS FOR CYBERNETIC ORGANISM, SOMETHING PART *HUMAN,* AND PART *MACHINE.*

④

"SO, NOT BEING ABLE TO CONTROL HIS ME-CHANICAL PARTS, CYBORG FELL...

"...STIFF AS THE TIN MAN IN THE 'WIZARD OF OZ.'

YOU SEE, CYBORG, IT WAS ONLY A MATTER OF TIME BEFORE *ONE* OF YOU TITANS FELL.

MY FATHER MADE CERTAIN I WOULD BE *STRONGER* THAN YOU.

AND NOW, TO FINISH THINGS OFF WITH A *FLOURISH*...

...I DISRUPT THE FLOW OF *WATER* IN THOSE RUSTY OLD *PIPES*...

...AND IN LESS THAN TEN MINUTES, BOTH OF YOU WILL *DROWN*--

--WHILE I REPORT BACK TO MY *FATHER*.

HE'LL BE PLEASED WITH MY *SUCCESS*. I'M SURE HE'LL BE *VERY* PLEASED.

I CAN'T MOVE...

THE PLAY'S UP TO *YOU*, MAN...DON'T LET ME *DOWN*.

CHANGELING! CHANGELING! YOU *HEAR* ME?

C'MON, BUDDY, OPEN YER EYES... *GET UP*... *GET UP!!*

UNHHH...

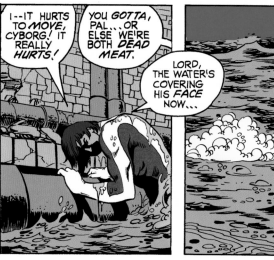

I--IT HURTS TO *MOVE*, CYBORG! IT REALLY *HURTS!*

YOU *GOTTA*, PAL...OR ELSE WE'RE BOTH *DEAD MEAT.*

LORD, THE WATER'S COVERING HIS *FACE* NOW...

NO MATTER *HOW MUCH* IT HURTS...

I GOTTA *DO SOMETHING!* I GOTTA SAVE *CYBORG!*

5

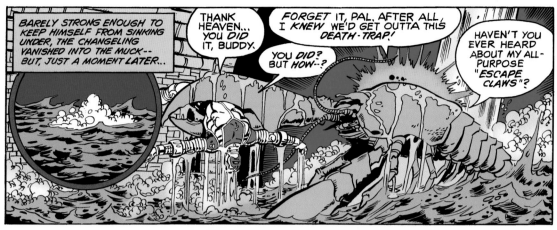

BARELY STRONG ENOUGH TO KEEP HIMSELF FROM SINKING UNDER, THE CHANGELING VANISHED INTO THE MUCK-- BUT, JUST A MOMENT *LATER...*

THANK HEAVEN... YOU *DID* IT, BUDDY.

YOU *DID?* BUT *HOW--?*

FORGET IT, PAL, AFTER ALL, I *KNEW* WE'D GET OUTTA THIS *DEATH-TRAP!*

HAVEN'T YOU EVER HEARD ABOUT MY ALL- PURPOSE *"ESCAPE CLAWS"?*

WHAT CAN I *TELL* YOU, MOM AND DAD? THE CHANGELING JUST HAS NO *SHAME.*

BUT I'M NOT REALLY GETTING TO THE *POINT* OF THIS LETTER, AM I?

IT'S SOMETIMES *HARD* WRITING DOWN YOUR INNER- MOST THOUGHTS AND EMOTIONS. BUT IF I CAN'T TELL *YOU* ABOUT 'EM, WHO *CAN* I TELL?

CHANGELING AND CYBORG HAD LOST THE DISRUPTOR'S *TRAIL* AND SO THEY RETURNED TO TITANS' TOWER ...

..."ESCAPE CLAWS," *GET* IT?

HE CHANGED CHANGELING BACK TO *HUMAN,* FROZE MY *MECHANICAL PARTS,* AND SOMEHOW OPENED THOSE *SEWER PIPES.*

ROBBIE, HE WON'T BE EASY TO *STOP.*

BLAST. I DON'T *LIKE* THIS, CYBORG.

HE'S *OUTGUESSED* ME AT EVERY TURN.

INSTEAD OF SOME *HERO,* I FEEL LIKE A *STUPID KID.*

BUT WE *ALMOST* HAD HIM, ROBIN.

PEOPLE HAVE LOST *FORTUNES* BETTING ON *"ALMOSTS,"* STARFIRE.

I SHOULD HAVE HAD THIS ALL *FIGURED OUT* BY NOW. WHAT'S *WRONG* WITH ME THESE DAYS?

6

WHAT'S WITH THIS *SELF-DEPRECATION* BIT? YOU KNOW YOU'RE *GOOD*.

DO I? I WISH I *DID*, WONDER GIRL. WITH *YOU* GUYS IT SEEMS LIKE I'M *HOT STUFF*... A *KNOW-IT-ALL*...

...BUT I'VE BEEN BACK WITH *THE BATMAN* AGAIN, AND NEXT TO *HIM* I FEEL LIKE I'M A STUPID KID REPEATING *FIFTH GRADE*...

...FOR THE *THIRD TIME*.

AND NOW *THIS*. THE DISRUPTOR'S AS YOUNG AS *WE* ARE. WHY HAVEN'T I FIGURED HIM OUT BY NOW. *WHY?*

YOU KNOW, I ALWAYS THOUGHT OF ROBIN AS SOMEONE *INFALLIBLE*...

...SO MUCH *BETTER* THAN ME, ALWAYS WITH EVERY *ANSWER* RIGHT AT HIS FINGERTIPS.

IT CAME AS QUITE A *SHOCK* TO DISCOVER THAT, JUST LIKE ME, HE SOMETIMES HAS *FEET OF CLAY*...

I GUESS SOMETIMES WE'RE ALL *INSECURE* ABOUT OURSELVES. BUT IF *ROBIN'S* WORRYING SURPRISED ME, *WONDER GIRL'S* SENT ME FOR A LOOP...

SHHHHH. HE'S COMING.

HEY! WHERE *IS* EVERYONE? WHY'RE THE *LIGHTS* OUT, MAN?

SURPRISE!

HAPPY BIRTHDAY, TINHEAD!

WHAT IN THE WORLD? HOW'D YOU PEOPLE KNOW--?

Happy Birthday Victor with love The Titans

7

AW, LOOKIT 'IM, 'BORGY'S *SHY*, ISN'T HE?

C'MON, RUSTY, JOIN THE *FUN*. IT'S ALL FOR *YOU!*

THIS IS A *WONDERFUL* IDEA. WE DON'T HAVE *BIRTHDAY PARTIES* ON TAMARAN.

HAPPY BIRTHDAY, CYBORG.

YEAH, *THANKS*, STARFIRE.

SO, YOU'RE *NINETEEN* TODAY. JOIN THE *CROWD*.

NINETEEN? YOUNGSTERS! *CHILDREN!*

TERRY, YOU'RE JUST *JEALOUS* BECAUSE YOU'RE ALMOST *MIDDLE AGED*.

HEY! 29'S NOT MIDDLE AGED. *IS* IT?

OH, *HI*, RAVEN. HOW *ARE* YOU?

I AM *WELL*, WALLACE, AND *YOU?*

UH, OHH... GOOD.

"MAN, YOU COULD CUT THE *TENSION* BETWEEN US WITH A *DULLED-DOWN BUTTER KNIFE*."

YOU DON'T SEEM TO BE *ENJOYING* YOURSELF. SOMETHING *WRONG?*

NO. *EXCUSE* ME, WALLACE...

YEAH, SURE...

"TO TELL YOU ALL ABOUT *RAVEN* WOULD FILL UP A HUNDRED LETTERS...

"SO LET ME GET BACK TO THE PARTY, WHICH WAS FUN.

"AS USUAL, *CHANGELING* WAS MAKING A *JACKASS* OF HIMSELF..."

"...BUT HE WAS THE LIFE OF THE PARTY, HE REALLY KEPT THE PLACE HOPPING.

"AND THE ONLY ONE WHO WASN'T ENJOYING HERSELF THEN WAS *WONDER GIRL*. SHE WALKED OFF WITH *TERRY LONG*..."

"THAT'S THE GUY I TOLD YOU ABOUT. HE'S DIVORCED. A *COLLEGE TEACHER*, AND THEY SEEM TO *LOVE* EACH OTHER VERY MUCH.

8

...NO, TERRY, NOTHING'S WRONG. WHY DO YOU *ASK?*

BECAUSE, LOVE, I'M NOT *BLIND* TO YOUR LITTLE QUIRKS.

WANT TO *TALK?*

IT'S REALLY *INSIGNIFICANT,* TERRY.

GREAT! THEN WE'LL BE BACK TO THE PARTY IN *NO TIME.* SO--?

IT'S *BIRTHDAYS,* TERRY.

YOU DON'T *LIKE* BIRTHDAY PARTIES?

NO, JUST *BIRTHDAYS.*

I DON'T KNOW WHEN *MINE* IS. HOW *COULD* I WHEN I DON'T KNOW WHO I *AM?*

I DON'T KNOW MY *AGE,* OR EVEN MY *REAL* NAME.

I DON'T *THINK* ABOUT IT OFTEN, HONEY, BUT AT TIMES LIKE THIS... WELL, I CAN'T *AVOID* THINKING.

I'VE TRIED EVERYTHING TO GET TO THE TRUTH, AND I'VE *FAILED.*

AND SOMETIMES IT REALLY *HURTS* NOT KNOWING. SOMETIMES I WAKE UP *CRYING...*

CAN WE *GO,* TERRY? I'M NOT IN THE *MOOD* RIGHT NOW.

SURE, HONEY. BESIDES, I'VE GOT THAT LATE *SEMINAR* TO GO TO.

BY THE WAY, YOU TELL CYBORG THAT SARAH *SIMMS* CAME TO SEE ME?

YEAH, HE JUST NODDED AND *WALKED AWAY.*

HE DIDN'T SAY A *WORD.* JUST WALKED AWAY.

HAPPY BIR

Happy Birthday, Victor. Love, Sarah and the kids

BEFORE I TELL YOU ABOUT *SARAH SIMMS,* YOU HAVE TO KNOW MORE ABOUT *CYBORG.* HIS MOTHER *DIED* IN THE ACCIDENT THAT DESTROYED HIS BODY. HIS FATHER, WHO OUTFITTED HIM WITH HIS STEEL FORM, JUST *RECENTLY* DIED.

SARAH SIMMS IS A *GIRL* HE MET. SHE TEACHES *PARA-PLEGIC KIDS.* WELL, ONE OF OUR ENEMIES *KIDNAPPED* SARAH A FEW MONTHS BACK.

... AND CYBORG BLAMES *HIMSELF* FOR WHAT HAP-PENED. HE'S REFUSED TO *SEE* HER EVER SINCE.

9

IT'S STRANGE, BUT HEARING ALL THOSE *OTHER* PROBLEMS SORT OF BROUGHT OUT ALL OF MY *OWN*...

"FOR SO LONG I COULDN'T *DECIDE* WHETHER TO GO TO *COLLEGE* OR BE *KID FLASH* THAT I NEVER REALIZED I COULD TRY TO DO *BOTH*...

"AND THEN THERE WAS *RAVEN*.

"I TOLD YOU A *LITTLE* ABOUT HER. MAYBE YOU COULD TELL THAT I REALLY *LOVE* HER...

"...EVEN THOUGH THAT LOVE IS NEVER *RECIPROCATED*. NOT EVER IN ANY WAY..."

RAVEN, WHY DOES CYBORG'S BIRTHDAY MAKE ME THINK ABOUT *TAMARAN*?

IT'S BEEN ALMOST *SEVEN YEARS* SINCE I'VE BEEN BACK HOME.

I ACHE TO SEE MY *PARENTS* AGAIN. AND I LONG TO SEE MY LITTLE BROTHER, *RYAND'R*...

LITTLE BROTHER? HE MUST BE NEARLY AS OLD AS THE *CHANGELING*--IF HE'S EVEN *ALIVE*.

OH, RAVEN. YOU DON'T KNOW HOW IT *FEELS*. I--I DON'T EVEN KNOW IF TAMARAN STILL *EXISTS*.

"STARFIRE-- HER REAL NAME IS *PRINCESS KORIAND'R*-- IS FROM ANOTHER WORLD.

"BOY, TALK ABOUT *HARD LIVES*. SHE WAS KIDNAPPED AT TWELVE, BEATEN, TORTURED, HURT IN SO MANY WAYS IT HURTS TO EVEN *THINK* OF THEM...

"I NEEDED SOME FRESH AIR TO THINK THINGS OUT.

"I TOOK MY BINOCULARS TO LOOK AT NEW YORK'S SKYLINE AT NIGHT... IT'S SO *BEAUTIFUL*, MOM AND DAD...

"...SO UNLIKE THE FLAT PLAINS OF *BLUE VALLEY*. THAT'S WHEN I SAW *WONDER GIRL* GLIDING ACROSS THE CITY...

10

"I WATCHED HER FOR A WHILE, THEN SUDDENLY SHE CLUTCHED HER SIDE...

"BUT WHAT COULD HURT AN AMAZON?

"I COULD TELL SHE HAD BEEN BADLY HURT.

"I STARED IN HORROR --FOR TOO LONG, I THINK, THEN MY STOMACH SANK...

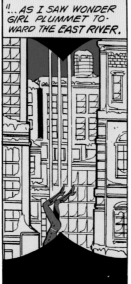

"...AS I SAW WONDER GIRL PLUMMET TO-WARD THE EAST RIVER.

"SHE FELL, AND THEN I SAW HIM. THE DISRUPTOR HAD RETURNED...

"WELL, I'M SURE I DON'T HAVE TO TELL YOU HOW I FELT AS I WATCHED THE LEERING, GRINNING GHOUL...

"...AND MAYBE I WAS STUPID IN NOT ALERTING THE OTHERS, BUT I TOOK OFF WITH ALL MY SUPER-SPEED...

"...I RAN SO FAST THAT I DIDN'T SINK INTO THE WATER, BUT INSTEAD SKIMMED OVER ITS SURFACE.

"LESS THAN THREE SECONDS LATER, I WAS SETTING UP A WHIRLWIND TO KNOCK THE DISRUPTOR ALL THE WAY FROM NEW YORK TO CINCINNATI!

11

"ONLY I HAD FORGOTTEN HOW *DANGEROUS* THE DISRUPTOR'S POWERS COULD BE.

WHOOM

"SOMEHOW HE HAD CHANGED THE *DIRECTION* OF MY WHIRLWIND. INSTEAD OF HITTING HIM...

"IT BLASTED RIGHT BACK INTO *ME!*"

I *DID* IT. I CAN'T *BELIEVE* IT, BUT I GOT *TWO MORE* TITANS.

CHANGELING AND CYBORG, WONDER GIRL AND NOW KID FLASH.

THERE'S ONLY THREE *LEFT.*

THIS WAY, SIR, HE IS *WAITING!*

DID YOU *SEE* THAT, HENRY? I KILLED *KID FLASH.*

DAD'S GOING TO BE SO *PROUD.*

DAD, HE'S *DEAD.* I SENT HIS WIND-FUNNEL RIGHT *BACK* AT HIM.

THERE'S NO WAY HE COULD HAVE *SURVIVED* ITS IMPACT.

YOU JERK, I COULD NAME A *DOZEN* DIFFERENT WAYS.

NEVER *UNDERESTIMATE* HIS KIND.

COME ON, DAD. I SAW HIM *FALL.*

DO YOU FORGET WHO I *AM,* MICHAEL? I AM *"BRAINS"* BELDON.

I HAVE BATTLED *THE BATMAN* TO A STANDSTILL.

I *KNOW* HOW THESE SUPER-POWERED SIMPLETONS PLY THEIR TRADE.

IF YOU DID NOT *PERSONALLY* SEE A DEAD BODY, HE IS NOT *DEAD.*

WHICH MAKES *YOU* AS MUCH AN IDIOT AS *THEY* ARE. HOW COULD YOU POSSIBLY BE MY *SON?*

BUT, DAD, I DID WHAT YOU *WANTED,* DIDN'T I? I WENT OUT TO KILL YOUR *ENEMIES.*

AND YOU *FAILED,* MICHAEL.

12

"OF COURSE I *WASN'T DEAD.* WHEN I SAW THE WIND *TURN,* I VIBRATED AT SUPER-SPEED*...* LET MOST OF IT PASS HARMLESSLY *THROUGH ME.*

"THEN AFTER I PULLED *WONDER GIRL* OUT OF THE WATER AND MADE SURE SHE WOULD BE *ALL RIGHT...*

"...I TOOK AFTER THE *LIMOUSINE.* NOW, I DIDN'T WANT TO ATTACK THIS 'BRAINS' BELDON CREEP OR HIS SON UNTIL I FOUND OUT WHAT THEY WERE AFTER...

"...SO I REMAINED PRACTICALLY *INVISIBLE* WHILE THE LIMO DROVE TO EAST HAMPTON, LONG ISLAND...

"A PLACE SO *POSH* THEY DON'T WASH DIRTY CARS -- THEY BUY *NEW ONES.*"

I'M *NOT* A FAILURE, DAD. I DO MY BEST, I *SWEAR* I DO.

I DON'T WANT TO *KILL* THE TITANS, BUT I'M DOING IT FOR *YOU.*

I'D DO *ANYTHING* FOR YOU, DAD, IF ONLY YOU'D SAY SOMETHING *NICE* TO ME... JUST *ONCE.*

MICHAEL, YOU ARE AN INCOMPETENT *NEANDERTHAL.* YOU MUST TAKE AFTER YOUR *MOTHER'S* FAMILY--

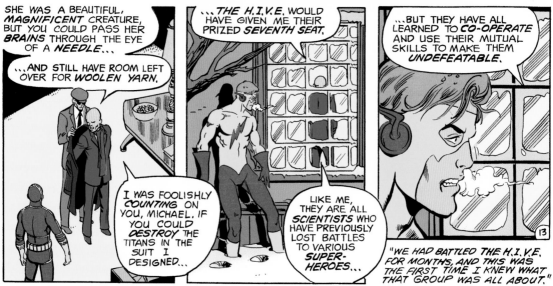

SHE WAS A BEAUTIFUL, *MAGNIFICENT* CREATURE, BUT YOU COULD PASS HER *BRAINS* THROUGH THE EYE OF A *NEEDLE...*

...AND STILL HAVE ROOM LEFT OVER FOR *WOOLEN YARN.*

I WAS FOOLISHLY *COUNTING* ON YOU, MICHAEL, IF YOU COULD *DESTROY* THE TITANS IN THE SUIT I DESIGNED...

...*THE H.I.V.E.* WOULD HAVE GIVEN ME THEIR PRIZED *SEVENTH SEAT.*

LIKE ME, THEY ARE ALL *SCIENTISTS* WHO HAVE PREVIOUSLY LOST BATTLES TO VARIOUS *SUPER-HEROES...*

...BUT THEY HAVE ALL LEARNED TO *CO-OPERATE* AND USE THEIR MUTUAL SKILLS TO MAKE THEM *UNDEFEATABLE.*

"WE HAD BATTLED THE *H.I.V.E.* FOR MONTHS, AND THIS WAS THE FIRST TIME I KNEW WHAT THAT GROUP WAS ALL ABOUT."

13

"SOMETIMES DAD HAS TOLD ME I DON'T *THINK* BEFORE I ACT. WELL, DAD, YOU'RE RIGHT. MAYBE I WAS GETTING COCKY...

"...BUT I DECIDED RIGHT THEN TO *GRAB* BELDON AND HIS SON *BY MYSELF.*"

WHAT?

"HIS BODYGUARD GRABBED FOR HIS GUN...

WHAM!

OKAY, BELDON, YOU'RE *NEXT.*

"...BUT BEFORE IT COULD CLEAR HIS HOLSTER, HE WAS *OUT* FOR THE NIGHT."

SO YOU *KILLED* HIM, DID YOU? THEN HIS BLASTED *GHOST* HAS RETURNED.

DO SOMETHING, YOU NITWIT. USE THAT SUIT'S *POWER.*

I... UHHHH...

MOM, I KNOW HOW YOU *GET* SOMETIMES, SO IF YOU'D PREFER NOT READING WHAT COMES *NEXT,* JUST SKIP TO THE NEXT PARAGRAPH. DAD, IF YOU'RE STILL *THERE...* WELL, I NEVER *FELT* THAT WAY BEFORE.

HE'S NOT GETTING THE *CHANCE,* BELDON.

BEFORE HE KNOWS WHAT *HIT* HIM, HE'LL BE--

AGGHHHH!

"OH, DAD, -- MY HEART SUDDENLY WENT *CRAZY.* I THINK MY BLOOD PRESSURE SHOT UP TO OVER *200.*

"I COULDN'T MOVE, COULDN'T *BREATHE...* COULDN'T FIGHT BACK AS THE DISRUPTOR POUNDED ON ME, SMASHED AT ME... IT WAS HORRIBLE."

14

I WOULD HAVE BEEN SO GLAD TO *DIE* JUST THEN IF ONLY TO STOP THE POUNDING *PAIN.* MY GOD, WAS IT *AWFUL.*

FORTUNATELY, PERHAPS, I WAS *UNCONSCIOUS* BEFORE MUCH LONGER. OKAY, TELL MOM SHE CAN START *READING* AGAIN.

ANYWAY, I WOKE UP SOON ENOUGH. MAYBE *TOO* SOON.

I DON'T *BELIEVE* THIS. THE *H.I.V.E.* -- AGAIN?

DON'T YOU JERKS *EVER* GIVE UP?

BELDON, YOU *FAILED* IN YOUR FIRST ATTEMPT AT SLAYING A TITAN.

YES, I KNOW MY *SON* FAILED. BUT WE'VE CAPTURED *KID FLASH*...

...AND THIS TIME I'LL MAKE SURE HE DOESN'T *SURVIVE.*

I WANT THAT SEVENTH *SEAT.*

AND HE'LL *GET* IT. THE DISRUPTOR'S PREVENTING ME FROM *RUNNING* OUT OF HERE...

...THOUGH THAT DOESN'T STOP ME FROM USING MY *SUPER-SPEED* POWERS...

...TO SET UP *VIBRATIONS* THAT WILL CARRY ALL THE WAY TO TITANS' TOWER...

...AND PRAY THEY DO WHAT ROBIN AND I SET UP SO LONG AGO IN CASE OF *EMERGENCIES* LIKE THIS.

TITANS' TOWER...

HE JUST HIT ME WITH THOSE *DISRUPTING* POWERS...

...AND I FELL LIKE YOUR PROVERBIAL *BRICK.*

AND WHAT OF *KID FLASH?*

HE WASN'T *THERE* WHEN I--

BOOM!

RAYEN, WONDER GIRL, STARFIRE -- THAT WAS A *SONIC BOOM.*

KID FLASH'S *SIGNAL,* ISN'T IT?

15

CYBORG HAS THE MOST EXTENSIVE *SCIENCE* BACKGROUND OF ANY OF US. HE USED HIS IN-BODY *COMPUTER* SENSORS TO TRACE MY SONIC BOOM'S *TRAJECTORY.*

BUT EVEN WITH THE TITANS' ABILITIES, IT STILL SEEMED TO TAKE *FOREVER* BEFORE--

C'MON, YA HEROES-- WE *FOUND* 'IM!

ARE YOU *ALL RIGHT?*

I AM *NOW,* WONDER GIRL... I CERTAINLY AM *NOW.*

THE *TITANS?* BUT, DAD, I *KILLED* MOST OF THEM.

THEY *CAN'T* BE ALIVE.

KA-THOOM!

YOU BRAINLESS DOLT, DON'T STAND THERE *WHIMPERING.* STOP THEM NOW AND *REDEEM* YOURSELF.

BUT I *KNOW* I KILLED THEM. I SAW THEM *DIE.* I DROWNED *TWO,* AND--

YOUR FATHER WAS *RIGHT,* DISRUPTOR-- YOU *ARE* A NITWIT.

YOU RELAXED YOUR *DISRUPTING* POWERS LONG ENOUGH FOR ME TO BREAK MY *BONDS...*

...AND PUT YOU ALL *OUT OF COMMISSION.*

HE DID IT *AGAIN.* STOPPED ME *COLD.* ONLY THIS TIME HE SEEMED TO DISRUPT THE *SYNAPSES* IN MY BRAIN. NO, MOM, IT *SOUNDS* WORSE THAN IT FELT.

IF FACT, I FELT *NOTHING...*

YOU HANDLE *HIM,* FLASHER, I GOT *THIS* ONE.

Y'SEE, PAL, I DON'T LIKE IT WHEN THUGS DRAW THEIR *GUNS!*

DON'T CALL ME *NITWIT!* I DON'T LIKE IT WHEN MY *FATHER* DOES-- --AND I *HATE* IT WHEN *YOU* DO!

AGHHH!

16

"NOT EVEN AS I FOUND MYSELF SPINNING SPASTICALLY ACROSS THE ROOM...

ROBIN...

...WATCH...

OOF!

KRAK!

...OU--

I'LL SHOW YOU *NOW*, DAD.

I'M IN *FULL* COMMAND OF THESE POWERS.

"IT WAS *TERRIBLE*, MOM AND DAD. WONDER GIRL'S LASSO WAS *UNCON-TROLLABLE*...

"... IT SNAPPED AROUND HER, *PINNING HER*...

"... WHILE CYBORG FOUND HALF THE MECHANISMS IN HIS ARM SUDDENLY *FLARE UP* AND *SHORT-CIRCUIT*.

"CHANGELING SPUN OUT OF CONTROL, UNABLE TO KEEP HIS *ANIMAL* SHAPES...

"... WHILE STARFIRE, THE *POOR* GIRL, FELT HER OWN *SOLAR* POWER EXPLODE WITHIN HER."

YOU *SEE*, FATHER? I TOLD YOU I WOULD KILL THE *TITANS!*

THE *H.I.V.E.* WILL LET YOU JOIN THEM *NOW*, DAD.

ALL BECAUSE OF *ME*.

NO, MICHAEL BELDON, YOU HAVE NOT SHOWN YOUR *STRENGTH* IN DEFEATING MY FRIENDS...

...YOU HAVE ONLY SHOWN WHY PEOPLE SUCH AS YOU ARE TO BE *PITIED*.

NOW YOU WILL SEE HOW *TERRIBLE* THE LIFE YOU HAVE SOUGHT TO LIVE CAN BE.

17

AND PERHAPS, MICHAEL BELDON, YOU WILL *CHANGE* YOUR WAYS BEFORE IT IS FAR *TOO LATE.*

"*I DON'T KNOW WHAT THE DISRUPTOR SAW, BUT I WILL NEVER FORGET THE LOOK OF UTTER HORROR TATTOOED ON HIS FACE.*

"*IT WAS AWFUL, HE SCREAMED AND SCREAMED...*

"*... AND THE SCREAMING NEVER SEEMED TO STOP.*

"*I KNOW NOW WHAT IT MUST BE LIKE TO FACE YOUR OWN HELL-- BECAUSE, GOD FORGIVE HIM, MICHAEL BELDON SURELY MUST HAVE SEEN HIS FATE...*

"*... A FATE THAT WAS TOO TERRIBLE TO ACCEPT. I STARED FOR A LONG TIME AT RAVEN, WONDERING HOW SHE, WHO PRACTICES AND PREACHES PACIFISM, COULD BE SO TOTALLY CRUEL. SHE MUST HAVE GUESSED WHY I WAS GLARING AT HER...*"

HE WOULD HAVE ALLOWED HIMSELF TO *KILL* JUST TO SATISFY HIS FATHER'S TWISTED *MADNESS.* I COULD NOT ALLOW THAT HATRED TO *FESTER* WITHIN HIM...

MY *OWN* FATHER IS ONE SUCH AS BELDON. CRUEL, EVIL, *MERCILESS.*

MICHAEL BELDON HAD TO LEARN HOW *TERRIBLE* THAT PATH COULD BE.'

HE HAD TO SEE OR HE MIGHT HAVE *EMBRACED* THE EVIL THAT I CHOSE TO *SPURN.*

"*MICHAEL BELDON HAD REMINDED RAVEN OF HERSELF AND TRIGON. IT'S THE FIRST TIME I EVER THOUGHT OF RAVEN IN THAT LIGHT.*

"*LORD, WHAT MUST IT HAVE BEEN LIKE FOR HER TO HAVE A FATHER WHO WAS A TOTAL FORCE FOR EVIL? EVEN NOW I SHUDDER TO THINK OF IT.*

IT WAS ALL *OVER*, AT LEAST THE *ACTION* PART OF THE STORY.

BUT WHAT REALLY *HURT* WAS WHAT HAPPENED *NEXT*.

"MICHAEL BELDON REFUSED TO *IMPLICATE* HIS FATHER. HE INSISTED THAT THE ENTIRE SCHEME WAS *HIS*, WE HAD NO *PROOF* WE COULD SHOW THE DISTRICT ATTORNEY, SO 'BRAINS' WENT *FREE*...

"...WHILE HIS SON TOOK A TEN-YEAR RAP, BELDON DID VISIT HIS SON THE DAY AFTER HE BEGAN HIS SENTENCE."

BECAUSE OF *YOU*, THE *H.I.V.E.* TURNED ME *DOWN*.

YOU'RE AN *EMBARRASSMENT*, MICHAEL. ONE I CAN NO LONGER *TOLERATE*.

BUT, DAD, I DID MY *BEST*. I TRIED FOR YOU, CAN'T YOU *SEE* THAT?

ALL I SEE IS A USELESS *FOOL* WHO HAS ROBBED ME OF MY GREATEST *DREAM*.

I NO LONGER WANT TO *KNOW* YOU. I NO LONGER WANT TO *ASSOCIATE* WITH YOU.

AND I NO LONGER WANT TO *SEE* YOU AGAIN.

NO, DON'T *SAY* THAT, DAD. PLEASE DON'T *SAY* THAT.

ALL I EVER WANTED WAS YOUR *LOVE*.

YOU CAN'T TURN YOUR *BACK* ON ME, DAD. PLEASE...DON'T *DO* THAT TO ME...

PLEASE, DAD...

I *LOVE* YOU, DAD...DAD, I LOVE YOU...

D...DON'T GO AWAY...DON'T LEAVE ME...PLEASE...

THEIRS WAS A FAMILY WITHOUT *LOVE*, AND THAT GOT ME TO *THINKING*.

I HAD JUST SEEN ROBIN DESPERATELY TRYING TO LIVE UP TO AN *IMAGE* RATHER THAN BEING *HIMSELF*...

WONDER GIRL DESPERATELY WANTING SUCH A SIMPLE THING-- HER OWN *IDENTITY*.

WHILE STARFIRE ONLY *WANTED* THE *JOY* OF KNOWING HER FAMILY MIGHT STILL BE *ALIVE*.

I'D NEVER REALLY *UNDERSTOOD* RAVEN'S *TRAUMAS* CAUSED BY *TRIGON*, OR CYBORG'S PROBLEMS WITH *SARAH SIMMS*...

19

I WAS ALWAYS SO WRAPPED UP WITH MY *OWN* PROBLEMS AND THINKING NO ONE *ELSE* HAD ANY. BUT THEY *DO*.

YOU TWO HAVE SHOWN ME THE *LOVE* MICHAEL BELDON NEVER HAD...

YOU ENCOURAGED ME TO BE *MYSELF*. YOU WERE THERE WHEN I *NEEDED* YOU, AND I ALWAYS FELT I COULD *TALK* TO YOU...

...and not be *threatened* by you. Because of you being there I grew up into a *full person* who wanted to say something I really haven't said *enough*. Mom and Dad, I *love* you so very much

"*LOVE*, WALLY."

AH, *THERE* YOU ARE, WALLY.

LISTEN, I'M HEADING INTO MANHATTAN. *NEED* ANYTHING?

WANT ME TO MAIL THAT *LETTER* FOR YOU?

MAIL IT?

NAH.

I THINK I'LL DELIVER IT *IN PERSON*.

A TITANS MINI-SAGA FOLLOWS!

WHILE *NEXT ISSUE*: THE TITANS' *GREATEST* FOE YET: **BROTHER BLOOD!**

A TITANIC TALE OF TITANS' TOMFOOLERY!

MEANWHILE, ON THE MYTHICAL WORLD CALLED EARTH-PRIME...

OH, LEN. I'M **DOOMED!** I'VE RUN OUT OF *TITANS'* IDEAS.

I HAVEN'T HAD A GOOD *DREAM* ABOUT THEM IN WEEKS!

ARTIST TO EDITOR! LEN, YOU THINK YOU CAN *HELP* WHAT'S-HIS-NAME?

SURE, GEORGE. GIMME A MINUTE.

FLUFFY, I'M SO SORRY ABOUT LAST NIGHT...

I HAVE TO INK *THIS?* OY, THOSE *BACKGROUNDS!*

OH, NO! IT'S TOO LATE! SOMETHING'S HAPPENING!

LEN! FOR HEAVEN'S SAKE--HELP!

SURE, GEORGE, GIMME A MINUTE.

CAN'T WE STILL BE *FRIENDS,* FLUFFY?

TH-THEY'RE GONE!

DON'T WORRY, ROMEO. THEY'LL BE BACK WHEN THE *PAYCHECKS* SHOW UP.

WH-WHERE *ARE* WE, GEORGE?

WELL, THIS SURE ISN'T THE *DC COMMISSARY!*

SOMETHING OTHER THAN THE *FOOD* STINKS HERE!

SO, YOU'VE *BEEN* TO EARTH-ONE BEFORE, EH?

THEN YOU KNOW WE MAD SCIENTISTS HERE HAVE ALL SORTS OF SCIENTIFIC-GOBBLY-GOOK *WEAPONS.*

SAVE A WATT

YOU *WRITE* AND *DRAW* THE TEEN TITANS. YOU WILL TELL ME ALL THEIR SECRETS!

NO WAY, JOSÉ, *NEVER!*

EEEP! ON THE OTHER HAND.!..

TOO LATE, FOUR-EYES!

WHAT HAVE YOU *DONE* TO MY GOOD BUDDY, MY PAL, MY TALENTED PARTNER--

DAISY, DAISY, GIVE ME YOUR ANSWER DO...

--AND THE CLOWN WHO *WROTE* ALL THESE LIES?

THE SAME AS I'LL DO TO *YOU,* CHUBS.

BOY, THIS'LL MAKE A GREAT *SPECIAL EFFECT* WHEN I WAKE UP.

I WILL WAKE UP, WON'T I?

2

GEORGE'S QUESTION IS ANSWERED SOON ENOUGH, AS...

DUH, MASTER, I DONE *STOLE* WHAT YOU SENT ME TO STOLE.

NOW, BEFORE I TURN YOUR BRAINS INTO *SPAGHETTI-O'S* -- WILL YOU *TALK?*

TALK? I'LL *SING!* I'LL *DANCE!* I'LL EVEN RECITE THE *KORAN!*

I DON'T KNOW WHERE WE *ARE*, BUT I'M SURE GLAD I DON'T HAVE TO DRAW THIS.

THIS, MY OVERWEIGHT GUESTS, IS MY TYPICAL MAD SCIENTIST'S *LABORATORY!*

TRAITOR! YOU'D RAT ON THE *TITANS* JUST TO SAVE YOUR *LIFE?*

YEP! SURE! IN A SEC! OF COURSE! BETTER BELIEVE IT!

EXCELLENT, MY FAITHFUL CRO-MAGNON!

I GOT IT AT A *DISCOUNT* FROM "*KIRBY, INC.*"!

DON'T *WORRY.* YOU WON'T HAVE TO *TALK!*

EEEP!

SPACE FOR RENT

OH, NO. IT--IT CAN'T BE--*THEM!*

WELL, YOU'RE *RIGHT.* IT'S NOT '*THEM*', IT'S *US!*

WE FOLLOWED YOUR *GOON,* IGORIGORIGOR-IVICH--

--RIGHT AFTER HE STOLE THAT *WHATEVER-IT-IS.*

I WANT YOUR CAPTIVES *FREED.*

ROBBIE, HIS NAME'S NOT '*FREED.*' IT'S--

SIGH! SOMETIMES I WONDER WHY I GOT *INTO* THIS BUSINESS.

PEREZ DEBRIS

NOT WELCOME

HI, GUYS. I WAS JUST *KIDDING* BACK THERE.

HONEST INJUN, I WASN'T *REALLY* GOING TO TALK.

YOU'LL STILL *SAVE* ME, WON'T YOU? *PLEASE?*

WOLFMAN, YOU'RE *DESPICABLE!* /3

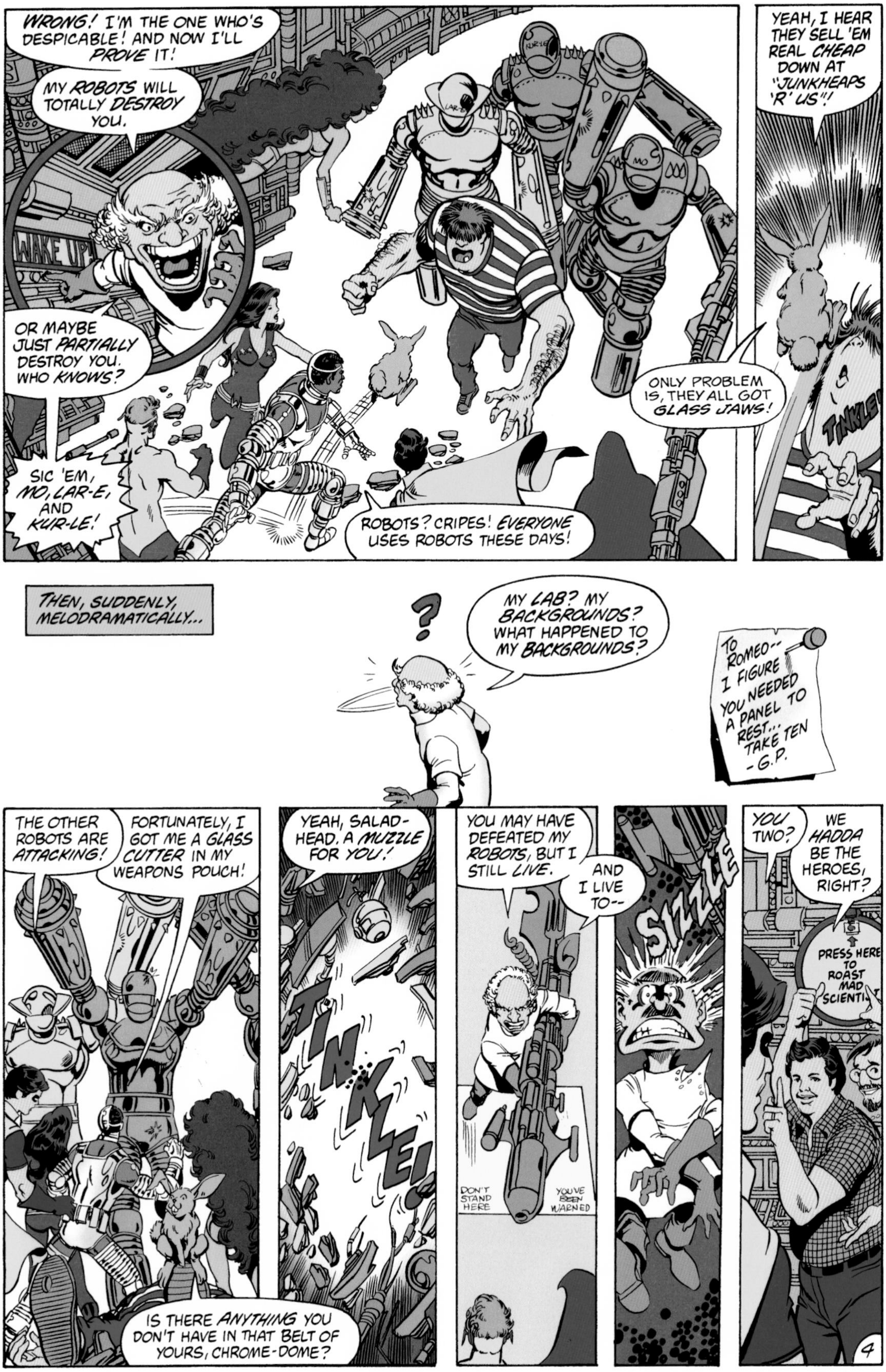
WRONG! I'M THE ONE WHO'S DESPICABLE! AND NOW I'LL PROVE IT!
MY ROBOTS WILL TOTALLY DESTROY YOU.
WAKE UP!
OR MAYBE JUST PARTIALLY DESTROY YOU. WHO KNOWS?
SIC 'EM, MO, LAR-E, AND KUR-LE!
ROBOTS? CRIPES! EVERYONE USES ROBOTS THESE DAYS!
ONLY PROBLEM IS, THEY ALL GOT GLASS JAWS!
YEAH, I HEAR THEY SELL 'EM REAL CHEAP DOWN AT "JUNKHEAPS 'R' US"!
TINKLE!
THEN, SUDDENLY, MELODRAMATICALLY...
?
MY LAB? MY BACKGROUNDS? WHAT HAPPENED TO MY BACKGROUNDS?
TO ROMEO-- I FIGURE YOU NEEDED A PANEL TO REST... TAKE TEN -G.P.
THE OTHER ROBOTS ARE ATTACKING!
FORTUNATELY, I GOT ME A GLASS CUTTER IN MY WEAPONS POUCH!
IS THERE ANYTHING YOU DON'T HAVE IN THAT BELT OF YOURS, CHROME-DOME?
YEAH, SALAD-HEAD. A MUZZLE FOR YOU!
TINKLE!
YOU MAY HAVE DEFEATED MY ROBOTS, BUT I STILL LIVE.
AND I LIVE TO--
DON'T STAND HERE
YOU'VE BEEN WARNED
SIZZLE
YOU TWO?
WE HADDA BE THE HEROES, RIGHT?
PRESS HERE TO ROAST MAD
4

I'M GONNA MAKE A FORTUNE *RECYCLING* THESE INTO *LAMPS!*

IT'S REALLY A PLEASURE *MEETING* YOU. I JUST CAN'T *BELIEVE* IT.

I'M NOT SURE *WE* CAN, EITHER. JUST ONE QUESTION, THO'--

--WHO ARE YOU?

POST NO BILLS

HI!

I'M MARV!

HI!

I'M STARFIRE!

I'M A WRITER!

I'M A SUPER-HERO!

YOU'RE GORGEOUS!

HI, GEORGE.

BUT, JUST AS MARV'S SMILE FADES INTO A QUIVERING MASS OF RED JELLO...

ZAP!

ROBIN! THEY'RE *GONE!*

SOMEHOW, STARFIRE, I DON'T FEEL ALL *TOO BAD* ABOUT THAT!

WHAT'S *HAPPENING* TO US, GEORGE?

CAN'T YOU *GUESS?* WITH ONLY *FOUR PANELS* LEFT TO THIS STORY...

...WE'RE RETURNING *HOME.*

AND JUST IN TIME TO WATCH *"THAT'S RIDICULOUS"* ON *TV.*

I'M GLAD YOU'RE SO UNDERSTAND-ING, FLUFFY.

IT WON'T *EVER* HAPPEN AGAIN.

MARV. GEORGE. YOU'RE *LATE* ON YOUR NEXT TITANS STORY.

NO *PROBLEM,* KAREN. I GOT AN *IDEA!*

THIS ONE'S *FANTASTIC!* IT'S THE GREATEST IDEA SINCE *DC* PUBLISHED *"THE GEEK"!*

DON'T *WORRY,* GUYS...

I'LL MAKE SURE HIS STORY *WORKS...*

...AS *USUAL.*

AND I HAVE TO *COLOR* HIS BOOK, SHEESH!

I TELL YOU, GEORGE, I MUST BE *BRILLIANT* TO COME UP WITH THESE STORIES. YOU HEAR ME? *BRILLIANT!*

YES, MARV. *OF COURSE,* MARV.

POOR, DELUDED FOOL.

DEFINITELY THE END!

5

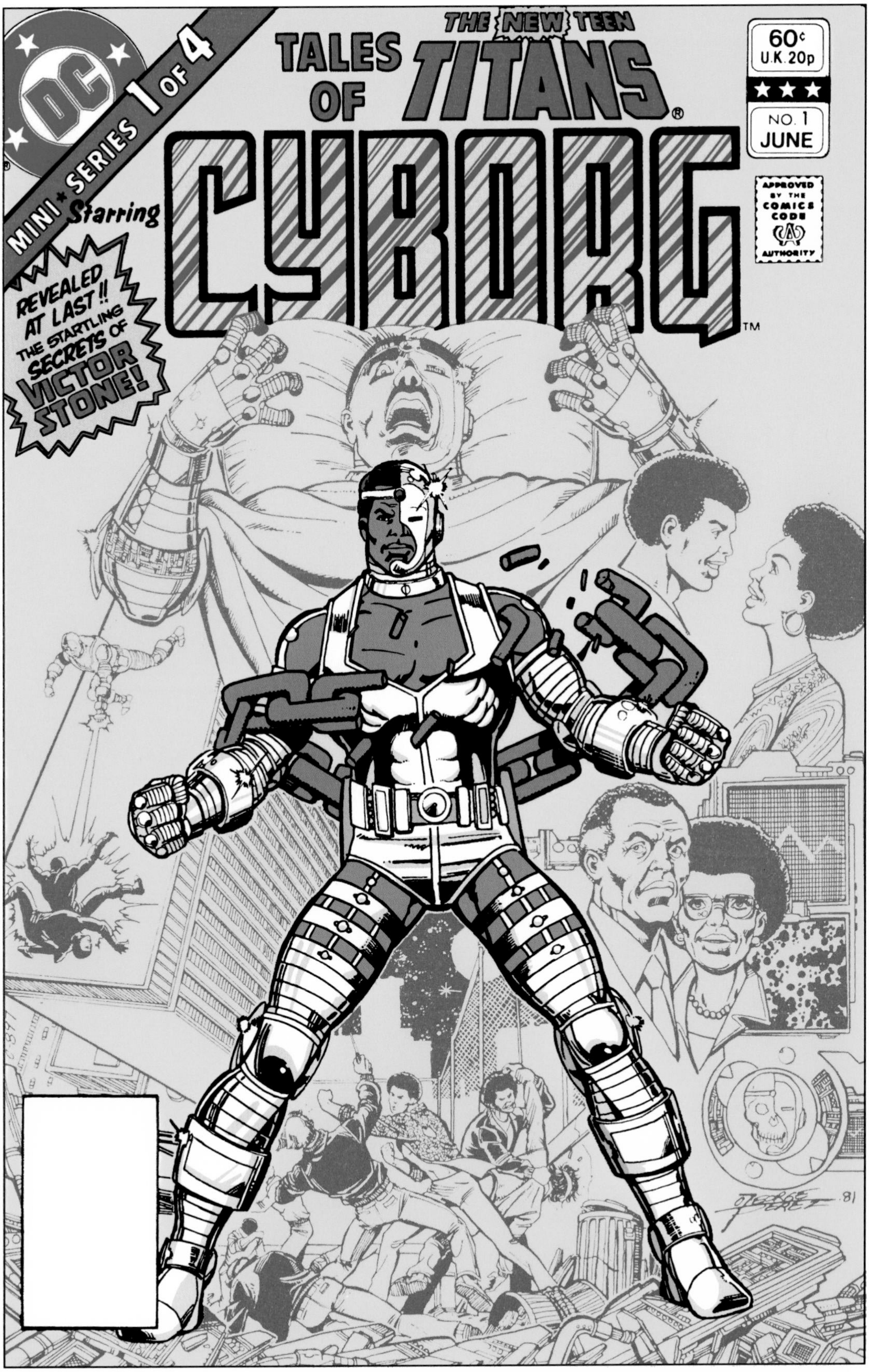

DC
MINI ★ SERIES 1 OF 4
THE NEW TEEN
TALES OF
TITANS®
Starring
CYBORG™
60¢
U.K. 20p
NO. 1
JUNE
APPROVED BY THE COMICS CODE AUTHORITY
REVEALED AT LAST!! THE STARTLING SECRETS OF VICTOR STONE!
GEORGE PEREZ '81

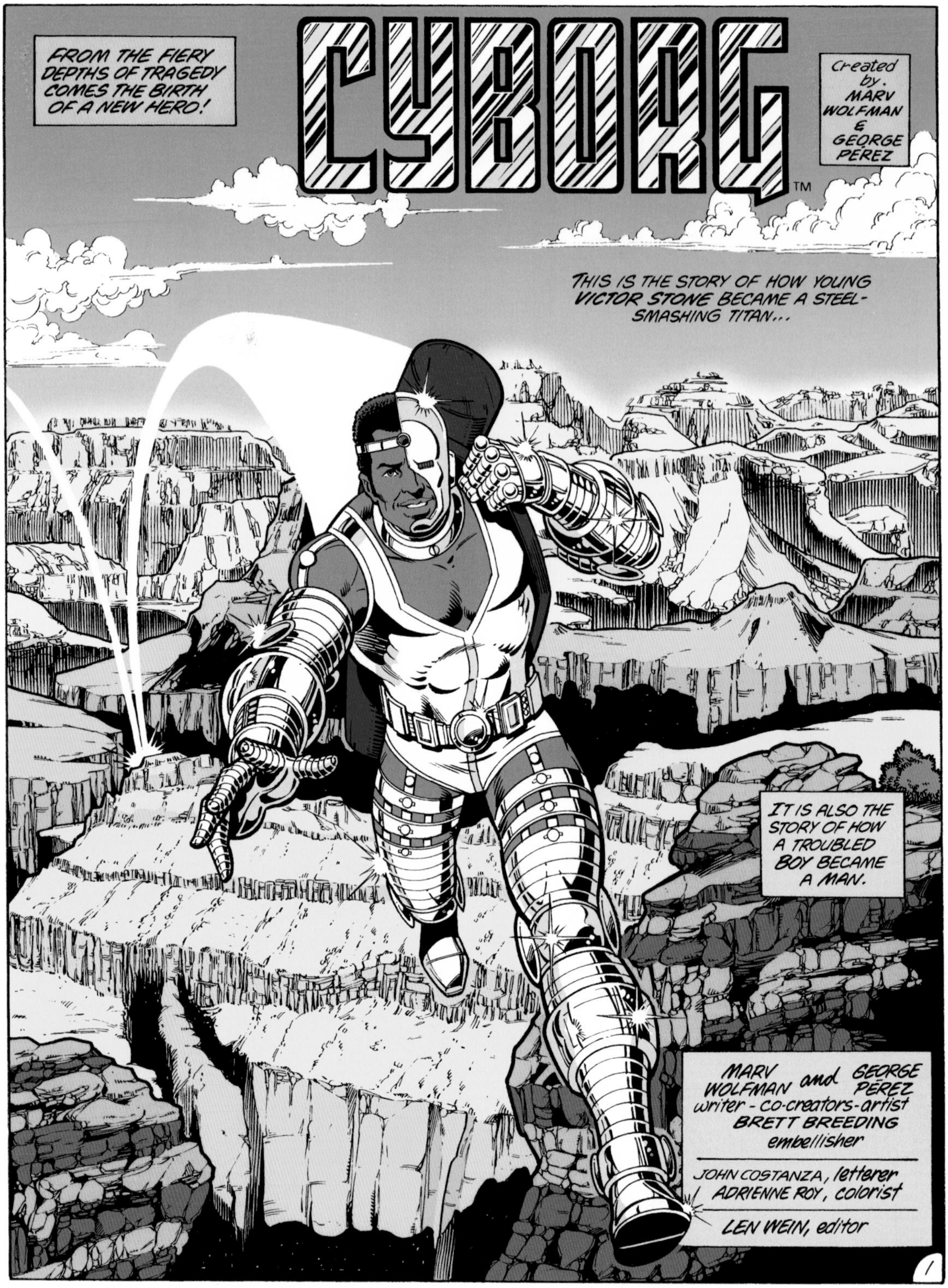
FROM THE FIERY DEPTHS OF TRAGEDY COMES THE BIRTH OF A NEW HERO!
CYBORG™
Created by. MARV WOLFMAN & GEORGE PÉREZ
THIS IS THE STORY OF HOW YOUNG VICTOR STONE BECAME A STEEL-SMASHING TITAN...
IT IS ALSO THE STORY OF HOW A TROUBLED BOY BECAME A MAN.
MARV WOLFMAN and GEORGE PÉREZ writer - co-creators-artist
BRETT BREEDING embellisher
JOHN COSTANZA, letterer
ADRIENNE ROY, colorist
LEN WEIN, editor
1

THE GRAND CANYON STRETCHES LONG AND WIDE BENEATH A DARK AND DUSKY COPPER SKY. THE AIR HERE IS FRESH, UNTAINTED BY CHEMICAL POLLUTANTS, AND THESE SIX YOUNG TITANS FEEL MORE ALIVE TODAY THAN THEY HAVE IN MONTHS...

MAN, THIS WAS ONE GOOD IDEA.

GARFIELD SUGGESTED THIS, VICTOR.

YEP! WE'VE BEEN SO *DEPRESSED* OF LATE, I THOUGHT SOMEBODY HADDA BECOME OUR OFFICIAL *CHEERLEADER.*

YOU'RE NOT GONNA HEAR NO FROM ME, PAL.

WE REALLY NEED SOME *FUN TIME* OFF.

C'MON, THE *T-JET'S* PARKED ON THE NEXT *BUTTE.*

YOU KNOW, WHEN WE WERE HERE THE *LAST* TIME, WE WERE TOO BUSY TO *EXPLORE* THIS PLACE.

BUT IT'S REALLY *LOVELY.* IN A WAY IT REMINDS ME OF *OKAARA.*

THE REST OF THE GANG'S *WAITING* FOR US THERE.

AND SOON...

SAY, WHERE'S *RAVEN?* I THOUGHT SHE'D BE *WITH* YOU?

WELL, IT TOOK *KORIAND'R* AND ME HALF THE MORNING TO CONVINCE HER TO *JOIN US...*

...AND THE *REST* BUYING HER SOME SUITABLE *CLOTHES.*

I JUST THINK SHE'S A LITTLE BIT *SHY* ABOUT--

I--I AM *HERE,* MY FRIENDS, I AM SORRY TO HAVE *DELAYED* YOU.

NO *PROBLEM,* RAVEN. I'M JUST GLAD YOU CAME.

HEY, YOU LOOK *GREAT* IN THAT.

TH-THANK YOU, WALLACE.

2

WELL, WAS I RIGHT OR WAS I *RIGHT*?

GETTING AWAY FROM IT ALL... *RELAXING.* NOW ISN'T THIS *BETTER* THAN BEATING UP ON *BAD GUYS*?

BESIDES, THE SCENERY HERE JUST CAN'T BE *BEAT*.

HOW'S THE *FIRE* DOING, DICK?

WELL, IT'S BEEN A WHILE SINCE I WAS A *BOY SCOUT.*

Y'KNOW, DONNA, I'M REALLY GOING TO *ENJOY* THIS WEEK.

CHOW TIME, GUYS AND GALS. FOOD'S GOING ON THE PIT.

SUCCULENT MORSELS COOKED THE WAY YOU *LIKE* 'EM...

...PROVIDING YOU *LIKE* 'EM THE WAY I *COOK* 'EM.

DID YOU ONLY BRING *MEAT*? I--I DON'T *EAT* THAT.

I-I'M SORRY, RAVEN, I DIDN'T *KNOW.*

LOOK, I'LL PICK UP SOME *VEGETABLES* AT *LEE'S FERRY*, OKAY?

IT'LL ONLY TAKE A *SECOND.*

NOW, I DON'T EXPECT *MEDALS* FOR COMING UP WITH THIS, BUT I GOTTA SAY THIS IS THE WAY FRIENDS *SHOULD* SPEND THEIR TIME, RIGHT?

FRIENDS...

Y'KNOW, WE'VE BEEN SO *BUSY* LATELY I HADN'T EVEN *THOUGHT* OF FRIENDS.

THOUGH I THINK WHEN I BECAME THIS GALVANIZED *FREAK*, I *LOST* ALL MY OLD FRIENDS.

YOU MUST BE *WRONG*, VICTOR. TRUE FRIENDS DON'T DESERT YOU BECAUSE OF AN *ACCIDENT.*

TRUE FRIENDS... YEAH, THEY *DON'T.* MAYBE I JUST NEVER *HAD* ANY TRUE FRIENDS...

3

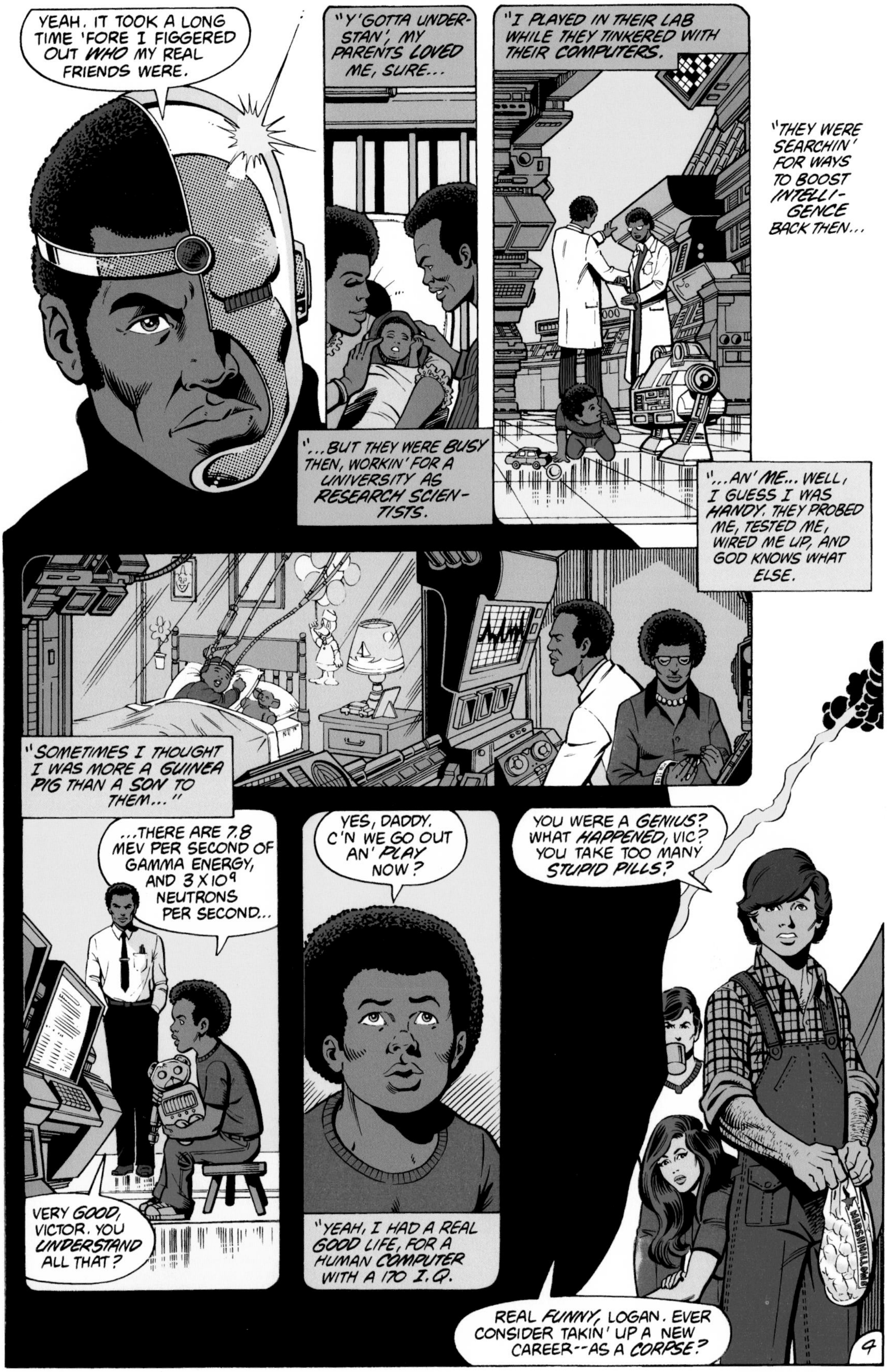
YEAH. IT TOOK A LONG TIME 'FORE I FIGGERED OUT WHO MY REAL FRIENDS WERE.
"Y'GOTTA UNDER-STAN', MY PARENTS LOVED ME, SURE...
"...BUT THEY WERE BUSY THEN, WORKIN' FOR A UNIVERSITY AS RESEARCH SCIEN-TISTS.
"I PLAYED IN THEIR LAB WHILE THEY TINKERED WITH THEIR COMPUTERS.
"THEY WERE SEARCHIN' FOR WAYS TO BOOST INTELLI-GENCE BACK THEN...
"...AN' ME... WELL, I GUESS I WAS HANDY. THEY PROBED ME, TESTED ME, WIRED ME UP, AND GOD KNOWS WHAT ELSE.
"SOMETIMES I THOUGHT I WAS MORE A GUINEA PIG THAN A SON TO THEM..."
...THERE ARE 7.8 MEV PER SECOND OF GAMMA ENERGY, AND 3 X 10⁹ NEUTRONS PER SECOND...
VERY GOOD, VICTOR. YOU UNDERSTAND ALL THAT?
YES, DADDY. C'N WE GO OUT AN' PLAY NOW?
"YEAH, I HAD A REAL GOOD LIFE, FOR A HUMAN COMPUTER WITH A 170 I.Q.
YOU WERE A GENIUS? WHAT HAPPENED, VIC? YOU TAKE TOO MANY STUPID PILLS?
MARSHMALLOWS
REAL FUNNY, LOGAN. EVER CONSIDER TAKIN' UP A NEW CAREER--AS A CORPSE?
4

I FEEL *SORRY* FOR YOU, VICTOR. ON TAMARAN LOVE IS *EVERY-THING.*

DIDN'T YOU EVER HAVE ANY *FUN* WITH YOUR PARENTS?

SURE I DID, SHORT-PANTS. I TOLD YOU, THEY *LOVED ME.*

WE *WENT* PLACES.

"I REMEMBER ONE YEAR IT WAS THE *CIRCUS.* ONCE OR TWICE A BALL GAME.

"BUT, ROBBIE, THOSE WERE REALLY EXCEPTIONS."

"NOW, THEY DIDN'T *DREAM* THEY MIGHT BE *HURTIN'* ME."

"BUT THEY KEPT PUSHIN', TEACHIN', AN' I KEPT LEARNIN': THAT WAS THE WAY IT MOSTLY WAS."

OKAY, GROUP, COME AND *GET* IT. DOGS AND BURGERS ALL *DONE.*

RAVEN, YOUR *SOY-BURGER'S* ALMOST FINISHED.

DID YOU *RESENT* YOUR PARENTS, VICTOR?

YEAH... AND *NO,* KORY.

GUESS I DIDN'T KNOW WHAT I WAS *MISSIN'!*

BESIDES, THEY DID SHOW THEIR *LOVE* TO ME, TOO.

STILL, IT SEEMS SO *SAD.*

A *CHILD* SHOULD ONLY BE BUBBLING WITH *HAPPINESS,* DON'T YOU THINK?

I THINK I KNEW IT AS I GREW *OLDER.*

5

"BY THE TIME I WAS *EIGHT*, I STARTED SNEAKIN' OUT AT NIGHT. JUST TO SEE WHAT I WAS *MISSIN'.*"

"DIDN'T KNOW WHAT I WAS *SEARCHIN'* FOR, AN' FRANKLY, I DIDN'T MUCH *CARE.*"

REVUE

DIRTY DINGUS McGEE
FRANK SINATRA
ALSO: WILLIAM HOLDEN
THE WILD BUNCH

BUS STOP

'Y'SEE, JUST BEIN' OUT WAS *FINE.*

"I HAD PRIVATE *TUTORS,* SO I NEVER WENT TO *PUBLIC* SCHOOL. NEVER MUCH WENT OUT AT ALL.

"AN' NOT *KNOWIN'* STUFF ALMOST PROVED THE *DEATH* OF ME. "

WATCH OUT, YOU CRAZY KID!

"I STOOD THERE LIKE SOME *FOOL* STARIN' AT THE *HEAD-LIGHTS.*

"I COULDN'T EVEN *MOVE,* I WAS SO SCARED.

"THEN I FELT SOMETHIN' *HIT* ME. I FELL BACK.

"TOOK A SECOND TO REALIZE IT WASN'T THE *CAR* THAT SMASHED INTO ME. "

MAN, YOU A FREAKIN' *JERK* OR SOMETHIN'? WHY YOU JUS' *STANDIN'* THERE, HUH?

C'MON, BOY, ANSWER ME.

YOU *SAVED* ME?

SURE, BOY, COULDN'T LET A BROTHER GO *SPLAT,* COULD I?

HEY, THE TAG'S *RON...* RON *EVERS.* WHAT THEY CALL *YOU,* BOY?

AND THAT'S HOW I MET MY FIRST FRIEND.

AND TO A RESTLESS, WITHDRAWN KID LIKE I WAS, *RON* SEEMED TO BE WHAT LIFE WAS ALL *ABOUT.*

HE MADE EVERY-THING *FUN.* SO NATCH, WHATEVER HE DID, I DID.

6

"TILL THE COPS CAUGHT ME."

I'M *SORRY*, MR. AND MRS. STONE. BUT HE AND HIS FRIENDS WERE FOUND *LOOTING A GROCERY STORE*.

"DAD DIDN'T SAY A **WORD** THE WHOLE TRIP HOME. HE JUST SENT ME TO MY ROOM.

"MAN, I HAD NEVER *SEEN* HIM LIKE THAT BEFORE. I WAS SO *SCARED* WONDERING WHAT HE WAS GOING TO *DO* TO ME.

"BUT HE NEVER *CAME* TO ME. ONLY MY *MOM* DID."

VICTOR--?   I'M *SORRY*, MOM. I REALLY *AM*. I WON'T DO IT *AGAIN*.

YOUR FATHER AND I *LOVE* YOU, VICTOR, WE HONESTLY *DO*. AND SOMETHING LIKE THIS IS SO... *DISAPPOINTING*.

PERHAPS WE'VE *PUSHED* YOU TOO MUCH...

NOT *YOU*, MOM, IT'S *DAD*. I DON'T *WANT* SCIENCE. I JUST WANT TO DO WHAT I *WANT*.

MOM, I DON'T KNOW ANY *KIDS*. DO I HAVE TO HAVE A *TUTOR*? CAN'T I GO TO *SCHOOL* WITH EVERYONE ELSE?

AND ALL WE WANT IS FOR YOU TO BE *HAPPY*. TO BE *GOOD*.

LOOK WHAT ASSOCIATING WITH OTHERS HAS ALREADY *DONE*, VICTOR. YOU'VE BECOME A *HOOLIGAN*.

BY GOD, SON. YOU'VE GOT THE STUFF OF *BRILLIANCE*.

WHY DO YOU INSIST ON *RUINING* YOURSELF?

I'VE HAD SUCH GREAT *DREAMS* FOR YOU.

I THINK THAT WAS THE FIRST TIME I TRULY FELT *HATE* FOR HIM. *HE* HAD DREAMS, BUT HE NEVER ONCE THOUGHT THAT MAYBE *I* HAD SOME, TOO.

7

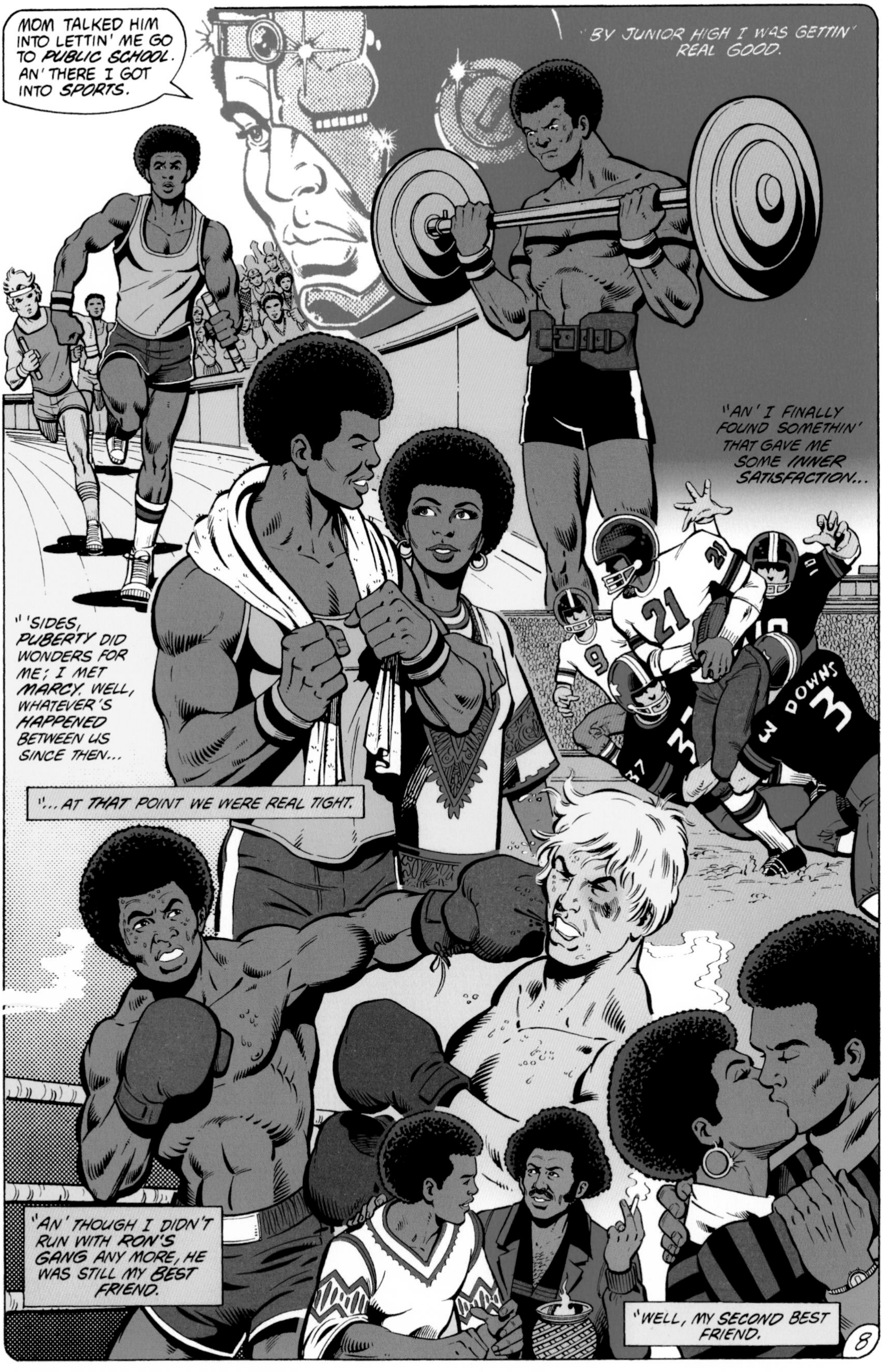
MOM TALKED HIM INTO LETTIN' ME GO TO PUBLIC SCHOOL. AN' THERE I GOT INTO SPORTS.
"BY JUNIOR HIGH I WAS GETTIN' REAL GOOD.
"AN' I FINALLY FOUND SOMETHIN' THAT GAVE ME SOME INNER SATISFACTION...
"'SIDES, PUBERTY DID WONDERS FOR ME; I MET MARCY. WELL, WHATEVER'S HAPPENED BETWEEN US SINCE THEN...
"...AT THAT POINT WE WERE REAL TIGHT.
"AN' THOUGH I DIDN'T RUN WITH RON'S GANG ANY MORE, HE WAS STILL MY BEST FRIEND.
"WELL, MY SECOND BEST FRIEND.
8

"OF COURSE, NOT EVERY-THIN' WAS GOIN' GREAT."

GOIN' OUT *AGAIN?* YOU'RE FALLING BEHIND IN YOUR *STUDIES.*

SO?

I DON'T *CARE*, DAD.

VICTOR, I *FORBID* YOU TO RUN WITH THOSE... *ANIMALS!* I DID NOT RAISE YOU TO BE *SHOT DOWN* ON SOME STREET CORNER.

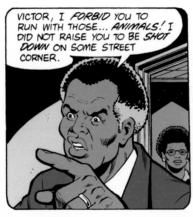

NO, YOU LISSEN TO *ME*, MAN. WHAT *YOU* SAY DOESN'T *MATTER* ANY MORE.

I SEE HOW YOU SUCK UP TO '*THE MAN*'! BUILDIN' THOSE WEAPONS FOR *S.T.A.R.*

VICTOR, I *FORBID*--

ME, I'M GOING TO DO THINGS *MY* WAY, AN' WHAT *YOU* SAY DON'T MATTER *NO HOW.*

SAVE IT, OLD MAN. I AIN'T *LISSENIN.'*

LORD, WHEN DID WE *LOSE* HIM?

WE'VE PUSHED HIM SO *HARD*, SILAS, NEVER ONCE WONDER-ING IF WE WERE DOING *RIGHT.*

BLACK POWER

I'M SO *AFRAID* OF HIM, ELINORE. YOU EVER *WATCH* HIM?

HE'S PURE BUNDLED-UP ENERGY WAITING TO *EXPLODE.*

HE HASN'T ANY *PATIENCE.* I--I DON'T THINK HE'LL EVER BE A *SCIENTIST*...

BUT HE'S GOOD AT *SPORTS.* HE *LOVES* THEM, TOO.

SPORTS? THAT'S A WASTE OF ALL THAT *BRIL-LIANCE*... AN UTTER WASTE OF ALL THAT *TALENT.*

"I HADN'T *SEEN* RON FOR A WHILE, DIDN'T EVEN KNOW HE WAS *BACK* FROM *REFORM SCHOOL,* UNTIL..."

HEY, VIC! HOW'S THINGS *GOIN' DOWN*, MAN?

RON? GOOD SEEIN' YOU, PAL. HOW YOU *BEEN?*

9

NOT *BAD,* M'MAN. BUT ME AN' THE BOYS COULD SURE USE YOUR *MUSCLE.*

WE GOT OURSELVES A *RUMBLE* GOIN' TONIGHT WITH A WHITE GANG CALLED *"THE HAWKS".*

RUMBLE? *NO THANKS,* PAL. NOT MY *STYLE* ANY MORE.

YOU *CHICKEN,* BOY? YOU FORGET YOU *OWE* ME?

WE'RE GETTIN' IT FROM *BOTH* SIDES, BOY-- EVEN THE *COPS* ARE COMIN' DOWN ON US 'CAUSE WE'RE *BLACK.*

I DON'T *BELIEVE* THAT, RON. THAT DOESN'T MEAN...

IT MEANS EVERY- THING, VICTOR-- *EVERYTHING!*

MY FATHER WAS PASSED OVER FOR *PROMOTION* FOR SOME *WHITE* DUDE.

THE COLOR OF OUR SKIN *MARKS* US, VIC. AN' LIKE MY FATHER *SAYS,* MAYBE WE SHOULD START *DOIN'* SOMETHING ABOUT IT.

I DON'T *KNOW,* HONEY. THIS ISN'T MY KIND A *FIGHT.*

BET YOU CAN GUESS WHAT *HAPPENED.* I WAS *INSULATED* AS A KID AND I DIDN'T GROW UP HATING ANYONE BECAUSE OF *COLOR*--

--BUT RON WAS MY *FRIEND,* AND MARCY WAS MY *GIRL.*

"'SIDES, I DIDN'T THINK A LITTLE *FIGHT* WOULD HURT ANYONE--

"-- TILL I GOT THERE AND SAW THEIR *KNIVES.*

"MAN, I FREAKED OUT WHEN I GOT *CUT* AN' SAW MY *BLOOD* DRIPPIN' OUT.

" I *FOUGHT BACK,* WITH EVERYTHIN' I HAD...

10

"PEOPLE DIDN'T MATTER THEN. COLOR DIDN'T MATTER.

"I JUST WANTED TO KILL.

TURN 'ROUND, BLACK BOY, AN'--

AN', NOTHIN', WHITEY.

RON?

GUESS YOU OWE ME 'GAIN, VIC, EH?

"I NODDED, NEVER THINKING I WOULDN'T HAVE BEEN THERE 'CEPT FOR RON.

"'COURSE, I DIDN'T HAVE TIME TO THINK, 'CAUSE JUST THEN..."

WEEOOOEEEOOOEEEO

SIRENS!

FORGET THE HAWKS! SPLIT!

"SOMEHOW I MADE IT BACK HOME...

"...LOOKIN' LIKE SOMETHING THE CAT WOULD'VE BURIED."

YOU ASKED WHY I'VE BEEN SO HARD ON HIM, ELINORE?

I SWORE I WOULDN'T CALL HIM MY SON IF HE WOUND UP THIS WAY...

...AND I MEANT IT!

WHY, VICTOR? FOR GOD'S SAKE, I THOUGHT ALL THIS WAS OVER.

HEY, IT'S HIS FAULT, MOM. ALWAYS PUSHIN' ME. ALWAYS PUTTIN' ME DOWN.

NO! DON'T BLAME YOUR FATHER. HE DIDN'T CUT YOU WITH THAT KNIFE.

YOU HAD FREEDOM OF CHOICE.

BUT, MOM--

11

DON'T DARE GIVE ME ANY 'BUTS,' VICTOR. NOBODY TOOK YOUR HAND AND *PUSHED* YOU INTO THIS. NOBODY BUT *YOU.*

...BUT YOU KNOW WHAT YOUR PROBLEM TRULY *IS?* YOU DON'T KNOW *WHAT* YOU WANT.

YOU WANTED PUBLIC SCHOOL, WE *GAVE* IT TO YOU. YOU WANTED SPORTS, WE DIDN'T *STOP* YOU.

YOUR FATHER WAS *RIGHT.* THERE IS *ANGER* INSIDE YOU.

BUT, DAMN IT, DON'T EVER AIM THAT ANGER AT *US,* VICTOR.

YOU COULD HAVE GONE *ANYWHERE,* DONE *ANYTHING...*

AIM IT WHERE IT BELONGS -- AT *YOURSELF,* FOR RUINING EVERY *OPPORTUNITY* YOU'VE HAD.

MOM WAS *CRYIN'* WHEN SHE SAID THAT, IT MUST'VE TORN OUT HER HEART TO GET *MAD* AT ME.

BUT BACK THEN ALL *I* GOT WAS *ANGRY.* I STOMPED OUT.

"MORE TIME PASSED. I WAS 17 NOW, AN' I GOT THIS CALL FROM RON TO HURRY OVER.

"HE LIVED IN THIS *TENEMENT* ON 126TH STREET."

DIDN'T THINK YOU'D *MAKE* IT, VIC. C'MON *IN.*

WHAT'S *UP,* RON?

FREEDOM, MAN. HOW WE DON'T *HAVE* NO FREEDOM. HOW THE HONKIES KEEP PUTTIN' US DOWN...

...HOW WE CAN'T GET *NOWHERE.* SO WE DECIDED TO TAKE OVER LITTLE MISS *WHITE LIBERTY--*

-- AN' TELL THE WORLD HOW *BAD* WE GOT IT... AN' HOW MUCH WE *WANT.*

AN' *YOU,* LITTLE BROTHER, YOU SPEAK *BETTER* THAN US. SO WE WANT *YOU* TO TALK FOR US.

NO, RON. I WON'T *DO* IT.

YOU'RE *WRONG* ABOUT ALL THIS.

AND *THIS* TIME I WON'T HELP YOU MAKE A *MISTAKE.*

12

YOU'RE LETTING YOUR OWN HATE *CONSUME* YOU, RON.

EASY FOR *YOU* TO SAY, MAN. YOU GOT A *SCHOLARSHIP* FOR COLLEGE YOUR OLD MAN ARRANGED... YOU GOT IT ALL.

JUST STOP IT RIGHT THERE, RON. NOBODY *GAVE* ME THAT SCHOLARSHIP. I WORKED DAMN *HARD* FOR THAT.

MY DAD *FOUGHT* ME, WOULDN'T GIVE ME A *PENNY* UNLESS I MAJORED IN *SCIENCE.*

BUT I *PROVED* MYSELF. I WORKED AN' GOT WHAT I WANTED.

ANYONE CAN DO THAT, RON -- AND THE COLOR OF YOUR *SKIN* DOESN'T MATTER ONE DAMN BIT.

YOU WALK OUTTA HERE AN' WE AIN'T *FRIENDS* NO MORE. YOU *HEAR* THAT, MAN? *YOU HEAR THAT?*

YOU HEAR THAT?

RON, I HEAR IT.

AND THAT'S *YOUR* DECISION, NOT *MINE.*

YOU REJECTED HIS *VIOLENCE.* YOU WERE GROWING UP.

MAYBE, RAVEN, BUT INSIDE I WAS SO MAD.

BUT I KNEW WHAT WAS RIGHT FOR ME.

WHAT *HAPPENED* TO THIS RON?

THE *COPS* GOT 'IM SOON'S HE CLIMBED THE STATUE.

HE SPENT ALMOST A YEAR IN *PRISON...*

...WHILE I WENT ON TO *COLLEGE...* WORKIN' MY BUTT OFF TO MAKE THE *OLYMPICS.*

13

"THEN, ONE DAY WHILE I WAS HEADING HOME AFTER DOIN' MY DAILY *TWENTY,* I DECIDED TO STOP AN' SEE MY MOM.

"GOD HELP ME, I DIDN'T KNOW THEN THAT I'D *NEVER* SEE HER *AGAIN...*"

YOUR PARENTS ARE UP IN THE *EIGHTH FLOOR* LAB.

THANKS, HANK.

"MY PARENTS WERE INVOLVED IN TWO DIFFER- ENT RESEARCH JOBS--ONE WAS A *WEAPONS SYSTEM* FOR THE ARMY...

"...THE OTHER WAS STRAIGHT RESEARCH ON *DIMENSION- PROBING* FOR S.T.A.R.

"HOW *FAR* THEY GOT IN BOTH AREAS I DIDN'T KNOW UNTIL I HAD OPENED THE LAB *DOOR...*

"I DIDN'T *SEE* MY MOM, BUT I KNEW SHE WAS THERE, SCREAMING OUT IN AGONY, HALF-CONSUMED BY THAT STINKING, FILTHY *THING--*

"--THAT DAMNED *BLASPHEMY* FROM ANOTHER DIMENSION.

"THE CREATURE-- GOD, IT *TURNED* TO ME, AND FOR THE FIRST TIME IN MY LIFE I WAS SO SCARED, SO VERY SCARED...

"THE FETID THING OOZED *OVER* ME. I FELT MY FLESH BURN AT ITS SLIMY TOUCH... I FELT MY BONES DISSOLVE RIGHT IN- SIDE MY BODY...

"MY FATHER LATER TOLD ME THAT HE CRAWLED IN STARK TERROR ACROSS THE LAB ROOM...

"...HE COULDN'T EVEN *THINK* STRAIGHT, BUT HE PUNCHED THE *RECALL* BUTTON ON THE COMPUTER...

"...THEN *BRACED* HIMSELF, AS THAT MURDERING CREATURE WAS SUCKED BACK INTO ITS OWN DIMENSION.

"THE COMPUTER *BLEW UP* AS IT SLIPPED *THROUGH.*

14

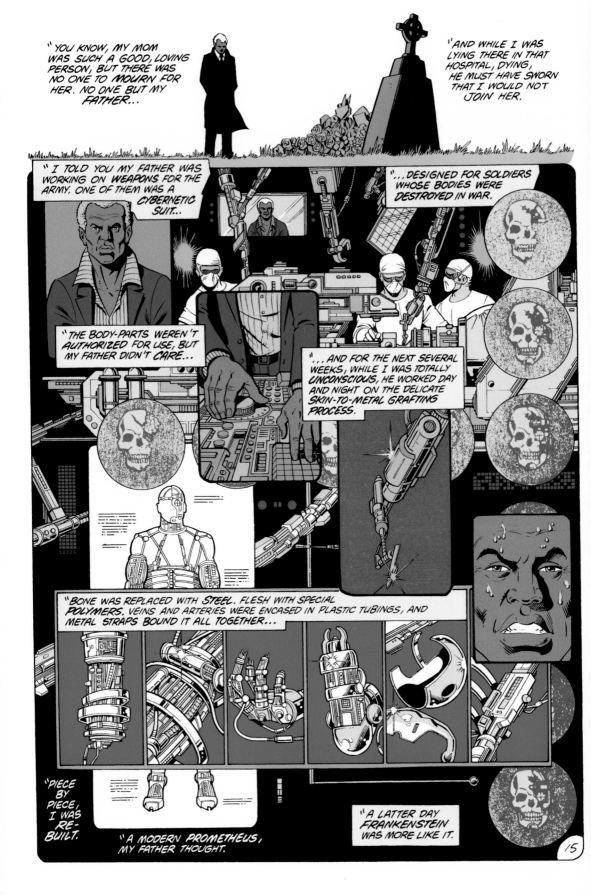

"YOU KNOW, MY MOM WAS SUCH A GOOD, LOVING PERSON, BUT THERE WAS NO ONE TO *MOURN* FOR HER. NO ONE BUT MY *FATHER*...

"AND WHILE I WAS LYING THERE IN THAT HOSPITAL, DYING, HE MUST HAVE SWORN THAT I WOULD NOT JOIN HER.

"I TOLD YOU MY FATHER WAS WORKING ON *WEAPONS* FOR THE ARMY. ONE OF THEM WAS A *CYBERNETIC SUIT*...

"...DESIGNED FOR SOLDIERS WHOSE BODIES WERE *DESTROYED* IN WAR.

"THE BODY-PARTS WEREN'T *AUTHORIZED* FOR USE, BUT MY FATHER DIDN'T *CARE*...

"...AND FOR THE NEXT SEVERAL WEEKS, WHILE I WAS TOTALLY *UNCONSCIOUS*, HE WORKED DAY AND NIGHT ON THE DELICATE *SKIN-TO-METAL GRAFTING PROCESS.*

"BONE WAS REPLACED WITH *STEEL*, FLESH WITH SPECIAL *POLYMERS*, VEINS AND ARTERIES WERE ENCASED IN PLASTIC TUBINGS, AND METAL STRAPS BOUND IT ALL TOGETHER...

"PIECE BY PIECE, I WAS *RE-BUILT*.

"A MODERN *PROMETHEUS*, MY FATHER THOUGHT.

"A LATTER DAY *FRANKENSTEIN* WAS MORE LIKE IT.

/15

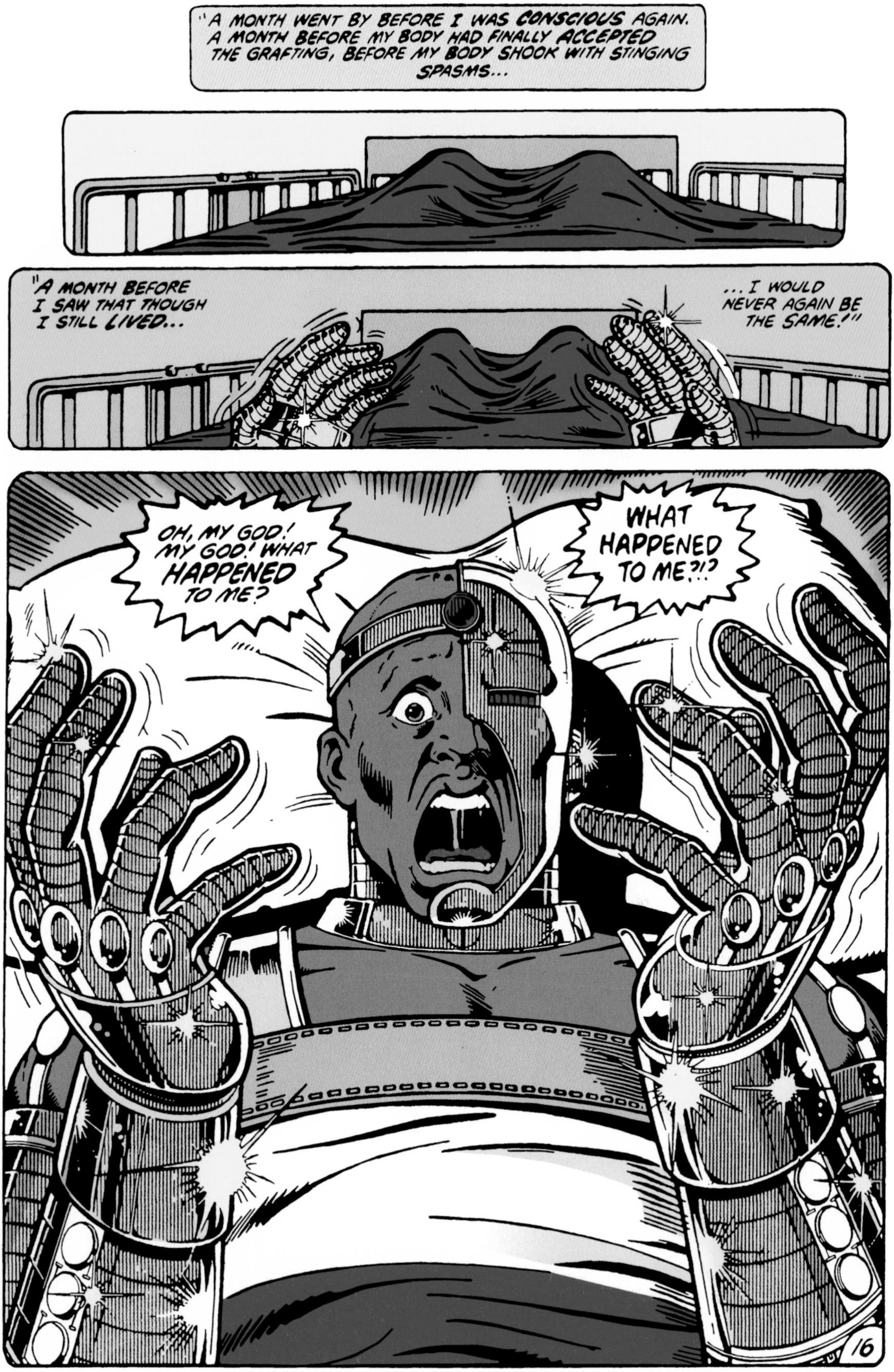
"A MONTH WENT BY BEFORE I WAS CONSCIOUS AGAIN. A MONTH BEFORE MY BODY HAD FINALLY ACCEPTED THE GRAFTING, BEFORE MY BODY SHOOK WITH STINGING SPASMS...
"A MONTH BEFORE I SAW THAT THOUGH I STILL LIVED...
...I WOULD NEVER AGAIN BE THE SAME!"
OH, MY GOD! MY GOD! WHAT HAPPENED TO ME?
WHAT HAPPENED TO ME?!?
16

I CAN *IMAGINE* WHAT YOU MUST HAVE BEEN *THINKING.*

WERE YOU VERY *FRIGHTENED,* VICTOR?

I DON'T THINK I CAN *DESCRIBE* HOW I FELT, GOLDIE.

THE *PAIN* MUST HAVE BEEN *TERRIBLE.*

"*PAIN?* NO, RAVEN. THERE WASN'T ANY PAIN. I WAS TOTALLY *NUMB.* NUMB AN' *ANGRY.*"

WHAT DID YOU *DO* TO ME?

I SAVED YOUR *LIFE,* SON. YOUR BODY WAS *HALF-DESTROYED.*

AND I GRAFTED YOU INTO AN EXPERIMENTAL *STEEL BODY.*

BUT, IF MY THEORY IS *CORRECT,* YOU'LL BE BETTER THAN *NEW* WHEN YOU--

'*THEORY*'? MY GOD, EVEN AFTER ALL THESE YEARS ALL I AM IS A DAMNED HUMAN GUINEA PIG!

YOU NEVER THOUGHT OF ME AS YOUR *SON,* DID YOU?

VICTOR, I--

JUST *SHUT UP,* OLD MAN. ALL MY LIFE YOU'VE *USED* ME, FORCED ME TO BE WHAT YOU *WANTED* ME TO BE.

AND ALL MY LIFE I *FOUGHT* YOU. BUT YOU *WON,* DIDN'T YOU?

CURSE YOU, MAN-- I'M *EXACTLY* WHAT YOU WANT NOW!

I *HATE* YOU, OLD MAN! I *HATE* YOU!

DAMN IT, WHY DIDN'T YOU LET ME JUST *DIE?*

WHY COULDN'T YOU LET ME *DIE!?!?*

17

"*FIVE MONTHS* I WAS IN THAT HOSPITAL! FIVE MONTHS FEELIN' LIKE SOME KINDA *FREAK!* EVERYTHIN' I ONCE KNEW I HADDA *RELEARN.* YOU IMAGINE WHAT I *FELT* LIKE HAVING TO FIGGER OUT HOW TO *WALK* AGAIN?"

"YOU KNOW WHAT IT'S LIKE NOT EVEN BEIN' ABLE TO HOLD SOMETHIN' WITHOUT CRUSHIN' IT?"

"I USEDTA RUN A MILE IN FOUR MINUTES, TWENTY. BUT NOW I COULDN'T EVEN WALK."

"I DIDN'T KNOW HOW TO ADJUST TO MY NEW STRENGTH."

"EVERYTHING WAS LIKE A LIVING HELL TO ME. RELEARNIN', READJUSTIN', STARTIN' FROM SCRATCH.

"FIVE MONTHS IT TOOK. FIVE LONG, LONELY MONTHS BEFORE I COULD HOLD AN EGG IN MY HAND AGAIN.

"FIVE MONTHS SPENDIN' EVERY HOUR WITH THE MAN I *HATED* MORE THAN ANYONE ELSE IN THE WORLD...

"...THE MAN WHO FORCED ME TO LEARN TO BE A *PERSON* ONCE AGAIN.

18

"FIVE MONTHS *BEFORE* I HAD THE *COURAGE* TO WALK OUT-SIDE. AN' WHEN I FINALLY *DID,* THINGS WERE NO *BETTER.*

FELT THEIR EYES BORING INTO ME. FEAR. *HATE.* IT HURT SO MUCH. BUT NEVER SO MUCH AS WHEN *KIDS* RAN AWAY FROM ME.

"*I* WAS A *MONSTER.* A BLASTED *FRANKENSTEIN.* AND I CURSED MY FATHER ALL OVER AGAIN FOR NOT LETTING ME *DIE.*

"FINALLY, I COULDN'T *TAKE* IT ANY LONGER..."

WHAT ARE YOU *DOING,* VICTOR?

GETTIN' *OUTTA* HERE, OLD MAN. *SEEIN'* YOU EVERY DAY MAKES ME HATE YOU AN' ME EVEN *MORE* THAN I ALREADY DO.

BUT WE'RE NOT FINISHED WITH YOUR *TRAINING,* VICTOR. THERE ARE STILL *TESTS*--

STUFF YOUR TESTS, OLD MAN.

I DON'T CARE IF MY BODY *REJECTS* THIS STEEL GARBAGE CAN YOU'VE TURNED ME INTO.

I DON'T CARE IF I *DIE.*

AND I DON'T CARE IF I NEVER *SEE* YOU AGAIN!

"HE SAID *NOTHING.* AND I HATED HIM EVEN *MORE* FOR THAT. OF COURSE I DIDN'T *KNOW* THEN HOW MUCH HE *CARED,* OR HOW MUCH HE REALLY *LOVED* ME...

"SO I *MOVED OUT.* MOVED TO HELL'S KITCHEN.

"IN A RATHOLE LIKE THAT, ONE MORE GODFORSAKEN LOSER WOULDN'T BE *NOTICED.* ⑲

"NOW, I'D STAYED PRETTY MUCH TO MYSELF FOR THE NEXT FEW WEEKS, UNTIL..."

NOK! NOK!

V·STONE

KEEP YER *SHIRT* ON!

AN' IF IT'S *YOU*, GREELY, YOU'LL GET MY RENT CHECK *NEXT WEEK*.

SO QUIT *HASSLIN'* ME, MAN.

"BUT IT WASN'T MY *LIQUOR-BREATHED* LAND-LORD...

RON? HOW'D YOU *FIND* ME, MAN?

HEY, *BRO'*, SOME WAY TO SAY HEY TO YOUR *NUMERO UNO AMIGO!*

HEARD YOU WENT THROUGH THE *WRINGER.* LOOKS BAD, BOY-- *REAL BAD.*

HURT, MAN?

ONLY WHEN I *LAUGH.* WHAT DO YOU *WANT*, RON?

ME? BRO, YOU GOT YOURSELF ONE SUSPICIOUS MIND. JUST AFTER *GOODNESS* AN' *JUSTICE*, MAN.

TALK ENGLISH AN' TALK *PLAIN.* I DON'T LIKE WASTING MY *TIME* ANY MORE.

OKAY, BOY, YOU GOT IT! IT WAS THE *MAN* THAT DID YOU IN. THE MAN DOES US *ALL* IN, BRO.

WELL, I TIED IN WITH SOME REAL GOOD FOLK NOW, --NO MORE TAKIN' OVER *STATUES.*

WE'RE GOIN' AFTER THE *BIG TARGET*, MAN--THE *UNITED NATIONS.*

AN' WE'RE GOIN' AFTER IT WITH *DYN-O-MITE!*

FIGGERED AFTER WHAT THE MAN *DID* TO YOU, YOU'D WANNA DO IT RIGHT *BACK*, BOY-- BACK WHERE IT *HURTS!*

YOU STUPID *IDIOT.* MY *FATHER* DID THIS TO ME, NO WHITE MAN. AND EVEN IF IT WAS A WHITE MAN-- *HE* WOULD BE THE GUY I'D GET--

--NOT *EVERYONE* JUST 'CAUSE 'A HIS *SKIN.*

'SIDES, I DON'T NEED *TROUBLE.* 'CAUSE VIC STONE'S COMIN' BACK.

DON'T *BELIEVE* IT, BOY. WHITEY'LL PUT YOU DOWN SO *FAST* YOU DON'T KNOW WHAT *HIT* YOU.

THEN YOU'LL COME BACK TO *ME*, BOY--TO YOUR *REAL* FRIEND.

20

'REAL FRIENDS'! RON LEFT AN' I FELT *ALONE.* FINALLY I DECIDED TO CALL *MARCY.*

'SCUSE ME, MARCY HOME? IT'S *VIC STONE.*

OH? YOU THINK SHE'LL BE 'ROUND FRIDAY NIGHT?

SATURDAY?

MEBBE *NEXT WEEK?*

UHH, YEAH, OKAY. LOOK, MEBBE I'LL *CALL BACK--*

YEAH... GOOD-BYE.

"I GOT THE *POINT.*

"*MARCY* WASN'T GOIN' TO BE *AVAILABLE* AGAIN.

"NOT FOR A *FREAK* WHO LOOKED LIKE *ME.*

"BUT I WASN'T GONNA BE PUT *DOWN.* I WAS CLIMBIN' *UP* AGAIN. I WENT BACK TO *SCHOOL.* "

WHAT DO YOU MEAN I'M NOT ON THE *TEAM* ANY MORE, COACH?

I WAS THE *BEST* YOU HAD. YOU SAID SO YOURSELF.

I'M *SORRY,* VICTOR. YOU CAN'T PLAY ON THE TEAM. YOU *KNOW* THAT.

YOU'RE NOT *NORMAL* ANY MORE. WITH THOSE STEEL ARMS AND LEGS-- YOU CAN OUTDO *ANYONE.* THE RULES COMMITTEE WON'T HAVE IT.

BUT IT'S *MORE* THAN THAT, VICTOR. IT'S ALSO YOUR *GRADES.*

BEFORE YOUR ACCIDENT THEY FELL TOO *LOW* TO CONTINUE YOUR *SCHOLARSHIP.*

I'M *SORRY,* VIC. I REALLY AM.

" YOU *BELIEVE* THAT? MY GRADES WERE TOO LOW! *ME!* I WAS CERTIFIED A *BLAMED GENIUS* WITH A 170 I.Q.

"EVERYTHIN' STARTED T'LOOK BAD. I DIDN'T KNOW *WHAT* TO DO. "

WHITEY CAME *DOWN* ON YA, HUH?

WELL, BOY, YOUR *REAL* FRIENDS WOULDN'T *DO* THAT. NO WAY, MAN.

WHAT DO YOU *WANT,* RON?

PAL, YOU LISSEN *CLOSE.* TONIGHT WE'RE MAKIN' *HISTORY!*

21

"I WENT TO GET *READY.*

"GET MY *STUFF* TOGETHER.

"I KNEW WHAT I HAD TO DO.

"AN' THERE WAS NO WAY *AROUND* IT.

"IT WAS 'BOUT THREE IN THE MORNING. GUARDS HAD COMPLETED THEIR TOUR AN' WERE ON THE OTHER SIDE OF THE BUILDIN'.

"NOW, I WAS *SUPPOSED* TO SHOW UP AT 3:15, BUT I WAS *EARLY.*"

"BUT THE OTHERS WERE ALREADY CLIMBIN' THE BUILDIN'. I DIDN'T *QUESTION* THAT THEN. MEBBE I *SHOULD'A.*

"NOT THAT IT WOULD'A MATTERED.

RON, THE BOMB'S *SET.* THIS IS GOOD EQUIPMENT.

MR. 'K' WOULDN'T HAVE ANY-THIN' *LESS,* PAL.

WE SET THIS THING TO *BLOW* SOON AS *VIC* SHOWS UP.

THEN WE *SPLIT*--

--AN' LET *HIM* BE OUR *SCAPEGOAT...*

...WHILE WE'RE *COOLIN'* OUR HEELS IN MR. K'S *COUNTRY.*

"USING *FOOT-GRAPPLERS* I CLIMBED THE OUTER WALL...

"...EVEN AS MY *EAR AMPLIFIERS* PICKED UP RON'S EVERY *TREACHEROUS* WORD.

"THOUGH NOTHING COULD HAVE *CHANGED.*"

HE'S *COMING.*

SET IT FOR *FIVE MINUTES,* THAT'LL GIVE US TIME TO GET *CLEAR.*

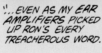

22

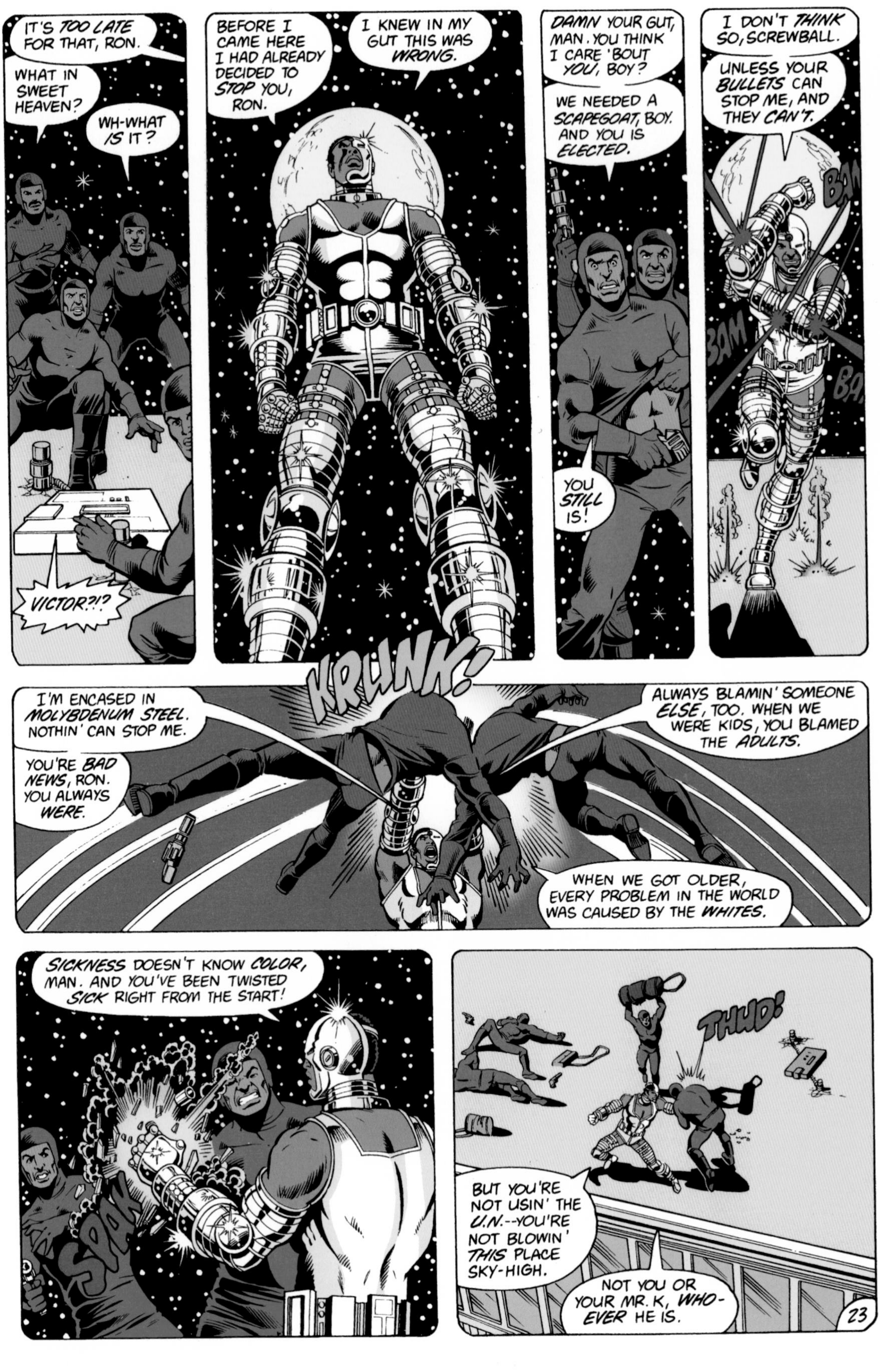
IT'S TOO LATE FOR THAT, RON.
WHAT IN SWEET HEAVEN?
WH-WHAT IS IT?
VICTOR?!?
BEFORE I CAME HERE I HAD ALREADY DECIDED TO STOP YOU, RON.
I KNEW IN MY GUT THIS WAS WRONG.
DAMN YOUR GUT, MAN. YOU THINK I CARE 'BOUT YOU, BOY?
WE NEEDED A SCAPEGOAT, BOY. AND YOU IS ELECTED.
YOU STILL IS!
I DON'T THINK SO, SCREWBALL.
UNLESS YOUR BULLETS CAN STOP ME, AND THEY CAN'T.
BAM
BAM
BA
KRUNK!
I'M ENCASED IN MOLYBDENUM STEEL. NOTHIN' CAN STOP ME.
YOU'RE BAD NEWS, RON. YOU ALWAYS WERE.
ALWAYS BLAMIN' SOMEONE ELSE, TOO. WHEN WE WERE KIDS, YOU BLAMED THE ADULTS.
WHEN WE GOT OLDER, EVERY PROBLEM IN THE WORLD WAS CAUSED BY THE WHITES.
SICKNESS DOESN'T KNOW COLOR, MAN. AND YOU'VE BEEN TWISTED SICK RIGHT FROM THE START!
THUD!
BUT YOU'RE NOT USIN' THE U.N.--YOU'RE NOT BLOWIN' THIS PLACE SKY-HIGH.
NOT YOU OR YOUR MR. K, WHO-EVER HE IS.
23

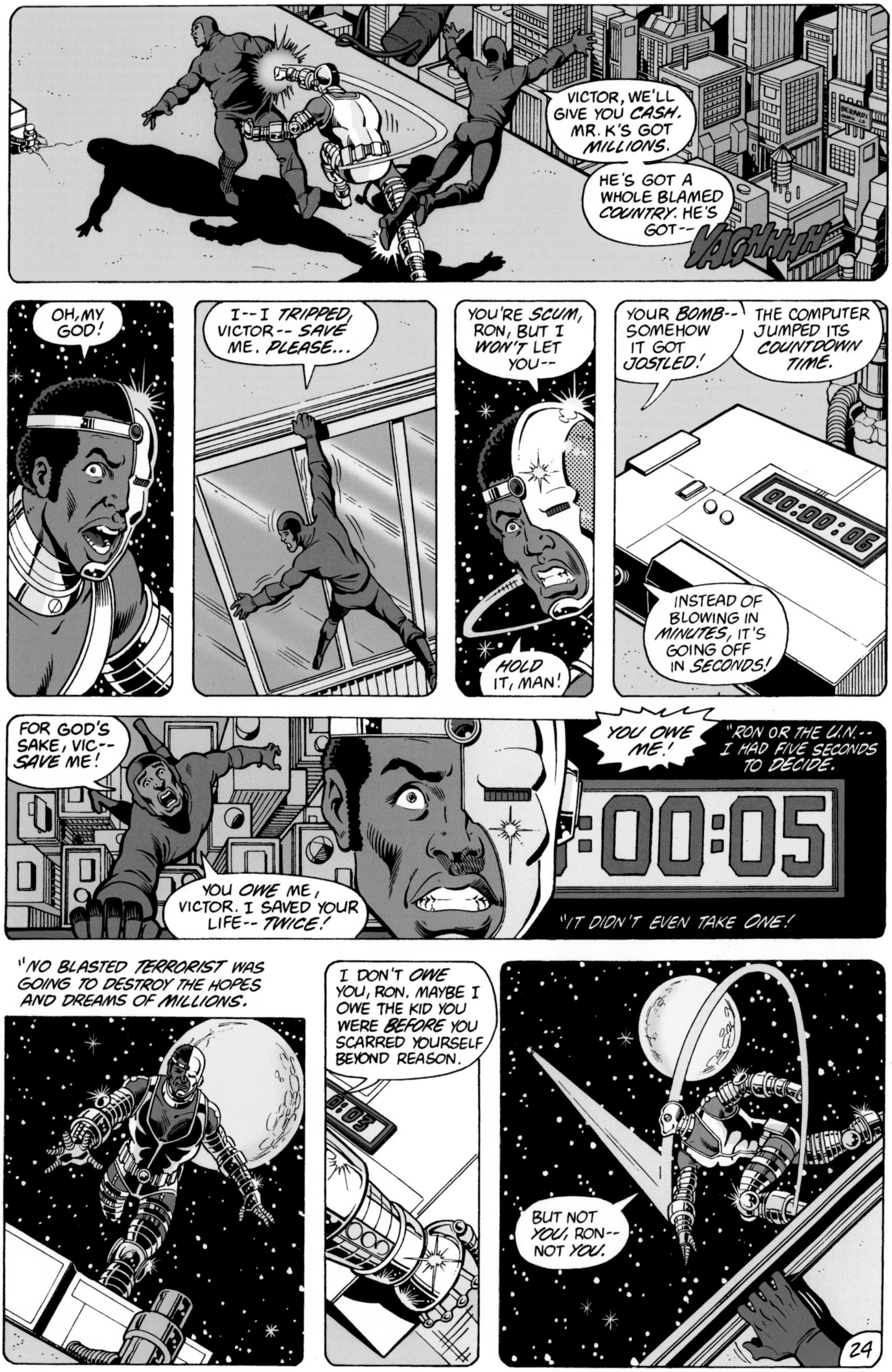

VICTOR, WE'LL GIVE YOU CASH. MR. K'S GOT MILLIONS.
HE'S GOT A WHOLE BLAMED COUNTRY. HE'S GOT--
YAGHHHH
OH, MY GOD!
I--I TRIPPED, VICTOR-- SAVE ME. PLEASE...
YOU'RE SCUM, RON, BUT I WON'T LET YOU--
HOLD IT, MAN!
YOUR BOMB-- SOMEHOW IT GOT JOSTLED!
THE COMPUTER JUMPED ITS COUNTDOWN TIME.
00:00:06
INSTEAD OF BLOWING IN MINUTES, IT'S GOING OFF IN SECONDS!
FOR GOD'S SAKE, VIC-- SAVE ME!
YOU OWE ME, VICTOR. I SAVED YOUR LIFE-- TWICE!
YOU OWE ME!
"RON OR THE U.N.-- I HAD FIVE SECONDS TO DECIDE.
:00:05
"IT DIDN'T EVEN TAKE ONE!
"NO BLASTED TERRORIST WAS GOING TO DESTROY THE HOPES AND DREAMS OF MILLIONS.
I DON'T OWE YOU, RON. MAYBE I OWE THE KID YOU WERE BEFORE YOU SCARRED YOURSELF BEYOND REASON.
BUT NOT YOU, RON-- NOT YOU.
24

"I INTENDED TO *SAVE* RON ONCE THE BOMB WAS CLEAR OF THE U.N....

"...BUT HE COULDN'T HOLD ON LONG ENOUGH.

"I'M CERTAIN HE *SCREAMED* AS HE FELL, BUT HE WAS *DROWNED* OUT BY THE ROAR OF THE *DRAGON*...

"...WHO *CONSUMED* ITSELF IN ITS OWN *FLAMING PYRE.*

THE COPS COMBED THE RIVER BUT COULDN'T FIND RON'S *BODY*, THOUGH I'M SURE HE *DIED* THEN...

...KILLED BY HIS OWN *HATE*, JUST LIKE MINE WAS KILLING *ME.*

UNTIL *YOU* PEOPLE FORCED ME TO LISTEN TO MY *FATHER.*

I--I HAD LET MYSELF *HATE* HIM FOR SO LONG-- PERHAPS THINKING THAT BECAUSE HE *WAS* MY FATHER HE SHOULD ALSO BE AN INFALLIBLE *GOD.*

AT LEAST, BECAUSE OF YOU, MY *TRUE* FRIENDS, I CAME TO *LOVE* MY FATHER...

...I LOVED HIM 'TIL THE MOMENT HE *DIED*. AS I WILL UNTIL I *JOIN* HIM.

SO YEAH, *REAL* FRIENDS ...I DIDN'T *HAVE* 'EM WHILE I WAS GROWIN' UP.

AN' SOMETIMES I GET A BIT *MISTY-EYED* 'CAUSE I CERTAINLY DO HAVE 'EM *NOW.*

AND WE SHALL *ALWAYS* BE YOUR FRIENDS, VICTOR.

HOW CAN WE *HELP* BUT LOVE ONE WHO IS SUCH A WARM AND LOVING MAN?

WARM AND LOVING...SO *STRANGE* TO HEAR THOSE WORDS...

NEXT:

25

...CONSIDERING MY WHOLE *LIFE* 'TIL NOW WAS SPENT BEING TAUGHT HOW *NOT* TO LOVE...AND HOW *NOT* TO EVER CARE.

THE STORY OF *RAVEN!*

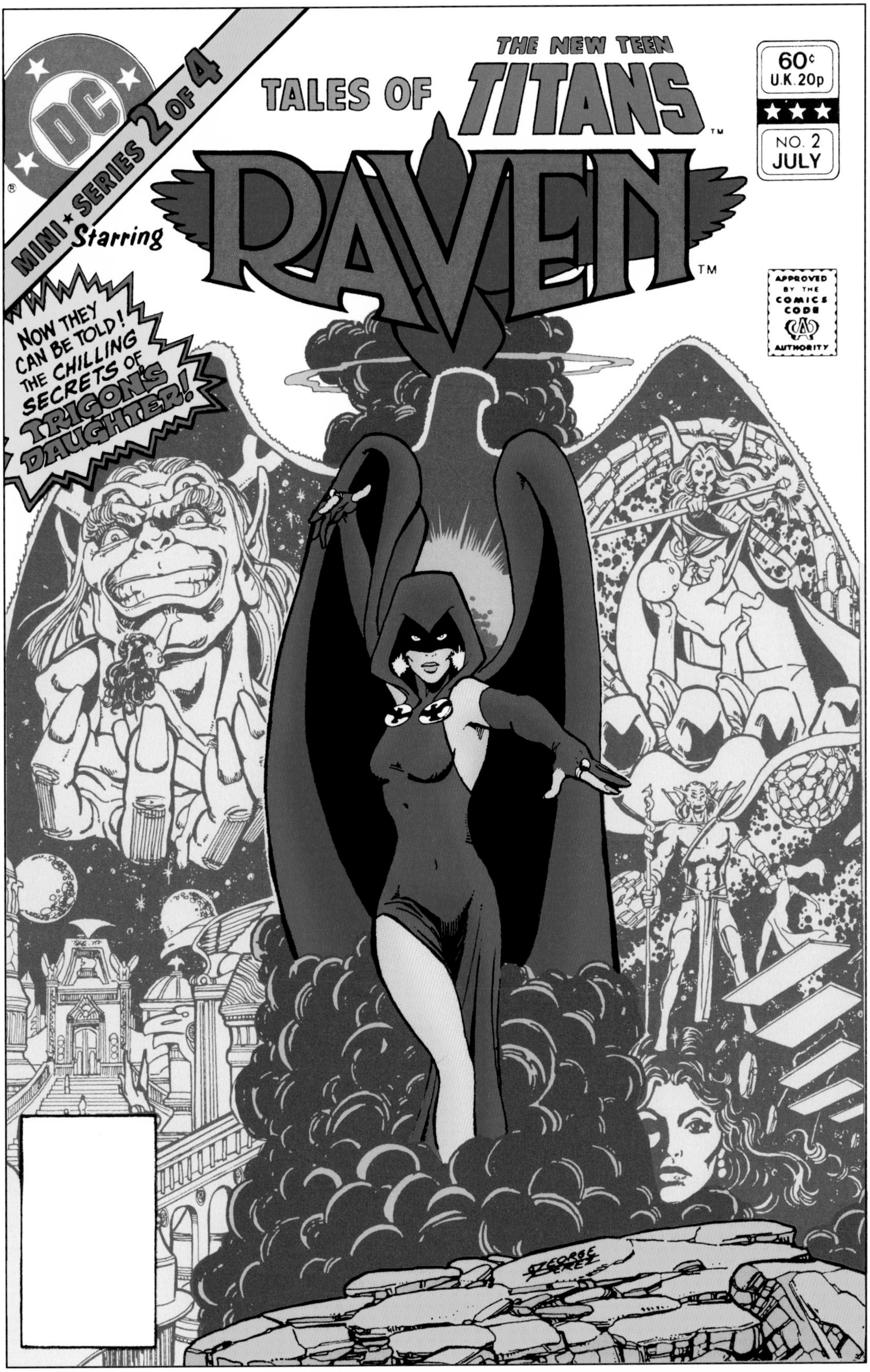
DC
MINI ★ SERIES 2 OF 4
Starring
TALES OF
THE NEW TEEN TITANS
RAVEN
60¢
U.K. 20p
NO. 2
JULY
APPROVED BY THE COMICS CODE AUTHORITY
NOW THEY CAN BE TOLD! THE CHILLING SECRETS OF TRIGON'S DAUGHTER!
GEORGE PEREZ

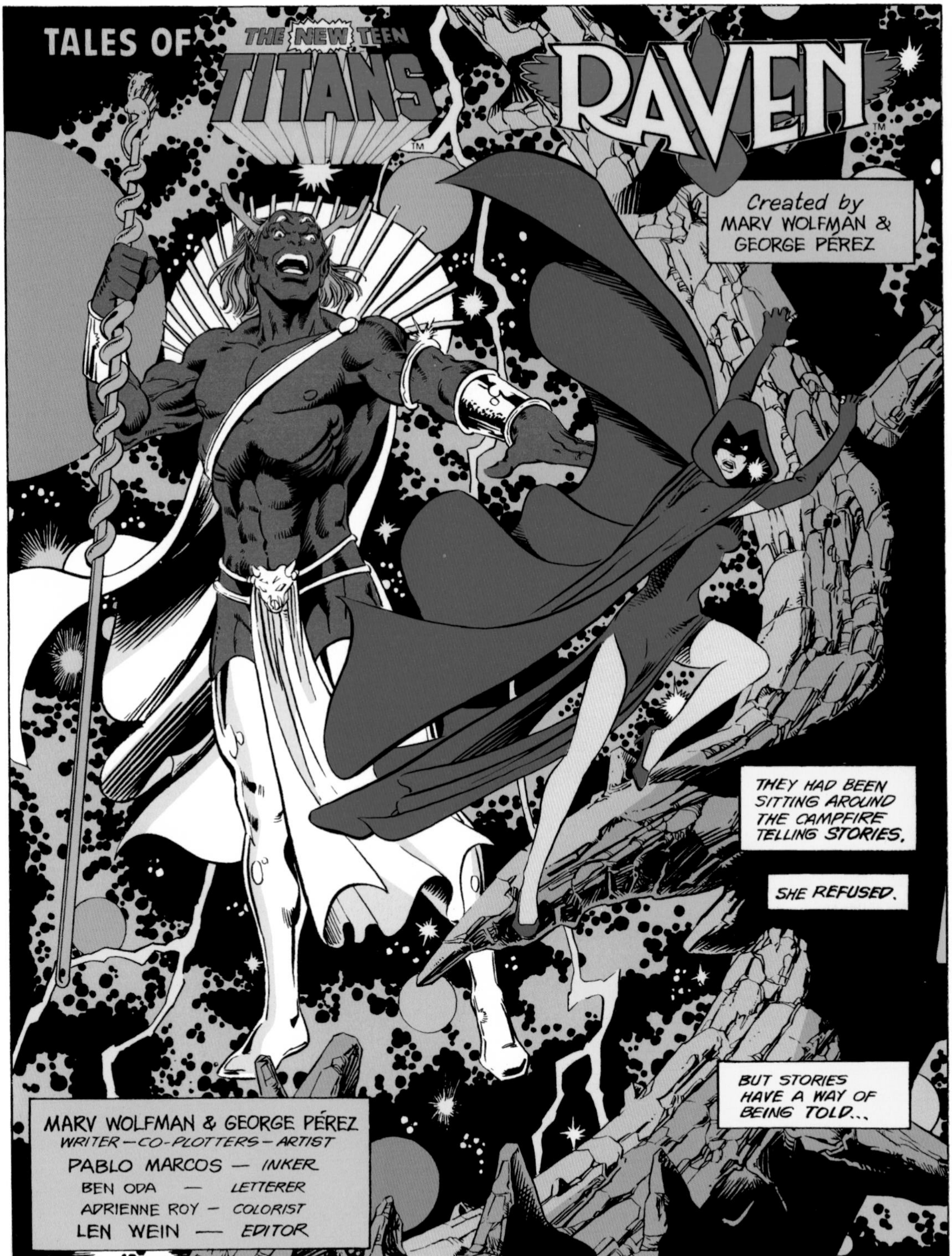
TALES OF THE NEW TEEN TITANS
RAVEN
Created by MARV WOLFMAN & GEORGE PÉREZ
THEY HAD BEEN SITTING AROUND THE CAMPFIRE TELLING STORIES.
SHE REFUSED.
BUT STORIES HAVE A WAY OF BEING TOLD...
MARV WOLFMAN & GEORGE PÉREZ
WRITER—CO-PLOTTERS—ARTIST
PABLO MARCOS — INKER
BEN ODA — LETTERER
ADRIENNE ROY — COLORIST
LEN WEIN — EDITOR

TRIGON, WHY ARE YOU *DOING* THIS TO ME?

WHY ARE YOU TRYING TO KILL YOUR *DAUGHTER?*

AND YOU'RE A PART OF *ME* THAT I'VE SPENT A LIFETIME TRYING TO *SUBMERGE!*

DON'T YOU UNDERSTAND, I'M *PART* OF YOU!

SPEAK TO ME, TRIGON! WHY DO YOU WANT TO *KILL* YOUR ONLY LIVING *CHILD?*

MY DAUGHTER, YOU WILL NOT *DIE.* I WILL NOT *PERMIT* IT.

MOTHER?!? THANK AZAR! HE WANTS ME *DEAD!*

NO, MY LOVING RAVEN, NOT *DEAD* --

-- HE SIMPLY WANTS THAT PART OF YOUR *SOUL* THAT IS RIGHTFULLY *HIS!*

AND I FEAR, MY CHILD, THAT NOT ONE OF US CAN *STOP* HIM!

HA! HA! HA! HA! HA!

NO! *NO!* MOTHER -- NOT *YOU!*

2

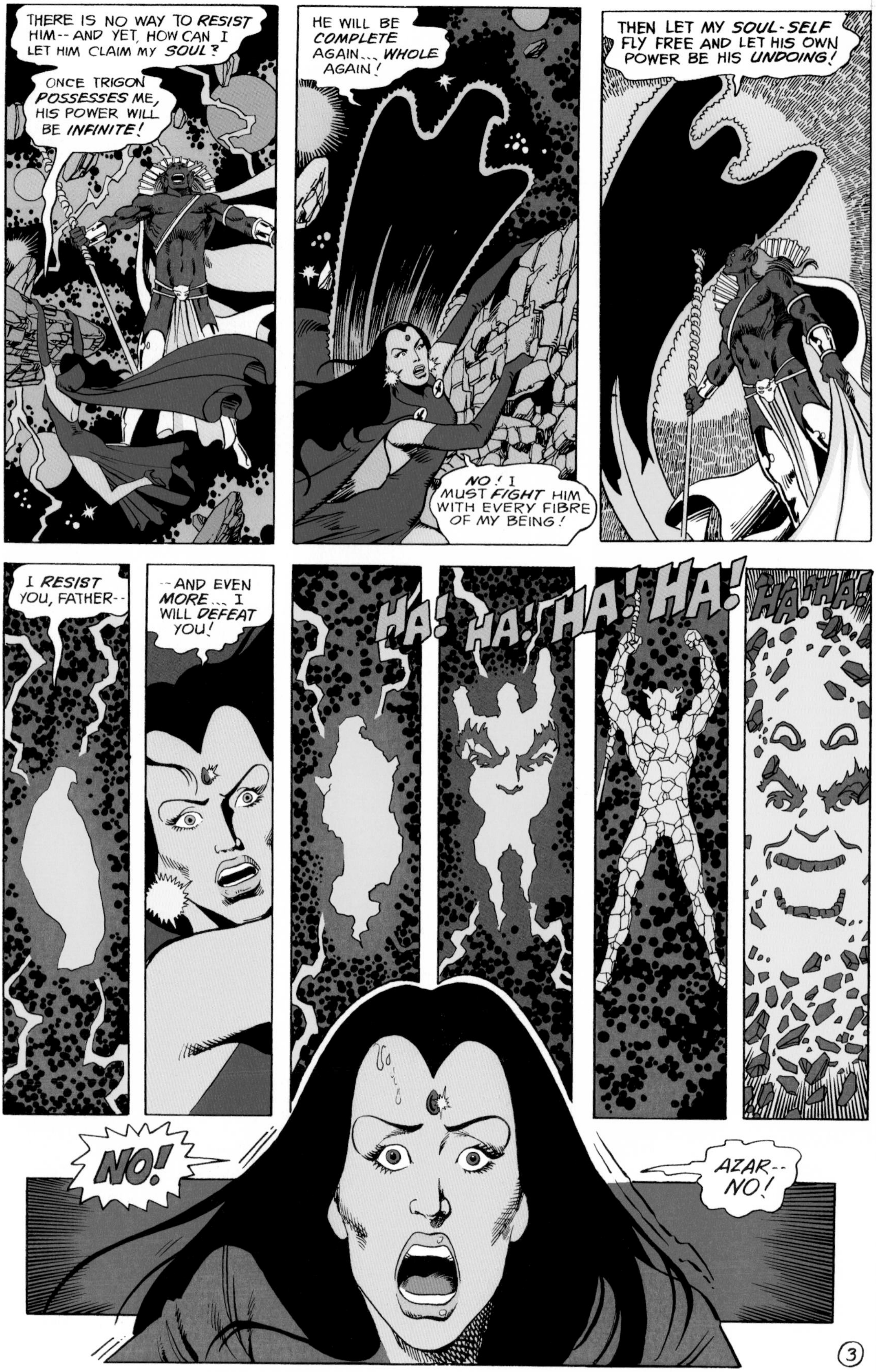
THERE IS NO WAY TO RESIST HIM-- AND YET, HOW CAN I LET HIM CLAIM MY SOUL?
ONCE TRIGON POSSESSES ME, HIS POWER WILL BE INFINITE!
HE WILL BE COMPLETE AGAIN... WHOLE AGAIN!
NO! I MUST FIGHT HIM WITH EVERY FIBRE OF MY BEING!
THEN LET MY SOUL-SELF FLY FREE AND LET HIS OWN POWER BE HIS UNDOING!
I RESIST YOU, FATHER--
--AND EVEN MORE... I WILL DEFEAT YOU!
HA! HA! HA! HA!
HA! HA!
NO!
AZAR-- NO!
3

MAN! WHAT WAS *THAT*?

THAT WAS *RAVEN'S* SCREAM! I'D KNOW IT *ANYWHERE*!

SOMETHING'S *HAPPENED* TO HER!

THE OTHERS CAN BARELY *BLINK* BEFORE WALLY WEST IS *GONE* AND STANDING AT THE SIDE OF THE WOMAN HE *LOVES...*

THOUGH HIS LOVE HAS NEVER *ONCE* BEEN RETURNED IN KIND.

WHAT'S *GOING ON* HERE?

RAVEN HAD A *DREAM*, I THINK.

PLEASE, RAVEN, JUST LET ME KNOW IF YOU'RE *ALL RIGHT*.

I AM... I WILL BE JUST *FINE*.

NO, RAVEN, THIS TIME YOU'RE *NOT* DISMISSING ME LIKE THAT.

YOU'VE KNOWN ALL ALONG THAT I *LOVE* YOU...

...YOU KNOW I JUST CAN'T GO BACK TO MY TENT AND *FORGET* THAT AWFUL SHRIEK.

YOU'RE *HURT*, RAVEN. YOUR FACE IS SO *PALE*. PLEASE, OPEN UP TO ME JUST *ONCE*.

RAVEN, WE'RE *ALL* YOUR FRIENDS. IF SOMETHING IS *TROUBLING* YOU, MAYBE WE CAN *HELP*.

AND EVEN IF WE *CAN'T*, SOMETIMES JUST *TALKING* ABOUT OUR PAINS MAKES THEM EASIER TO *BEAR*.

YOU ALL ARE MY FRIENDS, MY *ONLY* FRIENDS.

PERHAPS I HAVE *ERRED* IN KEEPING SO MUCH OF MY PAST A *SECRET*.

YOU'LL *TELL* US THEN? THANK GOD!

4

YOU KNOW ABOUT *TRIGON*...

KNOW HIM? MAN, HE ALMOST TURNED US INTO *HAMBURGER MEAT!*

GARFIELD-- *SHHHHH!*

I HAVE ALSO TOLD YOU HOW TRIGON MET MY *MOTHER*...

SHE WAS A WOMAN LOST IN HER OWN *CONFUSION* WITH NO CLEAR PRECEPTS OF HER OWN, SHE WAS SWAYED BY THOSE WHO STUDIED THE ARCANE ARTS.

...*SWAYED?* PERHAPS *'USED'* IS A FAR BETTER WORD, SHE ALLOWED HERSELF TO BE USED IN A DARK CEREMONY WHOSE PURPOSE WAS TO RAISE THE *DEVIL* HIMSELF...

"... BUT THIS TIME THE CEREMONY BROUGHT TO THEM SOMETHING FAR *DIFFERENT.*

"MY MOTHER TOLD ME HE WAS SO HANDSOME, HIS EYES WERE FLECKED WITH GOLD AND DANCED WITH SUNLIGHT...

"...HIS TOUCH WAS WARM, AND SHE MELTED INTO HIS ARMS AND FOUND HERSELF SWEPT ACROSS THE DIMENSIONS.

"SHE BECAME HIS LOVER AND *BRIDE*, AND MY MOTHER...

"...WHO HAD NEVER BEFORE KNOWN LOVE -- WAS TOTALLY ENTHRALLED...

"... UNTIL SHE SAW BEYOND THE IMAGE TRIGON HAD CONJURED--

"...AND SAW THE DEMON AS HE TRULY WAS!

5

"BUT IT WAS ALREADY *TOO LATE.* HIS *SEED* HAD BEEN PLANTED.

"HIS *CHILD* WOULD BE BORN, AND SO TRIGON SIMPLY CAST MY MOTHER BACK TO EARTH WHERE SHE WOULD BE *SAFE* FROM MY FATHER'S *ENEMIES.*

...BUT ALL THESE CHILDREN WERE *SLAIN* UPON BIRTH. MANY BY TRIGON'S *FOES,* THE OTHERS BY THEIR OWN *MOTHERS...*

...WHO THEN TOOK THEIR *OWN* WRETCHED LIVES AS WELL.

BUT THIS TIME TRIGON HAD PICKED HIS WIFE *WELL.* HE KNEW MY MOTHER WAS TOO *WEAK* A PERSON TO *SLAY* HIS CHILD.

SHE DESPERATELY SOUGHT *LOVE*... EVEN THE LOVE OF THE *DEVIL'S OWN.*

THIS TIME, TRIGON WAS CERTAIN, AFTER A HUNDRED ATTEMPTS AND MORE, HIS *OFFSPRING* WOULD *LIVE.*

I'M SORRY, RAVEN, BUT I DON'T *UNDERSTAND.* SHE KNEW WHAT WAS GOING TO *HAPPEN,* DIDN'T SHE?

SHE *DID.*

WASN'T SHE *SCARED?* WASN'T SHE *AFRAID?* SHE *HAD* TO BE.

"TRIGON HAD MANY WIVES *BEFORE* MY MOTHER.. ALL BORE HIM *CHILDREN...*

INDEED, GARFIELD, THE *HORROR* OF WHAT WAS GROWING INSIDE HER TOOK MY MOTHER FAR OVER THE BRINK OF *DESPAIR.*

"*FINALLY,* SHE COULD STAND IT NO LONGER. SHE TOLD ME SHE TOOK TOO MANY *PILLS* AND THEN SHE LAY DOWN TO DIE...

"...AND SHE WAS SO CERTAIN THAT *NIMBUS* OF *LIGHT* THAT APPEARED IN THE *ALLEYWAY* WAS MERELY A MAD *DELUSION...*

"... AND THE *FIGURE* THAT STEPPED FROM *IT* WAS A *MESSENGER* FROM *GOD* TAKING HER TO THE *REALM* BEYOND.

"HE SEEMED SO *PEACEFUL* AS HE REACHED OUT FOR HER.

"SHE TOOK HIS HAND EVEN AS SHE HAD TAKEN *TRIGON'S...*

"...AND THAT WAS THE *LAST* TIME SHE EVER SET FOOT ON THE *PLANET* OF HER *BIRTH.*

6

"HOW CAN I POSSIBLY DESCRIBE *AZARATH* WHEN I HAVE NEVER *TRULY* *SEEN* IT? AT LEAST NOT THE WAY IT LOOKED *BEFORE* I WAS BORN.

"MY MOTHER SPOKE OF ITS GLORIOUS *MARBLE STREETS* AND *GOLDEN COLUMNS*, ITS *BLUE-GREEN SKIES* AND *CRIMSON CLOUDS*.

"IT MUST HAVE BEEN *MAGNIFICENT* THE DAY SHE FIRST ARRIVED."

WHERE *ARE* WE? I'VE NEVER SEEN ANYTHING *LIKE* THIS BEFORE.

AM I *DREAMING*, OR AM I *DEAD*? IS THIS *HEAVEN*?

NO, MY DEAR, THIS IS NOT *HEAVEN*. WE EXIST *BETWEEN* ALL DIMENSIONS.

LONG AGO WE FLED THE *VIOLENCE* OF EARTH AND CAME TO LIVE HERE IN ETERNAL *PEACE*.

WE INVITE YOU TO *FORGET* YOUR PAST AND *LIVE* WITH US.

WE ASK YOU TO *BEGIN ANEW* IN AZARATH ... TO EVEN TAKE ANEW A NAME *BEFITTING* YOU --

ARELLA, THAT WHICH MEANS *THE MESSENGER ANGEL*.

BUT WHY *ME*? WHY BRING ME *HERE*?

BECAUSE OF THE *CHILD*. BECAUSE MANKIND MUST BE *PROTECTED* FROM THE WRATH OF *TRIGON'S* DAUGHTER.

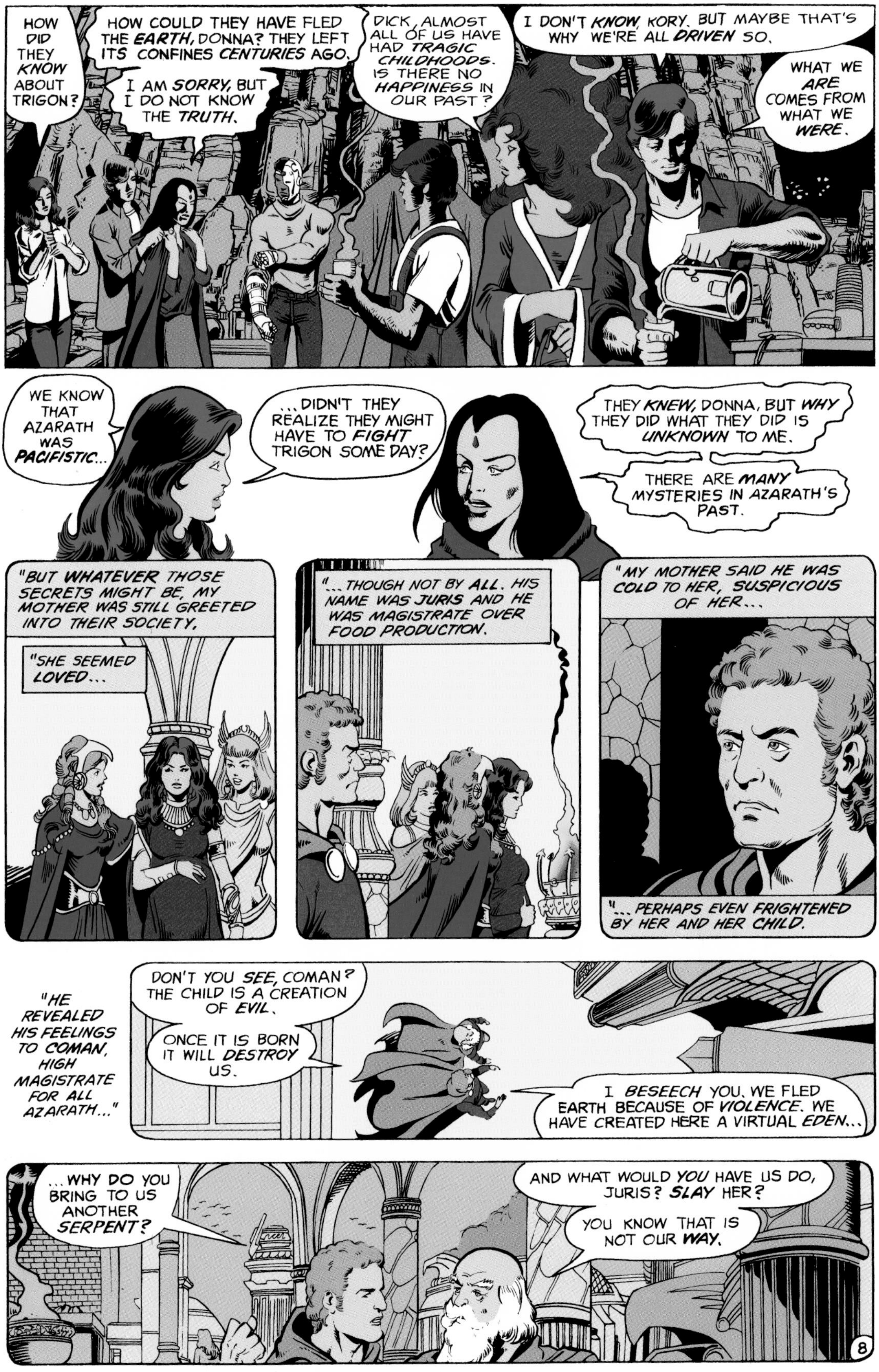
HOW DID THEY KNOW ABOUT TRIGON?
HOW COULD THEY HAVE FLED THE EARTH, DONNA? THEY LEFT ITS CONFINES CENTURIES AGO.
I AM SORRY, BUT I DO NOT KNOW THE TRUTH.
DICK, ALMOST ALL OF US HAVE HAD TRAGIC CHILDHOODS. IS THERE NO HAPPINESS IN OUR PAST?
I DON'T KNOW, KORY. BUT MAYBE THAT'S WHY WE'RE ALL DRIVEN SO.
WHAT WE ARE COMES FROM WHAT WE WERE.
WE KNOW THAT AZARATH WAS PACIFISTIC...
...DIDN'T THEY REALIZE THEY MIGHT HAVE TO FIGHT TRIGON SOME DAY?
THEY KNEW, DONNA, BUT WHY THEY DID WHAT THEY DID IS UNKNOWN TO ME.
THERE ARE MANY MYSTERIES IN AZARATH'S PAST.
"BUT WHATEVER THOSE SECRETS MIGHT BE, MY MOTHER WAS STILL GREETED INTO THEIR SOCIETY.
"SHE SEEMED LOVED...
"...THOUGH NOT BY ALL. HIS NAME WAS JURIS AND HE WAS MAGISTRATE OVER FOOD PRODUCTION.
"MY MOTHER SAID HE WAS COLD TO HER, SUSPICIOUS OF HER...
"...PERHAPS EVEN FRIGHTENED BY HER AND HER CHILD.
"HE REVEALED HIS FEELINGS TO COMAN, HIGH MAGISTRATE FOR ALL AZARATH..."
DON'T YOU SEE, COMAN? THE CHILD IS A CREATION OF EVIL.
ONCE IT IS BORN IT WILL DESTROY US.
I BESEECH YOU. WE FLED EARTH BECAUSE OF VIOLENCE. WE HAVE CREATED HERE A VIRTUAL EDEN...
...WHY DO YOU BRING TO US ANOTHER SERPENT?
AND WHAT WOULD YOU HAVE US DO, JURIS? SLAY HER?
YOU KNOW THAT IS NOT OUR WAY.
8

KILL HER? *NO*, BUT WE CAN CAST HER OUT *THE GREAT DOOR* INTO THE LIMBO BEYOND WHERE THE CHILD WILL NEVER CAUSE OUR *DESTRUCTION*.

WE *CANNOT*, JURIS.

INDEED, THE CHILD'S ONLY *HOPE* IS TO REMAIN IN AZARATH WHERE OUR TEACHINGS CAN *SUBMERGE* TRIGON'S DEADLY INFLUENCE,

I *WARN* YOU, JURIS-- DO *NOTHING* AGAINST ARELLA.

WE OF THE HIGH COUNCIL HAVE MADE OUR *DECISION*.

AND THE *REST* OF US WILL *DIE* BECAUSE OF IT.

IT WAS INTO THIS CLIMATE I WAS *BORN*.

"MONTHS PASSED, THEN MY MOTHER WENT INTO LABOR. AND, WITH A QUIET SIGH, I EMERGED INTO AZARATH.

"BUT FROM THAT MOMENT ON, AZARATH WAS FOR-EVER CHANGED. ITS EMERALD SKIES TURNED *BLACK* AS DEATH ITSELF.

"THE SWEET SMELL OF GOSSAMER BECAME THE PUNGENT ODOR OF *BRIMSTONE*.

"OUR WORLD SHOOK AND RUMBLED IN *PROTEST*.

"AND PEACE TURNED TO FEAR,

"LIFE BECAME *DEATH*.

"JURIS BELIEVED HE KNEW WHAT HAD TO BE DONE TO THE HELPLESS INFANT...

"...WHO HAD NOT *ASKED* TO BECOME THIS CATALYST OF TERROR..."

⑨

WHY DID EVERYTHING CHANGE, RAVEN? SURELY YOUR BIRTH *ALONE* WASN'T RESPONSIBLE...

IT *WAS*. I AM TRIGON'S *DAUGHTER*.

HE IS *PART* OF ME.

DON'T *SAY* THAT, RAVEN. *HE'S* A KILLER WITHOUT MERCY. *YOU* COULDN'T HARM A COMMON *FLY*.

DO NOT BE SO *CERTAIN* OF THAT, WALLACE.

EVERY DAY I MUST *CONTROL* THE FORCES THAT ARE CONTAINED WITHIN ME.

I AM AN *EMPATH* WHO THRIVES ON *EMOTION*, YET WHY DO YOU THINK I AM *NOT* PERMITTED ANY OF MY OWN?

"BUT I WANDER FROM MY TALE. *GALYA*, THE WOMAN WHOM I WAS ENTRUSTED TO FOR FEEDING, FOUND ME *MISSING*...

COMAN, RAVEN IS *GONE*, I'VE LOOKED *EVERYWHERE*.

THAT FOOL, *JURIS*.

THERE IS ONLY ONE PLACE HE WOULD HAVE *TAKEN* HER--

--THE *GREAT DOOR!*

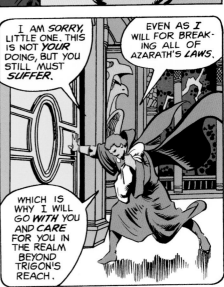

I AM *SORRY*, LITTLE ONE. THIS IS NOT *YOUR* DOING, BUT YOU STILL MUST *SUFFER*.

EVEN AS *I* WILL FOR BREAK-ING ALL OF AZARATH'S *LAWS*.

WHICH IS WHY I WILL GO *WITH* YOU AND *CARE* FOR YOU IN THE REALM BEYOND TRIGON'S *REACH*.

NO, JURIS--PLEASE DO NOT *DO* THIS.

YOU WERE ONE OF OUR *ORIGINALS*. HOW CAN YOU *IGNORE* OUR LAWS?

TO *KILL* IS OUR MOST HEINOUS *SIN!*

YOU THINK I DON'T *KNOW* THAT, COMAN? MY HEART IS *TORN* BECAUSE OF WHAT I MUST DO.

BUT, IF AZARATH AND THE WORLDS BEYOND ARE TO *LIVE*, I HAVE NO OTHER *CHOICE!*

10

"MY MOTHER TOLD ME THE DOOR *OPENED* AND A GREAT BLOOD-RED *LIGHT* SHONE THROUGH...

EEYYAAAHHHH—

THE DOOR *SLAMMED SHUT* ON ITS OWN. JURIS IS *GONE... DESTROYED.*

RAVEN--?

RAVEN! THANK AZAR SHE'S STILL *ALIVE!*

JURIS WAS THE *FIRST* TO DIE.

HOW MANY MORE WILL *FOLLOW?*

COMAN! BRING THE GIRL TO ME!

A-AZAR?!? SHE *CALLS!*

WE MUST *HURRY* TO HER.

"YOU MUST KNOW THAT AZAR WAS LIKE A GOD UNTO US."

"SHE LED US FROM EARTH TO *AZARATH* AND SHE TAUGHT AND GUIDED US FOR TWO HUNDRED YEARS,

"WHEN SHE *DIED,* HER DAUGHTER TOOK HER PLACE FOR THREE HUNDRED YEARS MORE...

"... AND HER DAUGHTER FOLLOWED HER.

"ALREADY *ANCIENT* WHEN I WAS BORN, *AZAR* WAS THE ONE WHO *CARED* FOR ME AS IF I WERE SOMETHING *SPECIAL.*"

I HAVE RECEIVED THE *WORD.* MY TIME IS COMING TO AN *END.*

WHEN *I* DIE, AZAR WILL BE NO MORE. THERE ARE NONE TO FOLLOW *ME* AS I DID MY MOTHER AND SHE *HERS.*

BUT I SUMMON YOU HERE FOR FINAL *GUIDANCE.*

11

WE HAVE BROUGHT INTO OUR MIDST THE GIRL NAMED *RAVEN*.

YOU ALL KNOW THE *REASONS* AND HOW THEY HAVE BEEN *DECREED*.

BUT STILL SOME OF YOU *DOUBT*. THUS LOOK TO THE ALL-REVEALING *ORBS*...

SEE THE WORLD OF OUR *BIRTH*, CALM AND SERENE IN BLISSFUL IGNORANCE.

NOW LOOK AND SEE WHAT WOULD HAPPEN IF THE GIRL WERE *CAST AWAY* FROM AZARATH.

I TELL YOU, SHOULD *EARTH* PERISH, THE REST OF THE UNIVERSE WOULD SOON *FOLLOW*.

ONLY THROUGH *OUR PRECEPTS* CAN THE DAUGHTER OF TRIGON *LIVE*.

ARELLA, GIVE TO ME *RAVEN*, FOR FROM THIS MOMENT ON SHE MUST BE *MINE* TO WORK WITH...

...MINE TO *TRAIN*.

MINE TO EXORCISE THE *DEMONS* THAT FOREVERMORE WILL TRY TO *CONTROL* HER.

DEMONS? WERE *YOU* POSSESSED LIKE THAT GIRL, *FRANCES KANE*?

NO, KORIAND'R. NOT *POSSESSED*.

THE DEMON IS MY *SOUL*...THAT PART OF ME WHICH IS *TRIGON*.

THAT PART OF ME I MUST ALWAYS *CONTROL*!

12

"I WAS TAKEN FROM MY MOTHER AND RAISED BY THIS ALMOST-GODDESS.

"SHE TAUGHT ME THE WAYS OF AZARATH, THE MEANINGS OF TRUE PACIFISM...

"...AND THE NEED TO SUBMERGE ALL MY BASIC EMOTIONS.

"SADLY, I SAW LITTLE OF MY MOTHER WHO WAS ASSIGNED TO TEMPLE FUNCTIONS ONLY...

"BUT I WOULD CATCH OCCASIONAL GLIMPSES OF HER BETWEEN MY LEARNING AND HER SOLEMN DUTIES.

"INSTEAD, I PRACTICED MY MEDITATIONS...

"...AND THE SECRETS OF INSTANTANEOUS TRAVEL.

"OH, I YEARNED TO BE AT HER SIDE, BUT THAT WAS NOT TO BE... AT LEAST NOT THEN AND NOT FOR MANY YEARS TO COME.

"I LEARNED HOW TO FLOW BETWEEN DIMENSIONS AND HOW TO CONTROL THE MYRIAD PATHWAYS TO MY DESTINATION.

13

"BUT MY GREATEST STUDIES CENTERED ON MY EMPATHIC ABILITIES, WHICH ONLY I IN ALL OF AZARATH POSSESSED."

RAVEN, THE BIRD IS DYING.

I KNOW, THERON. I SENSED ITS PAIN BEFORE YOU BROUGHT IT TO ME.

ITS AGONIES FLOW INTO ME...

...AND INTO MY SOUL. AHH, I FEEL IT HEALING.

IS THERE NO ONE I CANNOT CURE?

MY DEAR RAVEN, THERE ARE ONLY A VERY FEW YOU CAN CURE.

THOSE WHOSE PAINS AND AGONIES ARE TOO GREAT ARE BEYOND EVEN YOUR REDEEMING.

DISEASE IS BEYOND MY POWER TO DISPERSE. ONLY THE SIMPLEST OF PAINS CAN I CURE...

BUT THOSE PAINS, THOSE AGONIES, BECOME MY OWN AND THEY CAN ALMOST TEAR MY SOUL ASUNDER.

THE PAINS DON'T STAY WITH YOU, DO THEY?

OH, THEY STAY, KORIAND'R ...IN ALL TOO MANY WAYS THEY REMAIN WITH ME FOREVER.

STILL, YOU KNOW WE'RE ALMOST ALIKE. BOTH OF US WERE TRAINED TO USE OUR SKILLS.

YOU IN AZARATH, ME ON OKAARA.

ALIKE? PERHAPS, BUT YOUR POWERS COULD NOT DESTROY A UNIVERSE IF LEFT UNCONTROLLED.

MINE, DEAR KORIAND'R, CAN DO THAT-- AND MORE.

"BUT AGAIN I DIGRESS. YEARS PASSED AS I LEARNED AND MY MOTHER GREW MORE LONELY..."

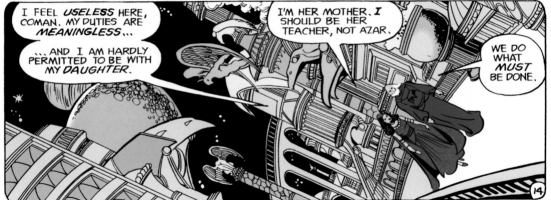

I FEEL USELESS HERE, COMAN. MY DUTIES ARE MEANINGLESS...

...AND I AM HARDLY PERMITTED TO BE WITH MY DAUGHTER.

I'M HER MOTHER. I SHOULD BE HER TEACHER, NOT AZAR.

WE DO WHAT MUST BE DONE.

14

IT HURTS SO MUCH NOT TO BE *WITH* HER.

I KNOW, COMAN, BUT I WANT TO BE HER *MOTHER*.

WHICH IS WHAT WE CANNOT *AFFORD*, ARELLA.

RAVEN IS NOT *ONE* OF US, NOR CAN SHE EVER TRULY *BE* OF OUR KIND.

SHE MUST NOT KNOW *LOVE* OR *HATE* OR *SORROW.* SHE MUST BE *DRAINED* OF ALL EMOTION.

YOU KNOW THE PENALTY SHOULD AZAR *FAIL.*

COMAN! ARELLA! WE *NEED* YOU!

WHAT *IS* IT, TYNAN?

AZAR IS *DYING.* SHE WANTS ARELLA AT HER SIDE.

ME? WHY *ME?*

AZAR *DYING?* WOULDN'T THAT HAVE *DESTROYED* AZARATH?

NO, WALLACE. AZAR WAS OUR *SPIRITUAL* LEADER BUT THERE WERE *MANY* WHO STUDIED AT HER *SIDE.*

HER LOSS, THOUGH, WAS *DEEPLY* FELT. WE LOVED HER AND ADMIRED HER.

MY MOTHER DID, HOWEVER, WONDER WHAT WOULD *BECOME* OF ME.

ARELLA, I TURN NOW TO *YOU...*

FOR *TRUST* AND FOR *LOVE...* TO DO BEST WHAT *MUST* BE DONE.

15

I'LL DO *ANYTHING* FOR YOU, YOU *KNOW* I WOULD.

RAVEN HAS BEEN *TAUGHT* WHAT SHE NEEDS TO *KNOW.*

HER EMOTIONS CAN BE *CONTROLLED* IF YOU DO NOT *TEMPT* HER.

BUT YOU MUST CONTINUE HER *EDUCATION,* ARELLA. TEACH HER THE *USE* OF ALL HER UNIQUE *POWERS.*

BUT, MORE *IMPORTANT,* ARELLA--HOW-EVER *COLD* THE GIRL MAY SEEM, NEVER *SHUN* HER, AND NEVER *FEAR* HER.

WHAT DO YOU *MEAN,* AZAR? HOW COULD I *FEAR* MY OWN *DAUGHTER?*

PLEASE, TELL ME WHAT YOU *MEAN--?*

"BUT, IT WAS *TOO LATE.*

"*AZAR'S* SPIRIT SOUL ROSE FROM HER AND *STRETCHED* OUTWARD TO THE *HEAVENS.*

"AND NEVER AGAIN WOULD HER LIKE BE KNOWN.

BEFORE SHE DIED, SHE GAVE ME THESE *RINGS* WHICH SHE HAD WORN, AS DID HER MOTHER AND *HER* MOTHER BEFORE HER.

THROUGH THESE RINGS AZARATH IS WITH ME *ALWAYS...*

AND SOMETIMES I FEEL *AZAR* HERSELF STILL LIVES TO *GUIDE* ME.

16

YOUR MOM TOOK OVER TEACHIN' *YOU* 'BOUT THE SAME TIME *MINE* STARTED DOIN' THE SAME THING.

'COURSE, *MINE* DID BECAUSE I HAD A *FALLIN' OUT* WITH MY *DAD.*

WHEREAS MY FATHER *TRIGON* AND I HAD NEVER EVEN *MET.*

NO, HE WAS WAITING FOR ME TO BECOME A *WOMAN,* HE WANTED HIS ONLY LIVING DAUGHTER TO RULE AT HIS *SIDE...*

BUT, AGAIN, I *HURRY* MY TALE. AZAR DIED WHEN I WAS BUT *TEN YEARS OLD...*

STILL LITTLE MORE THAN A *CHILD...*

...BUT I WAS NOT FILLED WITH THE *JOYS* OF CHILDHOOD. MY ACTIVITIES WERE NOT THOSE OF *PLAY...*

SOMETHING IS *WRONG* WITH HER, COMAN... SHE'S GIVEN UP HER PRAYERS AND TAKES TO *MEDITATION...*

EACH DAY FOR THE PAST THREE YEARS WHEN OUR STUDIES ARE OVER SHE RUSHES *HERE...*

SHE IGNORES ALL OTHERS, PREFERS *SOLITUDE* AND *QUIET.*

SHE NEVER *SPEAKS* TO ME UNLESS SHE *MUST.* COMAN, I TELL YOU, SOMETIMES I....I *FEAR* HER.

"MY MOTHER COULD NOT KNOW THAT ALL WAS AS AZAR DECREED BUT THEN I COULD NOT ENLIGHTEN HER AND BREAK MY WORD TO AZAR.

"STILL, SOMETIMES THE TRUTH HAS ITS OWN WAYS OF REVEALING ITSELF..."

EEYAAGGHH

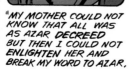

RAVEN? FOR AZAR'S SAKE-- *RAVEN!!*

"SHE RUSHED TO MY SIDE THINKING SHE COULD HELP ME. HOW WRONG SHE WAS... HOW TERRIBLY, TERRIBLY WRONG."

17

"YOU SEE, IT WAS THEN THAT THE NIGHTMARES BEGAN."

YOU ARE MINE, RAVEN-- MINE!

NO, NO! GO AWAY!

NO, DAUGHTER. I HAVE COME TO CLAIM WHAT IS MINE!

AZAR!

GET AWAY FROM HERE, TRIGON! LEAVE MY DAUGHTER ALONE!

FOR HEAVEN'S SAKE--OF ALL PEOPLE-- SPARE HER!

"MY MOTHER HAD CALLED UPON THE WRONG SIDE FOR PROTECTION...

"...BUT STILL HE WAS GONE, THOUGH HIS CHILL LINGERED ON."

ARE YOU ALL RIGHT, RAVEN? PLEASE ANSWER ME!

SO EVIL...SO VERY EVIL...

...HE SAID I WAS HIS DAUGHTER.

WHO IS HE, MOTHER? WHO IS HE?

"BUT MY MOTHER SAID NOTHING, THEN..."

AZARATH SHOOK, ARELLA... AND WE HEARD HIS VOICE.

IT WAS TRIGON, WASN'T IT? TELL THE TRUTH!

IT WAS TRIGON.

THEN, EVEN AFTER ALL THESE YEARS...WE ARE STILL NOT SAFE.

IT'S THE GIRL! SHE BROUGHT THE DEMON TO US.

YES, BUT WE ARE THE ONES WHO CREATED HIM!

18

"*I WAS BROUGHT TO THE TEMPLE AGAINST MY WILL, AND THOUGH I WAS NOT INTERESTED, I STILL LISTENED AS COMAN SPOKE.*"

CENTURIES AGO WE FLED THE *VIOLENCE OF EARTH* AND FOUNDED *AZARATH.*

BUT THE FORCES WE USED TO *PURGE* OUR EVIL NATURES DID NOT *DIE.*

THEY *MERGED,* THEY *GREW,* THEY FLOWED THROUGH THE ENDLESS DIMENSIONS OUTSIDE OUR *GREAT DOOR.*

AND, IN ANOTHER DIMENSION, THEY WERE *SUMMONED* DURING A MYSTIC *CEREMONY--*

--AND OUR EVILS WERE BORN AGAIN AS THE DEMON CALLED *TRIGON!*

"*AT THE VERY MENTION OF HIS NAME, THE ETERNAL FLAME FLARED BRIGHT...*"

"*...THEN DIMMED AND WAS EXTINGUISHED.*"

"*SUDDENLY, ALL ABOUT ME WERE SILENT.*"

"*THEN...*"

RAVEN!

"*I COULD NOT RESIST. I WAS BEING SUMMONED.*"

"*I STEPPED FROM THE OTHERS AND THEY MADE NO EFFORT TO STOP ME...*"

"*...NOR COULD THEY HAD THEY BEEN ABLE.*"

"*TRANSFIXED, I MADE MY WAY TO THE GREAT DOOR, A PLACE FROM WHICH I HAD BEEN FORBIDDEN.*"

19

"*THEN, THE DOOR SWUNG OPEN BY ITSELF.*"

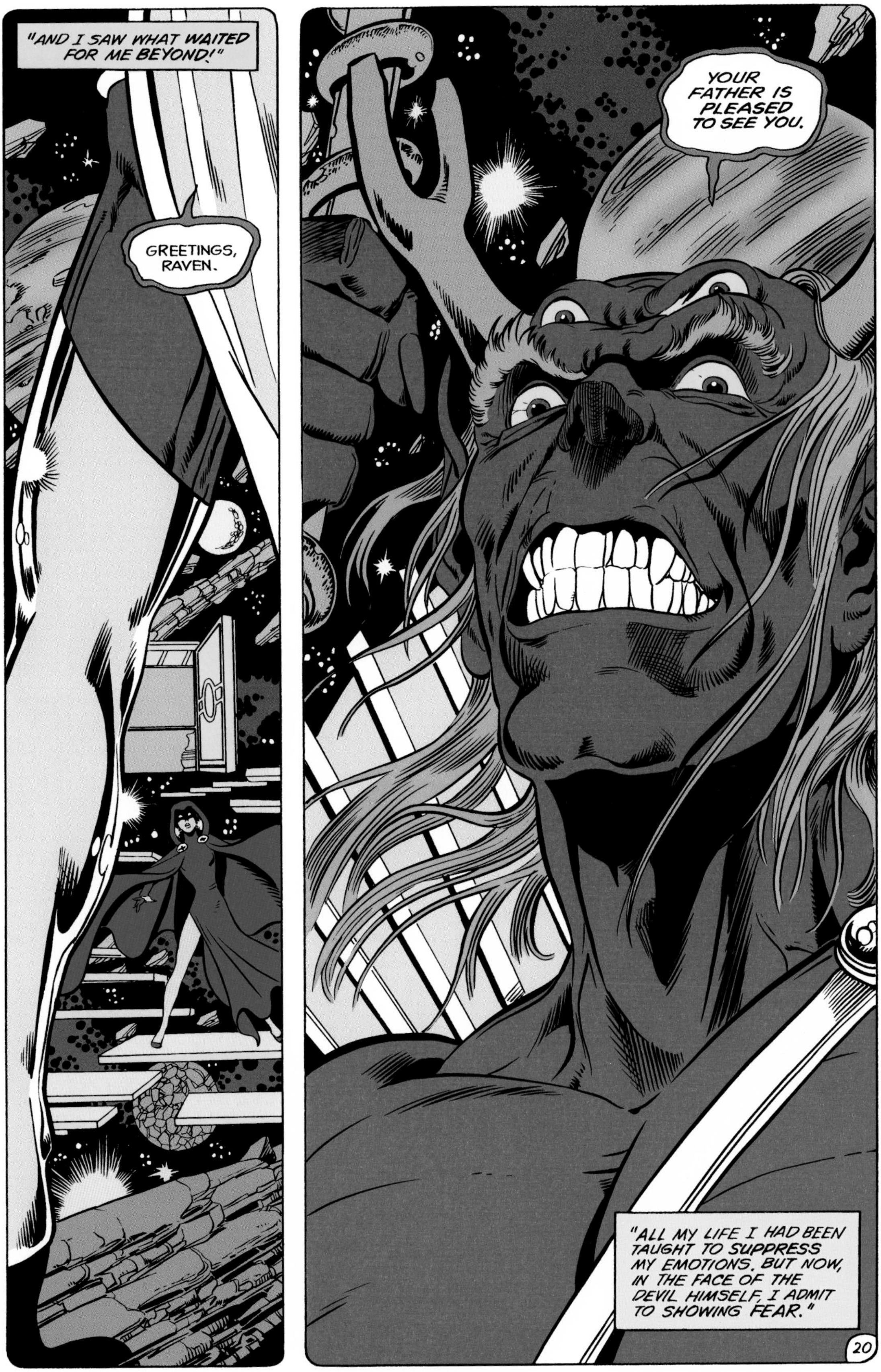
"AND I SAW WHAT WAITED FOR ME BEYOND!"
GREETINGS, RAVEN.
YOUR FATHER IS PLEASED TO SEE YOU.
"ALL MY LIFE I HAD BEEN TAUGHT TO SUPPRESS MY EMOTIONS. BUT NOW, IN THE FACE OF THE DEVIL HIMSELF, I ADMIT TO SHOWING FEAR."
20

YOU ARE MY *CHILD.* THE ONLY ONE TO HAVE EVER *SURVIVED.*

I HAVE WAITED *LONG* TO BRING YOU TO ME,

TO TAKE YOU *HOME,* TO HAVE YOU RULE *BESIDE* ME.

HOME? I AM TO GO WITH *YOU?*

"*I* HAD *WONDERED* WHY I WAS BRED AS AN *EMPATH. NOW I* KNEW THE *ANSWER.*"

GO WITH *YOU...* GO WITH MY *FATHER?* I...I--

N-NO...I SENSE EVIL... TERRIBLE *EVIL* IN YOU.

I SENSE *DEATH...* CRUEL, HEARTLESS *MURDER.*

NO! YOU MIGHT BE MY *FATHER* BUT I COULD NEVER STAND *BESIDE* YOU.

I HAVE BEEN BORN TO *PEACE.* YOU WALLOW IN *DESTRUCTION.*

CHILD, YOU HAVE BEEN *LIED* TO ALL THESE MANY YEARS.

I ORDAINED THAT AZARATH ADOPT YOU FOR I KNEW THERE YOU WOULD BE *SAFE* UNTIL I *NEEDED* YOU.

UNGHH!

I KNEW THEY WOULD NOURISH YOUR *POWERS* IN A WAY I COULD EASILY *SUBVERT.*

I *WANT* YOU, DAUGHTER!

BUT SHE'S NOT *YOURS* ANY MORE, TRIGON!

21

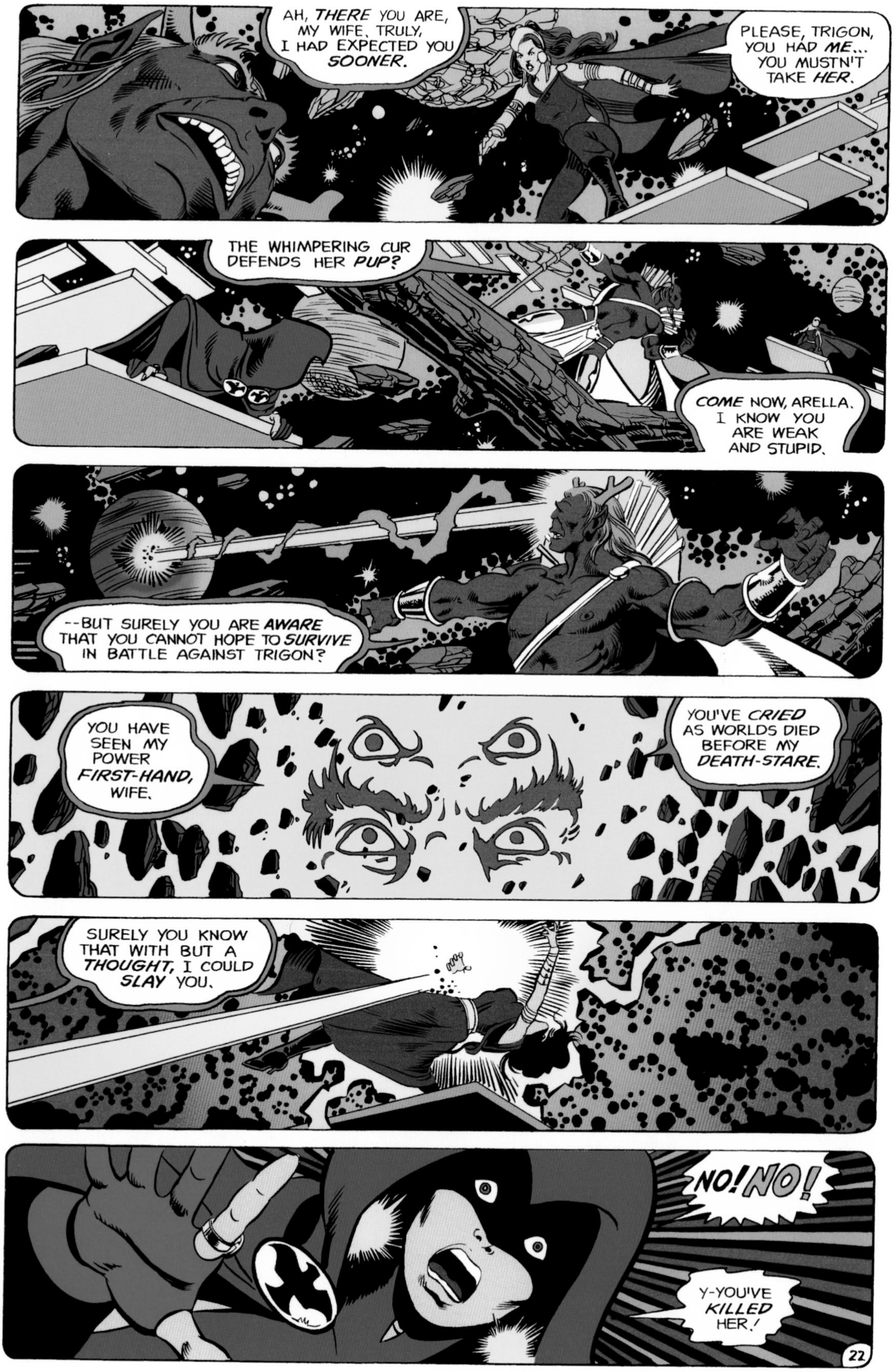
AH, THERE YOU ARE, MY WIFE. TRULY, I HAD EXPECTED YOU SOONER.
PLEASE, TRIGON, YOU HAD ME... YOU MUSTN'T TAKE HER.
THE WHIMPERING CUR DEFENDS HER PUP?
COME NOW, ARELLA. I KNOW YOU ARE WEAK AND STUPID.
--BUT SURELY YOU ARE AWARE THAT YOU CANNOT HOPE TO SURVIVE IN BATTLE AGAINST TRIGON?
YOU HAVE SEEN MY POWER FIRST-HAND, WIFE.
YOU'VE CRIED AS WORLDS DIED BEFORE MY DEATH-STARE.
SURELY YOU KNOW THAT WITH BUT A THOUGHT, I COULD SLAY YOU.
NO! NO!
Y-YOU'VE KILLED HER!
22

KILLED HER? *HARDLY,* DAUGHTER.

I STILL HAVE SEVERAL YEARS' *NEED* OF HER.

BESIDES, WHY *SLAY* SUCH A USELESS RAG--

--WHEN THERE IS MUCH MORE PLEASURE IN *HUMILIATING* HER.

TORTURE IS A FAR *BETTER* MEDICINE FOR THAT EXCUSE OF A WOMAN!

"HE LAUGHED AS MY MOTHER CRIED...

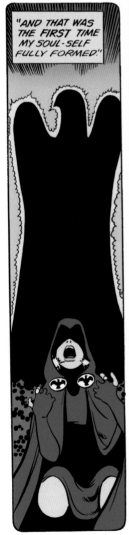

"...AND, FOR THE FIRST TIME IN MY LIFE, I WANTED ONLY TO *KILL.*

"AND THAT WAS THE FIRST TIME MY *SOUL-SELF FULLY FORMED.*"

AT LAST! AT VERY *LAST!*

YOU *DO* HAVE THE POWER I SENSED IN YOU!

YOU TRULY *ARE* MY CHILD.

DAUGHTER, THAT SOUL-SELF IS YOUR *DARKER* SIDE... THE PART OF YOU THAT IS *ME!*

I *BAPTIZE* IT NOW, RAVEN-- INSTILL IT WITH ALL *MY* ESSENCE.

THANK ALL THE DARK GODS, YOU ARE *MINE!!!*

... YOU ARE THE *DAUGHTER OF TRIGON!*

NO! NO! NO!

23

YOU CANNOT FOR-EVER *CONTAIN* WHAT YOU ARE.

THINK, DAUGHTER-- REMEMBER AZARATH AS IT *TRULY* IS.

THEY HAVE ALWAYS *HATED* YOU, GIRL.

THEY *FEAR* YOU, AS WELL THEY SHOULD.

AND, ALL ALONG YOU'VE *HATED* THEM FOR THAT, HAVEN'T YOU?

ADMIT IT, DAUGHTER. *ADMIT IT!*

N-NO... *FIGHT* HIM, RAVEN... FOR AZAR'S SAKE, *FIGHT* HIM...

THEY WANTED YOU DEAD, RAVEN. BUT *I* WOULD NOT *PERMIT* THAT!

I WAS THE ONE WHO STOPPED JURIS! *I* WAS THE ONE WHO *SAVED* YOU!

BUT *YOU* NOW HAVE THE POWER, DAUGHTER.

24

YOU CAN MAKE THEM *PAY* FOR THEIR HATREDS AND FEARS.

MAKE THEM *PAY!* ARE YOU *NOT TRIGON'S DAUGHTER?*

I ...I *AM!*

NO... RAVEN... *DON'T.*

I... IT IS *TOO LATE.*

SHE HAS TAKEN ON THE MANTLE OF HER *HERITAGE.*

THAT IS ALL I WISHED TO *KNOW.*

I HAVE NO FURTHER *NEED* FOR HER NOW.

"*THAT WAS ALL HE SAID. HE NO LONGER NEEDED ME.*"

"*THERE WAS A TERRIBLE, BLINDING FLASH OF LIGHT...*"

"*...AND MY MOTHER AND I FOUND OURSELVES BACK IN AZARATH.*"

WHAT *HAPPENED?*

I NEEDED TO KNOW IF YOU HAD THE *POWER.* I NEEDED TO KNOW IF YOU WERE TRULY MY *DAUGHTER.*

I NEEDED TO KNOW IF YOU COULD BE *CORRUPTED.* YOU CAN, RAVEN... YOU *ARE* MINE.

YOUR POWER WILL *GROW,* RAVEN. AND, WHEN YOU ARE A WOMAN, I WILL *RETURN.*

WE ARE SO MUCH *ALIKE,* DAUGHTER... SO VERY *MUCH ALIKE.*

MOTHER, WE *CAN'T* BE THE SAME... WE *CAN'T* BE.

"*BUT MY MOTHER SAID NOTHING. SHE SIMPLY HELD ME TIGHT AND CRIED.*"

MY MOTHER GAINED *STRENGTH* THROUGH THAT ENCOUNTER. AND *I*...

...AT LAST I *UNDERSTOOD* WHY AZAR WANTED ME TO *CONTROL* MY EVERY *EMOTION.*

WHEN I TURNED *EIGHTEEN* I SENSED TRIGON'S *RETURN,* AND THAT WAS WHEN I *LEFT* AZARATH AND SEARCHED FOR *YOU.*

GOOD GRIEF, RAVEN, WHY DIDN'T YOU TELL US THAT *BEFORE?*

ALL THAT TIME I THOUGHT YOU WERE JUST *SNUBBING* ME.

IN TRYING TO MAKE YOU *LOVE* ME, I COULD HAVE... MY GOD, WHAT COULD I HAVE *DONE?*

WHAT ARE *YOU* GRINNIN' ABOUT, SALAD-HEAD?

JUST SUDDENLY BEIN' GLAD THAT *MY* LIFE WASN'T THAT SCREWY!

WASN'T IT, CHANGELING? BE HERE *NEXT* ISSUE FOR:

THE DOOM PATROL!
THE OLD TEEN TITANS!
MENTO!
GALTRY!
THE ARSENAL!

AND A WHOLE LOT MORE!

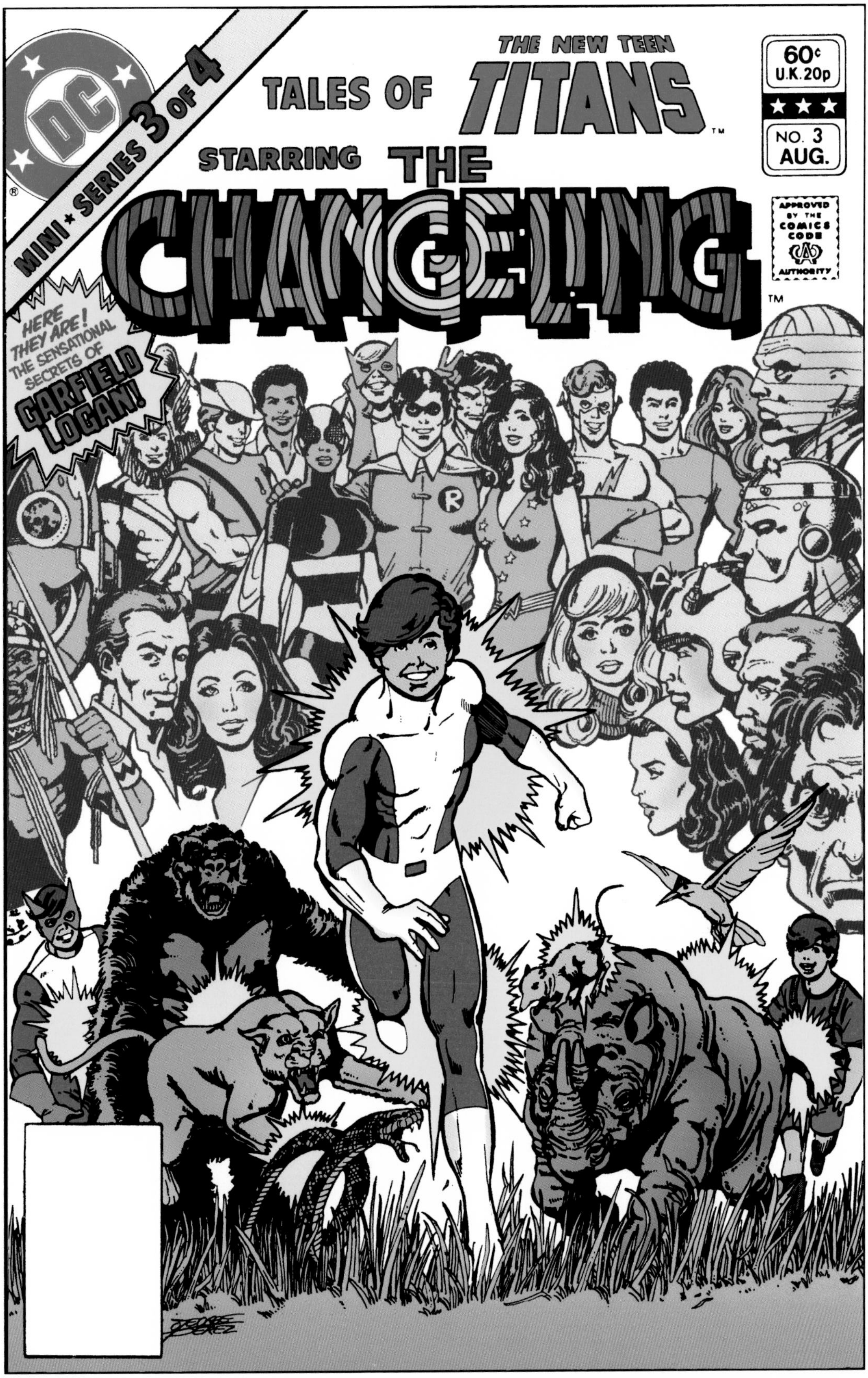
MINI ★ SERIES 3 OF 4
TALES OF
THE NEW TEEN
TITANS
60¢
U.K. 20p
NO. 3
AUG.
STARRING THE
CHANGELING
APPROVED BY THE COMICS CODE AUTHORITY
HERE THEY ARE! THE SENSATIONAL SECRETS OF
GARFIELD LOGAN!

MARV WOLFMAN writer • **GEORGE PEREZ** penciller • **GENE DAY** embellisher • **JOHN COSTANZA** letterer • **ADRIENNE ROY** colorist • **LEN WEIN** editor

THE CHANGELING

LADIES AND GENTLEMEN, BOYS AND GIRLS, SUPER-HEROES OF ALL AGES--

THEIR THIRD DAY HERE IN THE GRAND CANYON HAS COME TO AN EXHAUSTING CONCLUSION. HOURS OF RIDING RAGING RAPIDS AND CLIMBING TO HIGH CLIFF-DWELLINGS HAVE TAKEN THEIR TOLL...

...AT LEAST ON MOST.

TONIGHT, NO MORE OF WALLY'S TONGUE-SCORCHING, STOMACH-CHURNING, TEXAS-STYLE CHILI--

--TONIGHT WE DINE LIKE KINGS! 'OH, WHAT FOODS THESE MORSELS BE'!

TONIGHT, MOUTH-WATERING, SUCCULENT FRANKFURTERS FROM GOOD OL' RELIABLE NATHAN'S OF CONEY ISLAND.

SO ROUND, SO FIRM, SO FULLY-PACKED...

...NOT UNLIKE OUR OWN PRINCESS KORIAND'R OF TAMARAN.

HEROES AREN'T HARD TO FIND? N.C.

1

I THOUGHT *SUPER-HEROING* WAS TOUGH, BUT CLIMBING CLIFFS ALL DAY MADE ME USE MUSCLES I FORGOT I *HAD*.

CONEY ISLAND, HUH? MAN, I REMEMBER GOIN' DOWN THERE EVERY SUMMER...WALKIN' THE *BOARDWALK*...

...RIDIN' THE *CYCLONE!* IT SCARED ME HALF OUTTA MY WITS.

WE OUGHTTA DO THAT *AGAIN* SOMEDAY!

YOU'RE NOT SORRY YOU *OPENED UP* TO US, ARE YOU, RAVEN?

I THINK *UNDER-STANDING* YOU BETTER MAKES A DIFFERENCE.

IT IS *HARD* TO TALK ABOUT MYSELF, WALLACE. BUT NO, I AM NOT SORRY.

I KNOW YOU DON'T HAVE *HOT-DOGS* ON TAMARAN, BUT YOU'LL *LOVE* 'EM.

BUT ISN'T EATING DOGS *GRUESOME*, GARFIELD?

AW, THEY'RE NOT *REAL* DOGS... WE JUST *CALL* 'EM THAT.

OH, I KNOW. I WAS JUST *JOKING*.

I'M REALLY GLAD WE *TOOK* THIS VACATION. IT'S GIVEN US A CHANCE TO *KNOW* EACH OTHER BETTER.

I FEEL *CLOSER* TO ALL OF YOU.

YOU HADDA GO *SPOIL* THINGS, DONNA? LOGAN HERE'S *CHOMPIN'* AT THE BIT TO TELL US ABOUT *HIS* BAD OL' DAYS.

JUST KEEP IT *SHORT*, GREENIE. AN' DON'T BORE US *TOO* MUCH.

VPVPVP VP VPVP

SURE WOULDN'T WANNA DO *THAT*, VICTOR--

--NOT AFTER HAVING TO *FORCE* OUR-SELVES AWAKE DURING *YOUR* TALE OF WOE.

FACE IT, GUYS, HOW COULD *MY* STORY BE ANYTHING BUT A *GEORGE LUCAS* KIND'A SAGA?

IT'S GOT *EVERYTHING!* ACTION! GIRLS! TRAGEDY! GIRLS! LAUGHTER! GIRLS! AND LEST WE *FORGET*--

--GIRLS!

IT ALL BEGAN BACK IN *UPPER LAMUMBA*--DEEPEST, DARKEST, KING KONGEST *AFRICA*.

"*MY DAD, MARK LOGAN, WAS A SCIENTIST WITH MORE DEGREES THAN A FAHRENHEIT THERMOMETER...*"

MARIE! GET THIS BRAT *OUT* OF HERE! HE'S JUST RUINED A *WEEK'S* WORK.

2

"LIFE WAS *GREAT* BACK THEN, EX-CEPT THAT I SORTA GOT A LITTLE *SICK!*"

GARFIELD'S COME DOWN WITH *SAKUTIA*--A DEADLY DISEASE THAT ONLY *ANIMALS* CAN SURVIVE.

BUT MY *WORK* HERE HAS ISOLATED THE COMMON *GENETIC CODE* BETWEEN HUMANS AND ANIMALS.

MARK, THAT COULD *KILL* HIM IF YOU'RE WRONG.

SO WILL *SAKUTIA.* MARIE, WE'VE GOT *NO CHOICE.*

"WELL, *ONE* THING YOU CAN SAY ABOUT MY *DAD.*

"WHEN HE *GOOFS...*

"...HE GOOFS *BIG!*

"YEAH, HIS *MAD-SCIENTIST'S THINGIE* SAVED MY *LIFE,* BUT NOT QUITE THE WAY HE *THOUGHT* IT WOULD.

HOW WOULD *YOU* LIKE TO SPEND YOUR *"WONDER YEARS"* BEING CONFUSED WITH *'SPROUT,'* THE JOLLY GREEN GIANT'S *NEPHEW?*

WELL, AT LEAST NOBODY THOUGHT I WAS THAT *DAVID BANNER* GUY FROM TV.

SO THERE I WAS, A HUMAN *KERMIT THE FROG...* ALL READY TO GROW UP TO BECOME POSTER BOY FOR *"THE LAWN DOCTOR"!*

EXCEPT MY MOM WANDERED BY THIS *BLACK MAMBA,* A SNAKE SO MEAN ONLY *DARTH VADER* COULD LOVE 'IM.

SOMETHING CAME OVER ME AND I BEGAN TO *CHANGE...* INTO A *MONGOOSE.* WELL, EXIT ONE *SNAKE.*

"YEARS PASSED. THEN MY PARENTS... THERE WAS AN *ACCIDENT...*

"*LORD,* IT STILL *BOTHERS* ME EVEN NOW. I HAD ALL THESE *POWERS,* BUT I DIDN'T KNOW HOW TO *SAVE* THEM."

IT WASN'T YOUR *FAULT,* GAR. YOU WERE A *KID.*

YEAH, I KNOW, BUT IT DOESN'T MAKE THE *HURT* GO AWAY.

I CRIED FOR A *MONTH* IT HURT SO MUCH.

3

"BEFORE HE *DIED*, MY DAD BECAME FRIENDS WITH *KING TAWABA*, CHIEF OF THE LOCAL TRIBE. TAWABA TOOK ME *IN* AND MADE ME PART OF HIS *FAMILY*."

"BETTER TELL YOU, THAT REALLY TICKED OFF *MOBU*, THE TRIBE'S *WITCH-DOCTOR*. Y'SEE, MOBU *HATED* MY DAD..."

"...AND HE WASN'T VERY FOND OF *ME*, EITHER, AS I SOON *LEARNED*..."

YOU COME TO STEAL *SACRED* JEWELS. BUT I WILL *LEAD* YOU TO THEM...

...IF YOU *KILL* ONE SMALL BOY FOR ME.

"LIKE I SAID. J.R. EWING HAD NOTHING ON *MOBU*."

WELL, I FOLLOWED HUEY, DEWEY AND SCREWY AN' TRIED TO *STOP* 'EM..."

A GREEN LEOPARD? *KILL HIM!*

"I WAS HIT *BAD* AND TURNED BACK INTO THE HANDSOME JOCK YOU SEE BEFORE YOU NOW."

JUST 'BOUT THEN THE *TEMPLE* START- ED TO COLLAPSE. MOBU *DIED* THERE BUT THOSE CREEPS *RESCUED* ME...

...FIGURED THEY COULD USE MY POWERS TO HAVE ME *STEAL* THINGS FOR THEM.

SO THAT'S HOW I BECAME GARFIELD LOGAN, THE *F.B.I.'S MOST WANTED EIGHT-YEAR- OLD.*

"WELL, THOSE TWO JERKS FINALLY *KILLED* EACH OTHER, BUT THAT'S WHEN *GALTRY* FOUND ME."

"YOU REMEMBER WHAT I SAID ABOUT THAT BLACK MAMBA AND MOBU? THEY WERE *PIKERS* COMPARED WITH GRUESOME."

"HE WAS APPOINTED MY *LEGAL GUARDIAN*, BUT ALL HE GUARDED WAS MY *DAD'S MONEY.*"

"OF COURSE, THERE WAS A *BRIGHT* SPOT IN MY LIFE, TOO. BACK IN THE U.S.A. I MET MY FIRST--☆ GIRL ☆ (YAY!). HER NAME WAS *JILLIAN*."

HEY, JILLIAN! YOU ALWAYS DATE *WALKING SALADS?*

WHY DON'T YOU GO OUT WITH A *REAL BOY,* JILLIAN?

"YEAH, NOW I HAD GIRLS, AND THOUSANDS OF FRIENDS, TOO."

4

"GIRLS, FRIENDS, AN' BETTER THAN ALL OF THAT-- *THE DOOM PATROL.* LORD, I MISS THE *CHIEF,* AND *NEGATIVE MAN.* CLIFF STEELE'S STILL LANKING AROUND AS *ROBOTMAN,* BUT I GUESS I REALLY MOST MISS RITA FARR, *ELASTI-GIRL.* WHEN SHE MARRIED STEVE DAYTON THEY *ADOPTED* ME... NOW I ONLY HAVE *DAYTON,* BUT AT LEAST WE'RE FINALLY HITTING IT OFF WELL."

"AFTER THE PATROL WAS *KILLED,* I SORTA DRIFTED ALONG, BECAME A MEMBER OF *TEEN TITANS WEST.* YOU REMEMBER 'EM, *DICK.*

"THERE WAS *GOLDEN EAGLE,* THE *BUMBLEBEE,* YOU, *DONNA* AND *WALLY.*

"*SPEEDY* WAS WITH US THEN. SO WERE *LILITH, GNARRK, MAL, AQUALAD* AND THE OTHERS... THOSE WERE *GOOD TIMES...*"

6

UHH, GARFIELD-- WERE YOU PLANNING ON EATING YOUR *STICK*?

OOPS! GUESS I WAS *TALKING* TOO MUCH, HUH?

BUT DON'T WORRY. I'M AN *EXPERT* ON HOT-DOG COOKING!

WAS *LIZZIE BORDEN* YOUR TEACHER?

MAYBE YOU'D BETTER EAT AND *FORGET* THE STORIES TONIGHT.

LOGAN NOT *BRAG*? FORGET IT, DONNA. YOU'D HAVE A *JEWISH POPE* BEFORE THAT HAPPENS.

LAUGH IF YOU *WILL*, MY SKEPTICAL COHORTS, BUT HOW MANY OF *YOU* WERE MAJOR TV STARS? C'MON. LINE UP *ALPHABETICALLY*.

OH, THAT'S *RIGHT*. YOU WERE ON *"SPACE-TREK: 2022."*

YOU WERE ON *TELEVISION*?

BELIEVE IT, RAVEN. HIT NUMBER-ONE SHOW. BIG BUCKS! STARLETS BEGGING TO *DATE* ME. YEAH, I HAD IT *ALL!*

...*PLEASE*, TIFFANY?

WELL, Y'KNOW, LIKE I GOT THIS HERE AGREEMENT WITH *ROCKY*, OUR PRODUCER. WE'RE LIKE RILLY COMMITTED TO SHARING OUR SPACE.

YEAH. SHE SHARES THAT SPACE WITH *90%* OF *HOLLYWOOD*.

SURE, TIFFANY. I UNDERSTAND. NO *HARD FEELINGS*.

THAT'S *GOOD*, TAR.

NO VISITORS ON SET

THAT'S *GAR!*

EVERYONE-- ON THE *SET*.

TIM HERE, CAPTAIN OF "THE CORPORATION," HAS WANDERED INTO THE *DEMILITARIZED ZONE* AND WAS CAPTURED BY THE KLAMULONS.

J.S., AM *I* A KLAMULON?

YEAH, LEONARD. NOW *SHUT UP!*

EVERYONE IN PLACE. THIS IS A TAKE!

ACT SEVEN: SCENE FOUR

TAKE 2

7

CAPTAIN, MY HEART, IT CANNA TAKE THE *STRAIN!*

CALM DOWN, TORK. LISTEN, KLAMULON, YOU WON'T HOLD US FOR LONG. WE'VE GOT A SPECIAL *RESCUE ENSIGN* ON HIS WAY TO SAVE US.

I BEG TO *DIFFER*, CAPTAIN. THE ENSIGN WON'T *MAKE IT.*

WHAT? WHY *NOT*, TORK?

HE'S *DEAD*, TIM.

OH, WELL. EASY COME, EASY GO.

I GUESS IT'S UP TO *YOU*, TORK, TO STOP THAT KLAMULON *SNAKE-IN-THE-GRASS.*

GET IT? HUH?

YES, I *DO*, CAPTAIN. AS THE SHIP'S *METAMORPH*, I'LL PUT THE *SQUEEZE* ON THIS KLAMULON CREEP!

UGH! STOP! I GIVE!

STOP! STOP THE ACTION!

LOGAN, YOU THIRD-RATE FOUL-UP. YOU MISSED YOUR *MARK.*

YOU WERE *OFF CAMERA* AND WHAT'S WORSE, YOU SQUEEZED LEONARD SO HIS *REAL FACE* SHOWED THROUGH THAT FLIMSY MASK.

"*THE TV SCENE WAS GREAT, GUYS. I WAS A BIG STAR AND WAS TREATED LIKE ONE...*"

"*...BUT ONE DAY OUR SHOOTING WAS INTERRUPTED...*"

LOGAN, I'VE COME FOR *YOU.*

AND I'VE COME TO *KILL* YOU.

KRAK

"*SUDDENLY THIS ARMORED PEA-BRAIN SHOWS UP, SMASHING HIS WAY ONTO THE SOUND-STAGE, INTENDING TO TURN ME INTO DAISY FERTILIZER...*"

8

"*NATCH, I WAS* READY, *HERO THAT I ALWAYS AM. I FOUGHT BACK WITH A* FEROCITY *YOU GUYS HAVE NEVER SEEN...*"

DON'T *RUN*, YOU FOOL-- I'LL FIND YOU WHEREVER YOU *HIDE!*

FOR NOW AND FOREVER-- *THE ARSENAL RULES SUPREME!*

SKRAK!

"*THE* ARSENAL! SUDDENLY I REMEMBERED HEARING ABOUT HIM. HE WAS ONE OF THE GOOFBALLS THE *DOOM PATROL* ONCE FOUGHT.*"

MY BIO-SUIT HAS BEEN TOTALLY *REBUILT*, LOGAN.

SPING!

NOTHING CAN ESCAPE ME!

WANNA *BET*, UGLY? YOU MAY BE HOLDING *ONE* END'A THIS CABLE, CRETIN--

--BUT GOOD OL' *JUMBO* HERE'S GOT THE *OTHER!*

KRASH

"*ER, GARFIELD, YOU'VE DONE IT* AGAIN!*"

HMMM. OBVIOUSLY THE FIRE'S TOO HOT FOR *ONE* HOT DOG.

WHY DON'TCHA ORDER IN SOME "*CHICKEN DELIGHT*"?

NOPE! WE DO THINGS *MY* WAY.

WOULD YOU LIKE *ME* TO COOK THAT FOR YOU, GAR?

I'M AN *EXPERT*, M'LOVE. I KNOW WHAT I'M *DOING.*

THIS'LL *WORK.*

9

NOW THEN, WHERE *WAS* I? OH, YES. WE KEPT DUKING IT OUT.

THE ARSENAL WAS *GOOD*, BUT OF COURSE, I WAS A *PRO*.

WHAT WAS HE *AFTER*, GAR?

HEROES AREN'T HARD TO FIND N.C.

THAT'S THE *FUNNY* THING, WALLY...

WHEN HE *FIRST* ATTACKED THE DOOM PATROL THERE WASN'T ANY *REASON* FOR HIS ACTIONS.

IN FACT, HE TURNED OUT TO BE A *MIDGET*, SOMEONE THE PATROL NEVER EVEN *MET*.

ALL THEY KNEW WAS THEY KEPT GETTING *MYSTERIOUS* TIPS WHICH WOULD LEAD 'EM TO HIS ARMORSHIP. BUT EVEN *THEN* THEY DIDN'T UNDERSTAND *WHY* HE WANTED THEM DEAD.

"OF COURSE, I FOUND OUT..."

THIS BATTLEGROUND IS TOO *CONFINING*, LOGAN.

I WANT ROOM TO *DESTROY* YOU!

AND I WANT YOU TO *SUFFER*.

SCRIPT #2073
GARFIELD LOGAN

WE'LL MEET *AGAIN*, LOGAN--

--BELIEVE ME, WE WILL DEFINITELY MEET *AGAIN!*

LOGAN, THAT WAS *GREAT!* BUT CAN WE GET ANOTHER *TAKE?*

"I WANTED TO *KILL* THE DIRECTOR!"

10

"I DIDN'T HAVETA BECAUSE OUR SHOW WAS *SUED*, THEY SAID, FOR RIPPING OFF "STAR TREK" AND "SPACE: 1999".

"I TELL YA, SOME PEOPLE WILL SUE OVER *ANY STUPID THING.*

"BUT I HAD NO PROBLEM. OFFERS PILED IN."

H. SHELTON DRUM

CASTING DIRECTOR

NO!

GIBSON agency

CYNTHIA GIBSON
ENOLA GIBSON

NO!

...AND STILL *NO!*

"BUT I HAD ALREADY DE- CIDED *ACTING* WASN'T MY BAG..."

"SO I RETURNED HOME TO MY SPRAWLING MANSION IN WEST HOLLY- WOOD. WE TV PEOPLE LIVE *BIG*, Y'KNOW."

"THINGS WERE JUST *GREAT*. I HAD FUN, AN' I HAD GIRLS CRAWLING OUTTA THE WOODWORK TO DATE ME."

ZELDA ZORETZ? HI, THIS IS GAR...

GAR *LOGAN.*

FROM *TV.*

WITH *GREEN SKIN.*

ZELDA?

ZELDA?

"IT WAS *PARTIES* EVERY NIGHT. ONE DAY IT WAS "THE STUDIO", THE NEXT, *CHER'S* HOUSE. AFTER THAT, *HEF'S* MANSION."

"I WAS HARDLY EVER *HOME.* BUT ONE NIGHT I TOOK A BREATHER FROM LIVING LIFE IN THE *FAST LANE*--

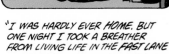

"--WHEN THERE CAME A *KNOCKING* AT MY *LIVING ROOM DOOR.*"

HI, GAR.

CAN I *COME IN*, GAR?

JILLIAN? OH, WOW! I DON'T BELIEVE IT. *WOW!*

OH YEAH-- OF COURSE. SURE.

I DIDN'T KNOW *YOU* WERE IN *L.A.* MAN, IT'S GREAT *SEEING* YOU.

YOU'RE LOOKING *WONDERFUL*, GAR.

I *AM?* OH, OF COURSE. SO ARE *YOU*, JILLIAN.

GOSH. SO ARE *YOU.*

"I WAS READY TO SETTLE DOWN WITH *ONE GIRL*. Y'KNOW, THE NOVELTY AND SUCH. AND JILLIAN WAS SUCH A *NICE* GIRL.

"WE PICKED UP WHERE WE HAD *LEFT OFF*. IT WAS GREAT.

"OH, I KNEW HER FATHER *HATED ME*. SEEMS HE WANTS GRANDCHILDREN, NOT *SALADS*, TO COMFORT HIM IN HIS OLD AGE.

"BUT WE DIDN'T WORRY 'BOUT HIM MUCH. WE JUST HAD *FUN*. I LOVED HAVING JILLIAN AROUND...

"...BUT I *DIDN'T* LOVE WHAT WAS GONNA *HAPPEN* SO VERY SOON."

I REALLY HAVE TO GO NOW, GAR, I HAVE *SCHOOL* TOMORROW.

WE'LL KEEP *SEEING* EACH OTHER, WON'T WE?

OH, I CERTAINLY *THINK* SO.

JILLIAN, NEXT WEEK THIS NEW *MOVIE'S* OPENING. "STAR WARS," I THINK IT'S CALLED. YOU WANNA GO?

I HEAR IT MAY BE *OKAY.*

OKAY.

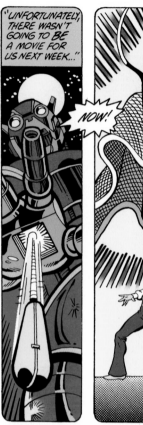

"UNFORTUNATELY, THERE WASN'T GOING TO *BE* A MOVIE FOR US NEXT WEEK..."

NOW!

GAR? GAR?!?

JILLIAN? OH, MY GOD!

HE'S GOT HER!

BUT HE *WON'T* TAKE HER FAR.

13

"GOTTA *TELL* YOU--IN MY *CONDOR SHAPE,* I FLEW FASTER'N I EVER FLEW BEFORE."

"I REALLY *HATED* THE ARSENAL. *ME,* MAYBE THE *SWEETEST* GUY WHO EVER SET FOOT ON THIS EARTH."

"I FOLLOWED THE FILTH NORTH TO THIS FANTASTIC *CASTLE* BUILT BY SOME CRAZY MOVIE STAR BACK IN THE THIRTIES."

"YOU MIGHT HAVE *SEEN* IT. THESE DAYS THEY USE IT ALL THE TIME IN THE *MOVIES.*"

"WELL, GRUESOME TOOK JILLIAN *INSIDE...*"

".".BUT ABSOLUTELY *NOTHING* WAS GOING TO KEEP ME FROM *RESCUING* HER."

LEMME *IN!* OPEN THIS *DOOR,* JERKO!

"GUESS I *SCARED* HIM, 'CAUSE HE DID WHAT I *DEMANDED.*"

WHUMP!

14

"I REMEMBERED SOMETHING *THE DOOM PATROL* TOLD ME 'BOUT *METAL-MIND--THE LAST FORTRESS* HE HAD WAS *JURY-RIGGED* WITH *DOZENS OF DEADLY TRAPS.*

"*NATCH, I WAS WARY. I CHECKED MY EVERY STEP...*

"WELL, MY EVERY *OTHER* STEP, AS IT TURNED OUT.

"HE BLASTED ME WITH THIS *SUN-GUN GIZMO,* INTENDING TO *ROAST* ME LIKE CHRISTMAS CHESTNUTS."

THE SAME WAY YOU'RE ROASTING THOSE *HOT-DOGS?*

SURE YOU DON'T WANT SOME *LEFTOVER CHILI?*

PLEASE SAY YES, GAR-- FOR THE SAKE OF ALL THOSE *INNOCENT* HOT DOGS YET TO BE *BORN.*

YOU *LAUGH,* HUMPH? WELL, HE WHO LAUGHS *LAST.* I'LL SHOW *YOU* WHO'S THE *JULIA CHILD* OF THE TITANS SET.

NOW, WHERE *WAS* I? OH, RIGHT...

"I WAS KINDA *STUNNED,* AND I DIDN'T *NEED* TO *GUESS* WHO'D *ZAPPED* ME..."

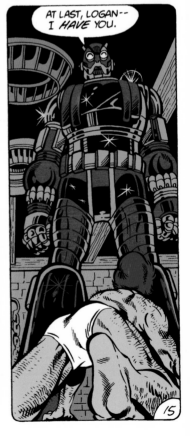

AT LAST, LOGAN-- I *HAVE* YOU.

15

JUST AS I HAVE YOUR LITTLE *GIRL FRIEND.*

JILLIAN?

HE HASN'T *HURT* ME, GAR. PLEASE DON'T *LET* HIM.

I'LL *KILL* YOU FOR THIS.

"*DO I HAVE TO TELL YOU I WAS TICKED OFF? SO I MADE THIS LIGHTNING-FAST METAMORPHOSIS...*

THUNK!

"*ONLY I KINDA FOUND THIS OBSTACLE IN MY WAY!*"

YOU DIDN'T TRULY THINK I'D ALLOW YOU *NEAR* ME, DID YOU, LOGAN?

OR DO YOU ONLY *ANSWER* TO *BEAST BOY* THESE DAYS?

"*SUDDENLY, THE BOTTOM OF ARSENAL'S MASK STARTED TO SLIDE UP.*

"*IT WAS OPENING.*"

YOU? I SHOULD'A *KNOWN* IT WAS YOU.

NOBODY ELSE COULD BE SO *SLIMY.*

"*GALTRY!*

"*MY EX-GUARDIAN DEVIL HIMSELF!*"

EVER SINCE I LOST *CUSTODY* OVER YOU AND YOUR FATHER'S *MILLIONS,* I'VE AWAITED THIS DAY.

IF YOU WANT HER *ALIVE,* GIVE ME THE *MONEY* YOU COST ME.

THAT'S WHAT IT COMES DOWN TO, BEAST BOY--YOUR *MONEY...*

...OR HER LIFE!

16

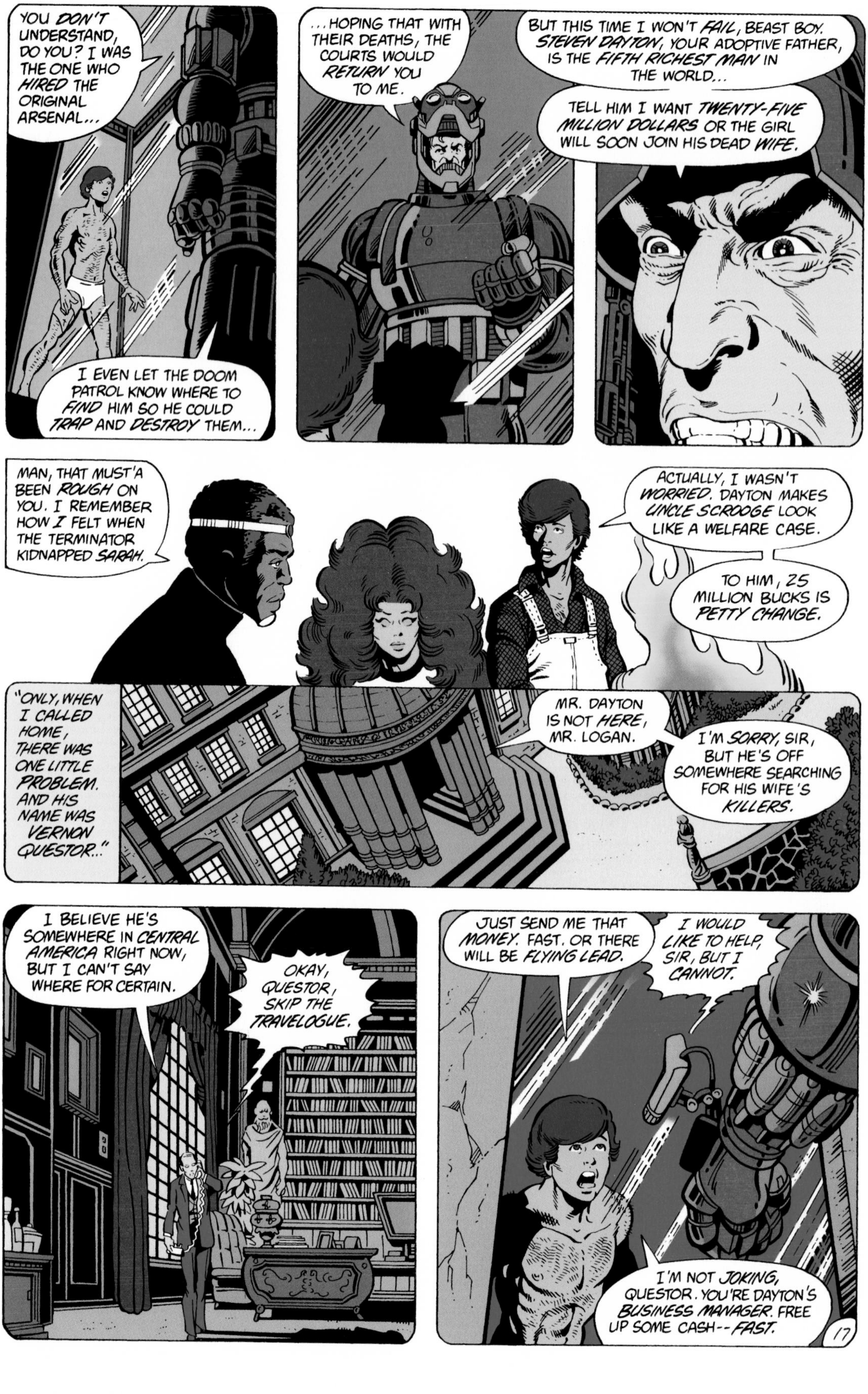
YOU DON'T UNDERSTAND, DO YOU? I WAS THE ONE WHO HIRED THE ORIGINAL ARSENAL...
I EVEN LET THE DOOM PATROL KNOW WHERE TO FIND HIM SO HE COULD TRAP AND DESTROY THEM...
...HOPING THAT WITH THEIR DEATHS, THE COURTS WOULD RETURN YOU TO ME.
BUT THIS TIME I WON'T FAIL, BEAST BOY. STEVEN DAYTON, YOUR ADOPTIVE FATHER, IS THE FIFTH RICHEST MAN IN THE WORLD...
TELL HIM I WANT TWENTY-FIVE MILLION DOLLARS OR THE GIRL WILL SOON JOIN HIS DEAD WIFE.
MAN, THAT MUST'A BEEN ROUGH ON YOU. I REMEMBER HOW I FELT WHEN THE TERMINATOR KIDNAPPED SARAH.
ACTUALLY, I WASN'T WORRIED. DAYTON MAKES UNCLE SCROOGE LOOK LIKE A WELFARE CASE.
TO HIM, 25 MILLION BUCKS IS PETTY CHANGE.
"ONLY, WHEN I CALLED HOME, THERE WAS ONE LITTLE PROBLEM. AND HIS NAME WAS VERNON QUESTOR..."
MR. DAYTON IS NOT HERE, MR. LOGAN.
I'M SORRY, SIR, BUT HE'S OFF SOMEWHERE SEARCHING FOR HIS WIFE'S KILLERS.
I BELIEVE HE'S SOMEWHERE IN CENTRAL AMERICA RIGHT NOW, BUT I CAN'T SAY WHERE FOR CERTAIN.
OKAY, QUESTOR, SKIP THE TRAVELOGUE.
JUST SEND ME THAT MONEY. FAST. OR THERE WILL BE FLYING LEAD.
I WOULD LIKE TO HELP, SIR, BUT I CANNOT.
I'M NOT JOKING, QUESTOR. YOU'RE DAYTON'S BUSINESS MANAGER. FREE UP SOME CASH--FAST.
17

I AM NOT *AUTHORIZED* TO MAKE SUCH A LARGE PER-SONAL WITH-DRAWAL.

MR. DAYTON DID NOT GIVE ME THAT *RIGHT.* THE BANKS WON'T ACCEPT MY *SIGNATURE.*

I AM TRULY *SORRY.*

"AT THAT MOMENT, I *HATED* DAYTON... MAYBE EVEN MORE THAN I DID *GALTRY.*"

IT IS *TOO LATE,* BEAST BOY. YOU *FAILED.*

AND YOU CAN NO LONGER *HELP* ME.

BUT THE *GIRL* POSSIBLY CAN.

HER FATHER ISN'T AS *WEALTHY* AS DAYTON, BUT HE IS A *MILLION-AIRE.*

HE'LL GIVE ME *EVERYTHING* FOR HIS LITTLE GIRL...*WON'T* HE NOW, JILLIAN?

AS FOR *YOU,* BEAST BOY, YOU'RE NOW A *DEAD MAN.*

THE WALLS ARE *ELEC-TRIFIED,* AND THE ROOM *AIR-TIGHT.*

YOU CAN'T BREAK FREE, WHICH MEANS YOU'LL *SUFFOCATE* FROM LACK OF *AIR.*

IN ABOUT *TEN MINUTES,* I'D SAY.

GALTRY! DON'T *DARE* HURT HER! GALTRY!!

I'LL SAVE YOU, JILLIAN. I'LL...

SKREEE!

DAMN!

18

UMMM...

DON'T *SAY* IT, KORY.

YOU'RE *GORGEOUS.* I'D LOVE TO LEAVE YOU WITH MY PERSONALIZED *HICKEYS*--

--BUT, IF YOU SAY IT, I COULD LEARN TO *HATE* YOU.

SO YOU HAD TO ESCAPE FROM A *LOCKED ROOM.* THAT'S *ROBIN'S* KIND OF TRAP. HOW'D YOU *GET OUT?*

IF ROBBIE'S SUCH AN *EXPERT,* HOT-SHOT, LET *HIM* FIGGER IT OUT.

BURROW OUT AS A *GOPHER?*

NOT EVEN *CLOSE.* THE FLOOR WAS *SOLID ROCK.*

ONE DOWN, NINE TO GO. ARLENE FRANCIS?

ASK HIM IF HE BECAME AN *ANT* AND SQUEEZED HIS WAY FREE?

NAH. HE SAID THE ROOM WAS *AIR-TIGHT.*

HMM. THE *FLOOR* WASN'T ELECTRIFIED SINCE YOU WALKED ON IT.

YOU TURNED INTO AN ELECTRIC EEL AND *SHORT-CIRCUITED* THE ROOM.

NO, NOT YET. OOH, I *LOVE* THIS, ROBIN, THE TEEN WONDER-- *STUMPED.*

WAIT! *WAIT!* KNOWING YOU, I THINK I *GOT* IT.

DON'T KEEP IT TO *YOURSELF,* DICK.

GAR TURNED HIMSELF INTO A *POR--*

HOLD IT! LET *ME* HAVE THE HONORS.

I HADDA SMASH THE GLASS WITHOUT *TOUCHING* IT.

SO GUESS WHICH MACHO HERO BECAME AN INSTANT *PORCUPINE...*

...AND *QUILLED* HIS WAY TO FREEDOM?

C'MON, GUESS. IT'S NOT *HARD.*

WHAT'S SHORT AND GREEN AND IRRESISTIBLY *CUTE?*

THE *FIRST* ONE WHO SAYS *'AVOCADO DIP'* IS IN SERIOUS TROUBLE.

19

"WHAM! I WAS OUT AND FREE..."

"FREE AND LEAPING LIKE A *LEOPARD* TO FIND THAT PAIN IN THE ARSENAL."

"HOLD IT, GAR. IT TOOK *ME* SEVERAL MINUTES TO FIGURE MY WAY OUT."

HOW'D *YOU* DO IT SO FAST?

OH, IT ISN'T HARD WHEN YOU'RE AS *GREAT* AS I AM.

OKAAAYY. THEY HAD A *TRAP* JUST LIKE THE ARSENAL'S ON "*SPACE TREK*." MY WRITERS USED THE SAME *PORCUPINE GIMMICK.*

SPOILSPORT.

GAR!

"NOW YOU KNOW WHENEVER I BECOME AN ANIMAL, I TAKE ON ITS CHARACTERISTICS."

"SO THERE I WAS SNIFFING MY WAY THROUGH HIS FORTRESS..."

"...UNTIL..."

YOU *ESCAPED*? YOU'RE *BETTER* THAN I HAD IMAGINED, BEAST BOY. BUT, IT WON'T *HELP*.

THE FIRST ARSENAL *DESIGNED* ALL THESE WEAPONS.

BEAST BOY, YOU CAN'T *POSSIBLY* ESCAPE.

WANNA *BET*, UGLY?

AND *STOP* CALLING ME BEAST BOY LIKE THE NAME IS *POISON!*

"FROM THE CORNER OF MY EYE I SAW JILLIAN. SHE WAS SO *TERRIFIED*.

"OBVIOUSLY, NOTHING LIKE THIS HAD *EVER* HAPPENED TO HER BEFORE.

20

"AND I WAS GOING TO MAKE CERTAIN IT *NEVER* HAPPENED AGAIN."

YOU ARE NO LONGER *GAR LOGAN* TO ME. YOU JOINED THAT *DOOM PATROL.* THEY *STOLE* YOU FROM ME WHEN THEY GAVE YOU THAT STUPID *NAME,* BEAST BOY.

I'LL *KILL* YOU, BEAST BOY. I'LL *DESTROY YOU!*

KRAK!

"WHAT CAN I TELL YOU? IF GALTRY EVER ENTERED THE MISS AMERICA PAGEANT, I'D LAY ODDS HE WOULDN'T WIN AS *MISS CONGENIALITY.*"

"WELL, I HAD TO *PLAN* MY ATTACK, SO I RAN..."

"... AT LEAST, I *PRETENDED* TO."

Y'KNOW SOMETHING, UGLY? YOU'VE *SPOILED* THAT NAME FOR ME. NOW I GOTTA *CHANGE* IT.

BY THE WAY, GALTRY--AM I BEING TOO MUCH OF A *BUTT-HEAD* FOR YOU?

POOM

GETTING YOUR *GOAT,* SO TO SPEAK?

THAT'S WHAT YOU GET FOR BEING SO GRUFF.

WHY DON'TCHA *LAMB* OUTTA HERE WHILE YOU STILL GOT THE CHANCE?

KRASH!

"GOLDIE, YOU WOULD'A *LOVED* THE FIGHT. I WAS ON THE OFFEN-SIVE--NO WISE CRACKS FROM YOU, STONE, ABOUT MY NEEDING DEODORANTS.

"*TROUBLE IS,* BOZO HAD A FEW *GIMMICKS* OF HIS OWN.

"I NEARLY BURNED OFF MY *TAIL FEATHERS...*

"...WHILE HE WAS MAKING IT A HOT TIME IN THE OLD TOWN TONIGHT. STILL, I GOT MY *FATHEAD* OUT OF THE FIRE, SO TO SPEAK.

21

"UNFORTUN-ATELY, CREEPO WAS READY. I TOLD YOU THE WHOLE PLACE WAS ONE BIG DEATH TRAP.

"MAYBE THAT SHOULD'VE MADE ME FEEL *IMPORTANT*, HIM SETTING ALL THAT UP JUST FOR *ME*--

"--BUT I WAS TOO BUSY TRYING TO SAVE MY READY-TO-WEAR *HIDE*."

NOW YOU'RE DOOMED, BEAST BOY. *POISON GAS* WILL DESTROY YOU.

"OKAY, MAYBE I'M *NOT* SUCH A BIG TIME *ESCAPE ARTIST* LIKE DICK OR THE BIG BAD BATMAN...

"BUT WE *SHAPE-CHANGERS* ARE FAR FROM *HELP-LESS.*

"I POOFED INTO A *WORM* AND SLITHERED *BELOW* THE GAS...

"..WHERE I CAUGHT MY BREATH AND PROVED ONCE AND FOR ALL HOW *STUPID* I CAN SOMETIMES BE.

HEY, GALTRY--YOO-HOO. *THIS WAY, STUPID!*

I WANNA MAKE A *LASTING IMPRESSION* ON YOU.

"*WHAP!* I CLUNG TO HIS FACE LIKE SARAN WRAP. I COULD TELL MY PAL WAS NOT EXACTLY *HAPPY.*"

YOU FOOL! I--I CAN'T SEE!

22

"YOU GOTTA REMEMBER, GALTRY WASN'T REALLY A TRAINED SUPER-BADDIE. HE DIDN'T QUITE KNOW HOW TO HANDLE THIS SITUATION."

"SO, LIKE THE NICE GUY HE IS, HE WENT BANANAS!"

YAGGHHH! I'M BLIND! WHAT HAVE YOU DONE TO ME!?

GET OFF ME! GET OFF ME!

KRASH!

"NATCH, I DIDN'T LISTEN. INSTEAD, I HELD ON TIGHTER THAN BROOKE SHIELDS' JEANS."

...UNTIL HE FELL INTO THE LAKE WHICH WAS BUILT IN THE CASTLE'S CENTER CLOISTER."

"LIKE I SAID, GALTRY WENT CRACKERS. HE WAS FLAILING ABOUT LIKE SOME THRASHING ANIMAL...

SPLASH!

FINALLY! NOW I CAN DESTROY YOU AT LAST.

"UNFORTUNATELY FOR HIM, I BECAME THAT ELECTRIC EEL DICK MENTIONED A WHILE BACK--

"--SHOT A COUPLE OF THOUSAND VOLTS THROUGH HIM AND HE WAS OUT!

SZZZRAKKKK!

23

"AND THE *BEST* THING IS CON EDISON DIDN'T EVEN SEND ME A *BILL* FOR ALL THAT ELECTRIC POWER. WELL, I TOSSED GRUESOME OUT OF THE *LAKE*...

"...*TOOK CARE OF HIS SUIT*...

"...AND WAS READY TO FINISH OFF *GALTRY* HIMSELF.

"I KEPT REMEMBERING ALL THE *BEATINGS* HE GAVE ME AS A KID...

...HOW HE TRIED TO *KILL* THE *DOOM PATROL*.

...HOW HE JUST TRIED TO KILL ME...

"...BUT, ABOVE IT ALL, HOW HE HAD *KIDNAPPED* AND *THREATENED* JILLIAN.

"AND I LET HIM KNOW JUST HOW *UNHAPPY* I WAS ABOUT IT ALL.

SPAMM!

"I STARED AT HIM FOR A LONG WHILE AS HE CRAWLED ON THE BEACH LIKE SOME FILTHY *WORM*. AND, YOU KNOW, FOR A WHILE, I FELT REAL GOOD.

"BUT THEN THAT CHANGED. GALTRY WAS NOTHING, BUT HE BROUGHT OUT AN *ANGER* IN ME THAT I DIDN'T LIKE.

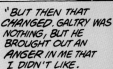

"THE ANGER THAT HAD BEEN *GROWING* WITHIN ME EVER SINCE THE *DOOM PATROL* HAD DIED.

"AN ANGER I VOWED TO GET RID OF. AND I *DID*, UNTIL WE FOUND THE PATROL'S *KILLERS*. THEN IT CAME BACK... IT ALL CAME BACK."

(24)

BUT IT'S *GONE* NOW. I HOPE *FOREVER.*

SO THAT'S THE STORY OF *GARFIELD LOGAN,* BOY HERO, GIRL CHASER, AND SUPER-HERO SUPREME.

YOU THINK I CAN SELL THE *MOVIE RIGHTS?*

MAYBE THEY'D GET *HARRISON FORD* TO PLAY ME? EH?

GARFIELD... OKAY! THESE HOT DOGS HAVE A *GRUDGE* AGAINST ME. MAYBE I ONCE ATE THEIR *COUSINS.*

I *GIVE UP!* I'LL *STARVE* TO DEATH. THAT'LL SHOW 'EM.

NAH. WHILE YOU WERE TALKING I COOKED THESE UP USIN' MY *INTERNAL GENERATOR.*

HAVE SOME, WILLYA?

'SIDES, WHILE YOU'RE EATING YOU CAN'T *TALK...*

AND BELIEVE ME, BROTHER--WE *ALL* NEED A REST AFTER THAT.

ONLY QUESTION *I* HAVE IS-- IF YOU *USED* TO BE SO GREAT, WHAT'S HAPPENED *SINCE?*

WEST?

YEAH, LOGAN?

YOU WANNA MAKE A CAREER OUTTA BEING THE *FASTEST CORPSE ALIVE?*

SIGH... ALL THAT REMI-NISCING...

...REMINDS ME OF *TAMARAN.*

I WONDER IF I'LL EVER SEE MY *HOMEWORLD* AGAIN?

NEXT: THE STORY OF STARFIRE!

25

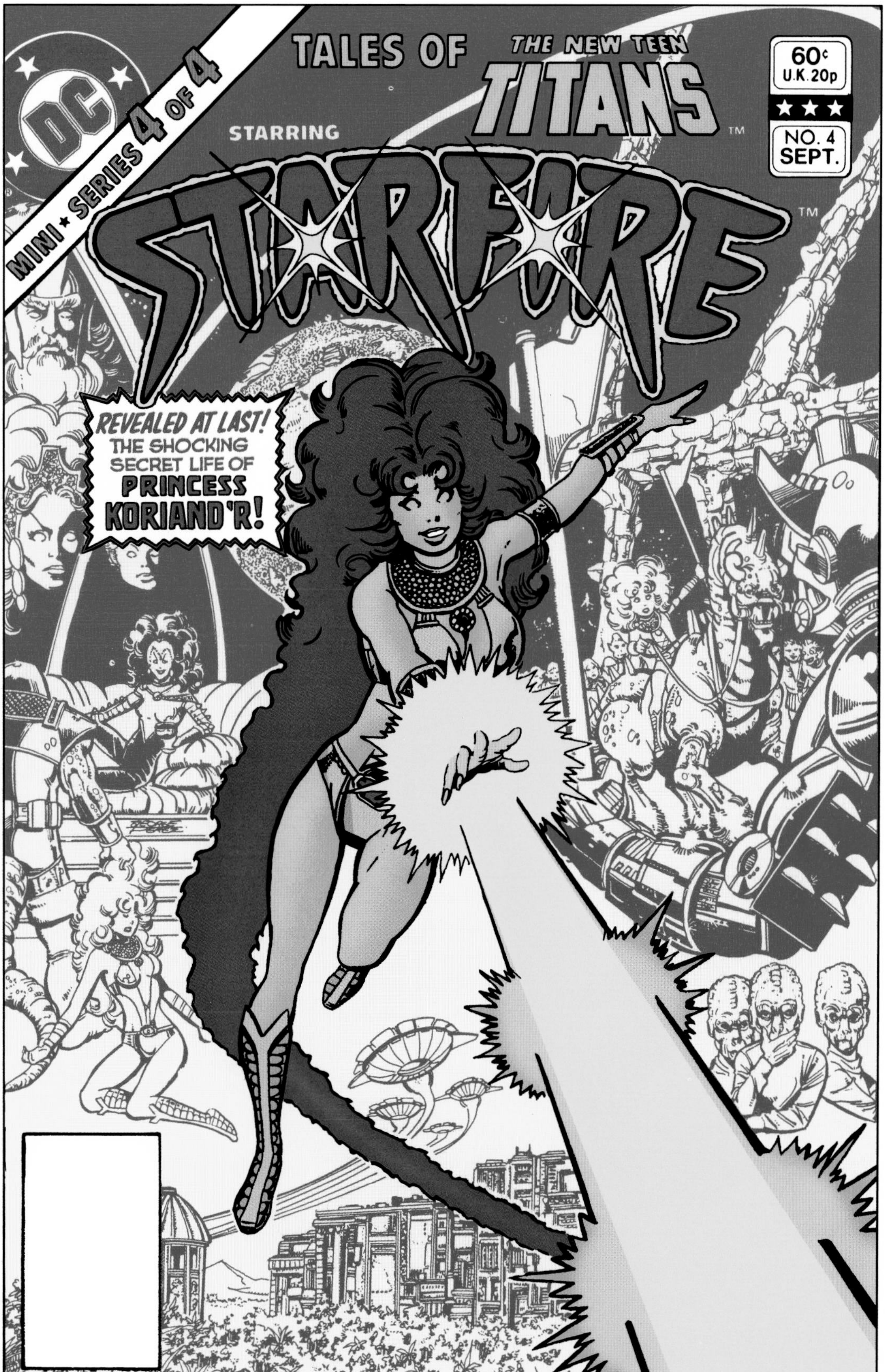
DC
MINI ★ SERIES 4 OF 4
TALES OF
THE NEW TEEN
TITANS
TM
STARRING
STARFIRE
TM
60¢
U.K. 20p
★★★
NO. 4
SEPT.
REVEALED AT LAST!
THE SHOCKING
SECRET LIFE OF
PRINCESS
KORIAND'R!

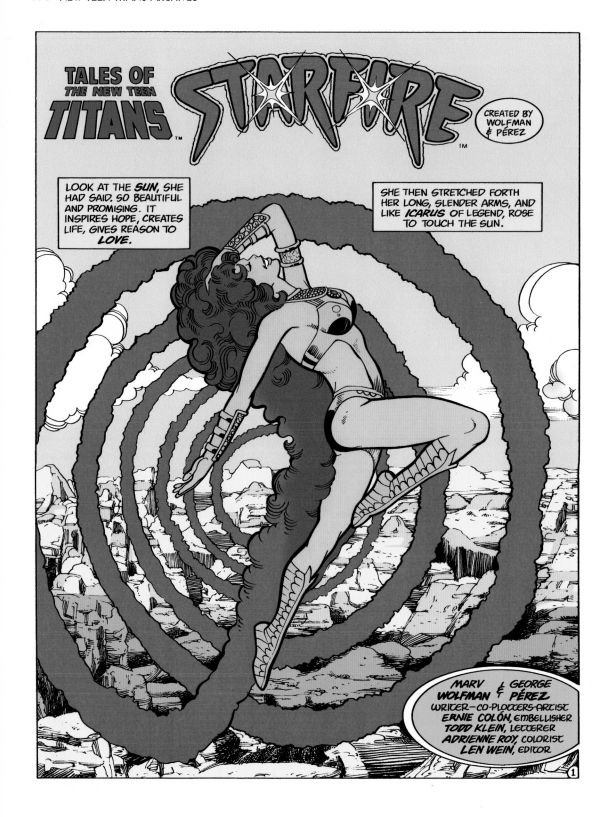

TALES OF THE NEW TEEN TITANS™ STARFIRE™

CREATED BY WOLFMAN & PÉREZ

LOOK AT THE *SUN*, SHE HAD SAID. SO BEAUTIFUL AND PROMISING. IT INSPIRES HOPE, CREATES LIFE, GIVES REASON TO *LOVE*.

SHE THEN STRETCHED FORTH HER LONG, SLENDER ARMS, AND LIKE *ICARUS* OF LEGEND, ROSE TO TOUCH THE SUN.

MARV & GEORGE *WOLFMAN* & *PÉREZ*, WRITER—CO-PLOTTERS-ARTIST
ERNIE COLÓN, EMBELLISHER
TODD KLEIN, LETTERER
ADRIENNE ROY, COLORIST
LEN WEIN, EDITOR

1

KORIAND'R'S AT *HOME* UP THERE, ISN'T SHE, DONNA?

IT'S WHERE SHE MOST COMES *ALIVE*, DICK.

I'VE WATCHED HER STARE AT THE SUN FOR *HOURS*, DRINKING IN ITS SPECIAL *WARMTH*.

MAN, I'M SORRY THIS TRIP IS *OVER*, BUT I'M GLAD WE'RE HEADIN' BACK TO *NEW YORK*.

YOU'RE *KIDDING*, VIC. FRANKLY, IT'S TOO *DIRTY* THERE FOR ME.

GIVE ME *BLUE VALLEY* ANY DAY.

C'MON, WALLY, THAT PLACE IS THE *ARMPIT* OF THE MID-WEST.

ME, I ♥ NEW YORK!

DO WE *REALLY* HAVE TO GO HOME, GUYS?

I *LOVE* IT HERE. THE AIR'S SO FRESH AND YOU CAN'T SEE *BUILDINGS* NO MATTER WHERE YOU LOOK.

WELL, *I'VE* GOT TO GET BACK. *INTERSESSION* ONLY LASTS SO LONG.

THAT'S RIGHT, DICK. YOU'VE GONE BACK TO COLLEGE.

OH, WELL. I GUESS ALL GOOD THINGS COME TO AN *END*.

BUT I DON'T THINK I'LL EVER *FORGET* THIS VACATION. IT WAS JUST *WONDERFUL*.

≋SIGHH≋ GOD CERTAINLY HAD HIS *ACT* TOGETHER WHEN HE FIRST ENVISIONED *KORY*.

EYES *IN*, SALAD-HEAD. SHE ONLY HAS EYES FOR *DICK*.

I CAN *DREAM*, CAN'T I?

I SENSED SUCH *HAPPINESS* IN YOU WHILE YOU WERE FLYING.

IT'S THE *SUN*, RAVEN. IT GIVES ME MY STRENGTH, MY *POWER*.

AND IT REMINDS ME OF MY *HOME*.

THE PLANET YOU CALL *TAMARAN?*

YES. BEAUTIFUL, GLORIOUS *TAMARAN*.

SOMETIMES I WONDER IF IT STILL IS *THERE*.

②

RAVEN, YOU SAID *AZARATH* WAS MAGNIFICENT. WELL, TAMARAN WAS SHEER *SPLENDOR* ITSELF.

WE'RE THE *EIGHTH* PLANET FROM OUR SUN, THE STAR YOU CALL *VEGA...*

"...BUT TAMARAN WAS STILL A *TROPICAL PARADISE.*

"THE AIR ALMOST SEEMED SCENTED WITH *PERFUME,* THE SKIES SHIMMERED WITH A GOLDEN GLOW.

"MAN AND NATURE STOOD SIDE-BY-SIDE *TOGETHER...*

"...AND THE ONLY ORDER ON TAMARAN WAS *LOVE.* OURS IS A PLANET RULED BY PASSIONS AND EMOTIONS...

"A PLANET WHERE *SCIENCE* SERVED ONLY TO HEIGHTEN OUR BEINGS, NOT TO FEED OUR GREED.

"WITH MORE THAN ENOUGH FOOD AND LAND FOR EVERYONE, THERE WAS NO NEED FOR *WARS.* AND OUR PALACES WERE NOT BUILT FOR *PROTECTION...*

"...BUT FOR *PEACE.*

"YES, IT WAS PARADISE. AND IT COULD NOT POSSIBLY LAST *FOREVER.*"

MYAND'R, HURRY! YOUR WIFE IS IN *LABOR.*

IS SHE ALL RIGHT? IS THE *MEDICOR* WITH HER?

HOW *IS* SHE, WOMAN? *TELL* ME!

"I WAS BORN AT *DAWN--* THE HOUR OF *INNOCENCE,* THEY SAY-- WHEN THE DAY IS YET TO BE AND STILL BRIMMING WITH HOPE AND POSSIBILITIES.

"MY FATHER, TAMARAN'S *KING,* SHOWED ME TO THE ASSEMBLY."

HER *FLESH* IS LIKE GOLD AND HER *EYES* ARE AS GREEN AS HER MOTHER'S.

LOOK, EVERYONE AT MY *PRIDE:*

HER NAME IS *PRINCESS KORIAND'R,* AND LIKE UNTO HER NAME, MAY SHE FOREVER SEE THE OPTIMISM OF *TOMORROWS.*

3

"ALL TAMARAN REJOICED AT MY BIRTH. ALL, THAT IS, BUT ONE: MY SISTER, KOMAND'R."

FROM THE MOMENT I WAS BORN, KOMAND'R DESPISED ME. SHE HAD BEEN SICKLY AT BIRTH, JUDGED UNFIT TO EVENTUALLY RULE.

I WAS GIVEN THE HONOR OF PRINCESS WHICH SHE SO COVETED.

ONE DAY I WOULD RULE, NOT SHE.

YOU MAKE HER SOUND LIKE LUCRECIA BORGIA AND DARTH VADER ROLLED UP INTO ONE.

MY SISTER IS EVIL. HER SOUL IS BLACK AS DEATH ITSELF.

EVEN WHEN WE WERE CHILDREN THE DIFFERENCES BETWEEN US WERE SO VERY APPARENT.

LUAND'R, LOOK. SHE LOVES HER PET.

I'D SAY THEY LOVE EACH OTHER.

"SNAR AND I WERE AS ONE. ALL DAY WE'D PLAY TOGETHER.

"UNTIL..." WHAT HAPPENED HERE, KOMAND'R? WHO KILLED THE DROR?

I DO NOT KNOW, MOTHER. IT WAS DEAD WHEN I FOUND IT.

"I NEVER BELIEVED HER. SHE HAD KILLED MY PET AS SHE TRIED TO KILL EVERYTHING THAT WAS MINE.

"BUT THERE WAS ONE THING I COULD DO THAT SHE NEVER COULD. BECAUSE OF HER SICKNESS, SHE WAS UNABLE TO HARNESS THE SOLAR WINDS AND SOAR UNFETTERED IN THE SKIES.

"THOSE WERE SUCH HAPPY DAYS FOR ME...

"...THOUGH DAYS KOMAND'R SPENT IN PLOTTING HER VENGEANCE, I AM SURE.

"HER HATE FOR ME AND FOR ALL TAMARAN GREW WITH EVERY PASSING YEAR."

④

WAS SHE *UNLOVED?* DID YOUR PARENTS *FAVOR* YOU OVER HER?

NOT AT FIRST, RAVEN. THEY LOVED US *BOTH.* BUT EVENTUALLY IT BECAME *IMPOSSIBLE* TO LOVE THAT TRAITRESS.

KEEP *TALKING,* KORY. I'M JUST PUTTING ON MY *ROBIN* UNIFORM. IT'S ALMOST TIME TO TAKE THE T-JET *HOME.*

HOW DID YOU AND KOMAND'R EVER *LIVE* TOGETHER UNDER THE SAME *ROOF?*

SHE WAS MY OLDER SISTER, WALLY. I *WANTED* HER TO LIKE ME.

BUT KOMAND'R ONLY *AVOIDED* ME.

I TOLD YOU TAMARAN BELIEVED IN *PEACE,* BUT WE ALSO KNEW THE *TRAGEDY* OF WAR.

"THE CITADEL WAS THE PLANET *CLOSEST* TO OUR SUN—AND FOR MORE THAN ONE HUNDRED YEARS THEY HAD SENT THEIR WARSHIPS AGAINST US. THEY NEEDED OUR *FOOD* TO SUSTAIN THEM. AND OUR PEOPLE TO BE THEIR *SLAVES.*"

SIRE, OUR SCANNERS HAVE PICKED UP *CITADEL* WARSHIPS.

IT'S ANOTHER *ATTACK.*

THEN, BY *X'HAL,* WE'LL BATTLE THOSE FILTH BACK TO THEIR *RINGED FORTRESS.*

COMMAND OUR SOLDIERS TO MAN ALL *FLIERS!*

"WE BELIEVED IN PEACE, BUT WE ACCEPTED THE *NECESSITIES* OF WAR.

"*LEFT ALONE,* WE CHERISHED THE JOYS OF NATURE. PROVOKED, WE LUSTED AFTER THE BLOOD OF *BATTLE.*

"SUCH WAS OUR *DUAL NATURE,* AND SUCH WAS THE WAY WE *LIVED.*"

⑤

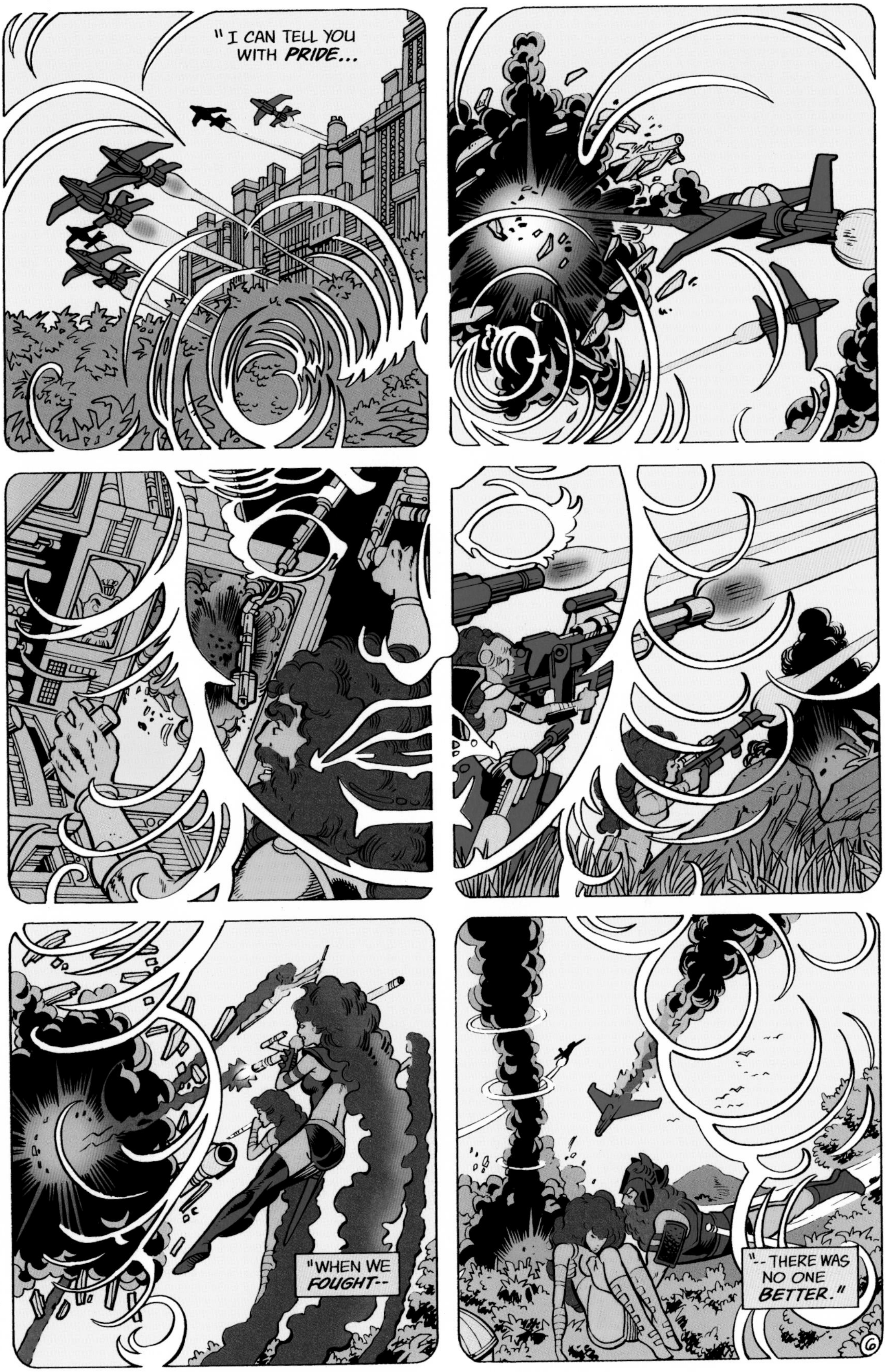
"I CAN TELL YOU WITH PRIDE...
"WHEN WE FOUGHT--
"--THERE WAS NO ONE BETTER."
6

"VICTORIOUS, WE SENT THE CURSED CITADEL SOLDIERS SCAMPERING LIKE DOGS TO THEIR *DEN.*

"AND THAT NIGHT THERE WAS *CELEBRATION* ACROSS ALL TAMARAN.

"BUT, WHILE OUR PARENTS *PARTIED...*"

KOMAND'R? WHAT HAVE YOU DONE TO *KORIAND'R?*

SHE LAUGHED AT ME BECAUSE I COULDN'T *FLY.*

I HAD TO *PUNISH* HER.

I *DIDN'T* LAUGH, FATHER. SHE *HATES* ME BECAUSE I *CAN* FLY.

HATE YOU? I DON'T *NEED* TO FLY.

"I HAVE ALL THE *POWER* I NEED HERE IN MY *FISTS,*" THAT'S WHAT SHE SAID. WE WERE *SISTERS,* BUT TOTAL STRANGERS WOULD HAVE HAD MORE IN *COMMON* THAN WE.

FOR YEARS WE INHABITED THE SAME PALACE, BUT WE NEVER *SPOKE* TO EACH OTHER.

"WE GREW UP AND *APART,* WITH KOMAND'R STAYING MORE AND MORE TO HERSELF. BUT THEN...."

WE CAN NO LONGER DELAY YOUR *TRAINING.* EACH MONTH THE CITADEL FORCES TRY TO BREAK THROUGH OUR NEW *DEFENSES.*

WE NEED MORE *WARRIORS,* AND EVEN THE DAUGHTERS OF KINGS MUST LEARN TO FIGHT...

...FROM THE *WARLORDS* OF OKAARA.

"WITH THE BIRTH OF OUR BROTHER *RYAND'R,* KOMAND'R GREW EVEN *MORE* RESENTFUL, MORE *HATEFUL.* YET FOR ONCE SHE SEEMED TO WANT TO *FOLLOW* OUR MOTHER'S DESIRES..."

THE *WARLORDS?* AT LAST! I HAVE BEEN *AWAITING* THIS DAY.

I AM *ANXIOUS* FOR THIS CHANCE, MOTHER. *VERY* ANXIOUS.

⑦

"OKAARA! THAT WORD WAS ALMOST *MYSTICAL* TO US."

"FOR YEARS, I, *TOO*, HAD WANTED TO MAKE MY PILGRIMAGE THERE. NOW I WOULD FINALLY GET THE *CHANCE.*"

IT'S *BEAUTIFUL,* MOTHER..., YOU CAN SEE ALMOST *FOREVER* OUT IN SPACE.

WHY DO WE HAVE TO *SHARE* THIS TRANSPORT SHIP WITH ALL THE DREGS OF OUR SOLAR SYSTEM?

LOOK AT THEM! WEAKLINGS, *ALL* OF THEM. THEY THINK THIS IS A *PARTY.*

DON'T THEY KNOW WE'RE GOING TO OKAARA TO LEARN TO *KILL?*

"THE *DREGS,* SHE CALLED ALL THE OTHERS. BUT LIKE US, THEY WERE THE CHILDREN OF *CHIEFTAINS.* THEY WERE THE *BEST* OUR PLANETARY SYSTEM HAD TO OFFER."

OH, MOTHER-- *LOOK.* IT'S OKAARA.

IT'S EVEN *MORE* MAGNIFICENT THAN THE HOLOGRAMS SHOWED.

"OKAARA WAS A PLANET THAT HAD *DIED* A MILLION YEARS BEFORE LIFE EMERGED ON ANY OTHER VEGAN WORLD..."

"SHE WAS A ROCKY HUSK ON THE OUTSIDE. BUT *INSIDE*...AHH, YOU WILL HAVE TO *SEE* IT SOMEDAY."

"*THERE WERE TUNNELS AND CAVERNS EVERYWHERE...*

"...AND THEY EACH *REFLECTED* THE LIGHT IN A DIFFERENT WAY. EVERY COLOR POSSIBLE WAS THERE. I WILL NEVER FORGET ITS *MAJESTY*... ITS *POWER.*

⑧

"I NEVER *SAW* X'HAL WHILE ON OKAARA, BUT I COULD *FEEL* HER PRESENCE AMONGST US. ANYWAY, THE *CHILDREN*-- KOMAND'R AND I WERE BUT *TWO*-- WERE BROUGHT BEFORE THE FABLED WARLORDS.

OKAARA WAS ALSO THE HOME OF X'HAL, OUR LIVING GODDESS.

YOU MEAN SHE WAS *REAL*, LIKE RAVEN'S *AZAR?*

REAL, OH *YES*. BUT ALSO *REMOVED* FROM ALL REALITY.

"I MUST ADMIT THEIR PRESENCE *FRIGHTENED* ME.

FOR MORE MILLENNIA THAN CAN EASILY BE COUNTED WE HAVE *TRAINED* THE CHILDREN OF OUR MOTHER STAR.

WE BRING YOU TO OKAARA TO TEACH YOU NOT ONLY THE ARTS OF *WARFARE*, BUT THOSE OF THE *HUMANITIES*.

THE TWO MUST BE FOREVER *ENTWINED*.

TEACH US TO *KILL*. THAT IS ALL THAT MATTERS.

TO KILL IS *NOTHING*. ANYONE CAN KILL. IT TAKES NO *SKILL* TO TWIST DAGGER THROUGH FLESH.

TO ACHIEVE *PEACE* IS THE GREATEST GOAL THAT CAN BE REACHED. BUT...

...WHEN ONE MUST *FIGHT* TO ACHIEVE THAT PEACE, ONE MUST FIGHT TO *WIN*.

BETWEEN RIGHT AND WRONG THERE CAN BE NO *COMPROMISE* ON THE FIELD OF BATTLE.

"HOW CAN I TELL YOU WHAT IT *FELT* LIKE, TRAINING ON OKAARA?"

"OUR FIRST YEAR WAS SPENT LEARNING TO *APPRECIATE* ALL THAT WAS ABOUT US, TO KNOW WHAT WAS *WORTH* FIGHTING FOR ..."

"...WHEN THERE WAS NO *ESCAPE* FROM BATTLE.

"THEN WE LEARNED THE ART OF *WARFARE*. EVERY MANNER OF FIGHTING WAS TAUGHT US.

"WE WERE SHOWN HOW TO LOVE OUR FRIEND AND HOW TO HATE OUR ENEMY. WE LEARNED OF *COMPASSION*--

"--AND *COMPROMISE*. BUT WE ALSO LEARNED THAT WHEN THEY FAILED, THERE WAS ONLY ONE RECOURSE: *WAR!*

"AND IN WAR, THERE COULD BE ONLY ONE OUT-COME: *VICTORY!*

"ON OKAARA I GREW FROM YOUNG CHILD INTO YOUNG *WOMAN*. AND SOON I WOULD RETURN HOME TO MY *PARENTS*.

"BUT FIRST THERE WOULD BE THE *TOURNAMENT*."

10

SO YOU WERE **USED** TO TOURNAMENTS? NO WONDER YOU DID SO WELL ON **PARADISE ISLAND.**

THE TOURNAMENT WAS A MANNER OF **GRADUATION EXERCISE.**

AND I EXCELLED IN ITS **FUNDAMENTALS.**

"KOMAND'R AND I WERE TO FACE EACH OTHER WITH **SOLAR LANCES.**

"A NEAR SWIPE WOULD **DISLODGE** YOUR OPPONENT FROM HIS MOUNT. THE ONE WHO FELL WOULD **LOSE.**

"WE WAITED FOR THE SIGNAL TO **BEGIN....**

"...AT LEAST **I** DID. KOMAND'R RUSHED FORWARD.

"OUR FIRST CHARGE WAS A **DRAW.** OUR LANCES CLANGED TOGETHER WITH NO WINNER OR LOSER.

"HER LANCE ARCED **DOWN** AND I SHOVED MINE **UP.** BUT SHE HAD THE UPPER HAND AND I FELT MYSELF ABOUT TO FALL.

"BUT KOMAND'R TOOK **ADVANTAGE** OF MY MOMENTARY WEAKNESS WITH AN ACT THAT ONLY DEMONSTRATES HER **SAVAGERY.**

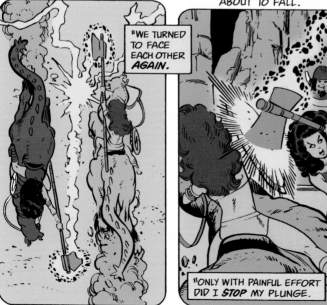

"WE TURNED TO FACE EACH OTHER **AGAIN.**

"ONLY WITH PAINFUL EFFORT DID I **STOP** MY PLUNGE.

"HER BLADE SLICED THROUGH MY MOUNT'S **LEG.**

11

"IT WAS AGAINST ALL THE RULES, BUT RULES MEANT **NOTHING** TO KOMAND'R. MY BEAST **DIED** AND I FELL HELPLESS TO THE GROUND."

SHOULD WE **STOP** THE FIGHT?

NO. I WANT TO SEE HOW KORIAND'R **FARES.**

YOU LOOK SO **PITIFUL**, SISTER.

I SHOULD **KILL** YOU FOR WHAT YOU DID.

YOU **SHOULD**, SHOULD YOU?

WELL, LITTLE SISTER, YOU HAVEN'T HALF THE STRENGTH TO **DO** THAT.

STILL, THIS IS MY CHANCE TO SHOW EVERYONE HOW **WEAK** YOU TRULY ARE.

COME ON, KORIAND'R...

...WE'RE GOING FOR A LITTLE **RIDE.**

"MY FLESH WAS TORN AGAINST THE JAGGED ROCK. STILL, I COULD DO NOTHING BUT **HOLD ON.** SURELY THE WARLORDS WOULD **STOP** THIS MADNESS...

"BUT THEY **DIDN'T.**"

VERY GOOD, SISTER. YOU HAVEN'T YET **CRIED OUT.**

LET US SEE HOW MUCH LONGER YOUR STOIC POSE CAN **LAST.**

"BUT THE PAIN HAD BECOME **TERRIBLE**...

"...AND SO, I REACHED FOR MY **SWORD**..."

⑫

"...AND *DREW* IT--

"--HACKING AT THE *ROPES* WHICH BOUND ME.

"FOR THE MOMENT I WAS *FREE*...

"...BUT KOMAND'R HAD NO INTENTIONS OF LETTING ME REGAIN MY *BREATH*."

STAY *AWAY* FROM ME, KOMAND'R.

I *DESPISE* YOU!

"MY *SHIELD* SLAMMED INTO HER BEAST'S LEGS AS PLANNED...

"BUT I THOUGHT IT WOULD MERELY FALL TO THE GROUND.

"IT *DIDN'T*."

OH, *NO!* KOMAND'R!!

"BOTH BEAST AND KOMAND'R FELL INTO THE *CREVASSE*. I FLEW IN *AFTER* HER.

"REMEMBER, MY SISTER COULD NOT *FLY*...

"...AND I WAS NOT ABOUT TO LET *HER* DIE. AT LEAST NOT *THEN*.

"OH, YES, I WAS A *FOOL*. BUT I *SAVED* HER.

⑬

"...NOT THAT SHE WAS *GRATEFUL*."

ARE YOU *ALL RIGHT*, KOMAND'R?

HOW DARE YOU *HUMILIATE* ME, KORIAND'R?

I WANTED YOU *DEAD*--

--AND YET YOU *SAVED* ME.

YOU ARE *WEAK*, SISTER. AND WORSE, YOU ARE A *FOOL*.

DIDN'T YOU *LEARN* ANYTHING HERE?

YOU NEVER LET AN ENEMY *SURVIVE.*

NEVER!

NO! THAT IS ENOUGH!

WHAT?

YOU ARE WITHOUT A *HEART* OR A *SOUL.*

YOU WALLOW IN YOUR OWN *HATE.*

YOU ARE NOT ONE OF US. *LEAVE* US NOW, KOMAND'R.

YOU ARE A *DISGRACE.*

OH, I WILL *LEAVE*, WARLORDS. AND I'LL GO WHERE I WILL BE *APPRECIATED.*

BUT I'LL BE *BACK.* TO SEE YOU ALL BURN IN *HELL!*

"SHE *LEFT*, WE ASSUMED, TO RETURN TO *TAMARAN*."

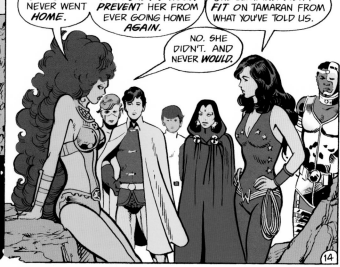

BUT SHE NEVER WENT *HOME.*

WHAT SHE DID WOULD *PREVENT* HER FROM EVER GOING HOME *AGAIN.*

SHE CERTAINLY DIDN'T *FIT* ON TAMARAN FROM WHAT YOU'VE TOLD US.

NO. SHE DIDN'T. AND NEVER *WOULD.*

14

"I SAID BEFORE THAT TAMARAN HAD INSTALLED NEW *DEFENSES* THE CITADEL COULD NOT BREAK THROUGH. BUT...."

WARSHIPS! BUT *HOW?*

MYAND'R, WHAT *IS* IT?

"MY FATHER *COULDN'T* GUESS, BUT *I* KNEW. KOMAND'R HAD FLED TO THE *CITADEL* AND REVEALED ALL OUR *SECRETS.* BECAUSE OF MY SISTER, TAMARAN WOULD BE *DEFEATED.*

"MORE THAN EVER BEFORE, I *HATED* KOMAND'R.

"AND I *SWORE* AT MYSELF FOR LETTING HER *LIVE.*

"BUT I *ALSO* SWORE THAT SHOULD WE EVER MEET AGAIN, SHE WOULD SURELY *DIE.*

"MORE THAN *FIVE MILLION* OF OUR PEOPLE DIED IN THAT FIRST ATTACK. MANY *MORE* WOULD PERISH IN THE WEEKS TO COME." (15)

IT WAS HORRIBLE. OUR WORLD HAD BEEN SO *LOVELY*, BUT NOW ALL YOU COULD SMELL WAS THE STENCH OF *BURNING FLESH.*

"...A TRUCE THAT DEMANDED A *SACRIFICE.* MY FATHER *REFUSED* IT AT FIRST, BUT THEN REALIZED HE HAD NO OTHER *CHOICE.*"

"ONE HUNDRED YEARS OF WARFARE HAD TAKEN ITS *TOLL.* HE HAD TO SUCCUMB OR TAMARAN WOULD BE COMPLETELY *OBLITERATED.*"

MYAND'R, WE HAVE *COME.*

SO *SOON?* I HAD HOPED IT WOULD BE *LONGER.*

FATHER... MOTHER... RYAND'R... I ...I *LOVE* YOU ...I LOVE...

PARADISE WAS *LOST*... BURIED BENEATH THE RUBBLE OF TOO MANY CITADEL RAIDS.

BUT, AT LAST, A *TRUCE* WAS CALLED...

TAKE ONE LAST *LOOK*, CHILD-- SINCE YOU WILL NEVER SEE YOUR FAMILY *AGAIN!*

FOR IF YOU SHOULD *RETURN* TO TAMARAN, THEY AND ALL THEIR PEOPLE WILL BE INSTANTLY *DESTROYED!*

"THE GORDANIANS WERE THE CITADEL'S *SLAVERS.*

"WE ALL HAD HEARD HOW *TERRIBLE* THEY COULD BE."

WELL, WELL-- IT HAS BEEN A *WHILE*, HASN'T IT, KORIAND'R?

I DON'T BELIEVE IT-- *YOU?*

WHO *ELSE*, SWEET SISTER?

WHO ELSE WOULD DEMAND THAT *YOU* BE TAKEN CAPTIVE? I HAVE *PLANS* FOR YOU, MY DEAR. (16)

"CITADEL SLAVERY WAS *UNLIKE* THE SLAVERY THAT EXISTED ON *YOUR* WORLD.

"WE WERE SOLD FOR *ONE YEAR.* AS LONG AS WE WERE NOT *KILLED,* OUR MASTERS COULD DO *ANYTHING* TO US.

"AT EACH YEAR'S END KOMAND'R WOULD *CLAIM* ME AGAIN. AND I ALWAYS SWORE I'D CLAIM MY *VENGEANCE.*

"I... CANNOT TELL YOU HOW *TERRIBLE* THOSE SIX YEARS WERE.

"I TRY NOT TO *THINK* ABOUT IT, BUT SOMETIMES AT NIGHT I... CANNOT *HELP* IT.

"BUT THERE WERE *MOMENTS...*

"...TIMES WHERE I EXACTED *REVENGE...* THOSE I STILL RE-MEMBER SO *VIVIDLY.*

"THE TORTURES AND THE DEGRADATIONS... THOSE ARE BEST *FORGOTTEN.*

"DURING THOSE YEARS I LOST MUCH OF MY *INNOCENCE;* I LEARNED HOW TO *HATE.*

⑰

"IT WAS HALFWAY THROUGH THE END OF MY FIFTH YEAR WHEN I *KILLED* MY LAST MASTER, A WORM WHOSE VERY TOUCH *SICKENED* ME. I WAS RETURNED TO THE GORDANIANS TO BE BROUGHT TO THE CITADEL FOR *TRIAL.*

"AT THIS POINT WHAT *HAPPENED* TO ME NO LONGER *MATTERED.* I HAD SWORN TO NEVER AGAIN GO THROUGH ANOTHER YEAR OF *SLAVERY.*

HERE SHE *IS.* I HAD TO *DRUG* HER INTO SUBMISSION.

KORIAND'R, WHAT AM I EVER GOING TO *DO* WITH YOU?

YOU KILLED YOUR *MASTER* AND THAT IS SOMETHING THAT CANNOT BE *PERMITTED.*

YOU'LL HAVE TO *DIE,* OF COURSE.

A *TOAST* THEN-- TO THE *AFTERLIFE.*

YOU DIE, AND THEN *TAMARAN* ITSELF WILL *FOLLOW.*

YOU'RE *SCUM!*

BUT I AM *ALIVE.* THAT IS ALL THAT *MATTERS.*

"BUT I WAS FATED NOT TO BE *BROUGHT* TO THE CITADEL. YOU SEE, THE PLANET I HAD BEEN SENT TO WAS AN *OUTWORLD POST...*

"...ONE WHICH HAD PERIODICALLY BEEN ATTACKED BY THE *PSIONS,* THE CITADEL'S DREADED *ENEMIES!*"

18

" THE PSIONS HAD BEEN AT *WAR* WITH THE CITADEL FOR MORE THAN A *MILLENNIUM*-- BUT JUST BECAUSE THEY *HATED* THE CITADEL, DO NOT THINK THEY WERE ANY *BETTER*. IN FACT, THEY WERE FAR *WORSE*, FAR *CRUELER*, IF THAT IS POSSIBLE.

"THOSE OF THE CITADEL WERE *BARBARIANS*, BUT THE PSIONS WERE *SCIENTISTS*.

"THEY WOULD STRIP OFF YOUR *FLESH* JUST TO SEE HOW *LONG* YOU WOULD LIVE.

"THEY *JUSTIFIED* ALL THEIR SICKNESS IN THE NAME OF SCIENCE. LIFE MEANT *NOTHING* TO THEM. OUTSIDE OF THEMSELVES, EVERYTHING ELSE EXISTED SOLELY FOR THEIR EVIL *TESTS*."

RESISTANCE? HOW SILLY OF YOU.

SQA, THE GORDANIANS ARE *WARM-WEATHER* CREATURES.

OBSERVE THE EFFECTS OF EXTREME *COLD* ON THEIR FRAGILE NERVOUS SYSTEMS.

THEIR *BLOOD VESSELS* WILL BLOAT AND EXPLODE. THEIR *HEARTS* WILL RUPTURE UTTERLY.

THEY WILL EXPERIENCE TERRIBLE *PAIN* BEFORE THEIR FLESH CRACKS.

STRANGELY ENOUGH, GORDANIANS WON'T DIE *IMMEDIATELY*. THEY *SUFFER* GREATLY BEFORE DEATH OVER-TAKES THEM.

DISSECT THE THING TO DISCOVER *WHY*. THE ANSWER MIGHT PROVE *ILLUMINATING*.

19

THEN AGAIN, IT MIGHT **NOT.**

LOOK, THIS ONE STILL **LIVES.** WELL, THAT WILL BE REMEDIED ONCE YOU BEGIN ITS **DISSECTION.**

CURIOUS RACE. AND SO **MINDLESS.**

WELL, LET US SEE WHAT **ELSE** MIGHT BE ON BOARD.

WHO KNOWS, WE MIGHT FIND **OTHER** LIVING CREATURES FIT FOR...

...EXPERIMENTATION.

TAMARAN- IANS? HOW **PERFECT.**

I BELIEVE I HAVE THE VERY EXPERIMENT THESE SUN-WORSHIPPERS MIGHT ACTUALLY **ENJOY...**

...BEFORE THEY **DIE.**

"UNCONSCIOUS, WE WERE STRAPPED INTO THEIR TERRIBLE MACHINES. WHEN I AWOKE I KNEW MY DEATH WAS **AT HAND.**"

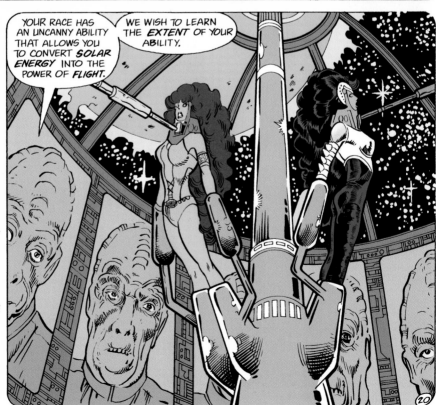

YOUR RACE HAS AN UNCANNY ABILITY THAT ALLOWS YOU TO CONVERT **SOLAR ENERGY** INTO THE POWER OF **FLIGHT.**

WE WISH TO LEARN THE **EXTENT** OF YOUR ABILITY.

20

WE WISH TO SEE *HOW MUCH* ENERGY YOU ARE CAPABLE OF CONVERTING.

DO YOUR *WORST*, PSION. IF I LIVE, I WILL *KILL* YOU.

TRUST ME. YOU *WON'T* LIVE.

NOW, *SOME* OF OUR SCIENTISTS THEORIZE YOU CAN CONVERT ONLY *MINIMAL* ENERGY BEFORE YOUR BODIES EXPLODE.

OTHERS PLACE THE LIMIT FAR *HIGHER*.

UNTIL NOW OUR RESEARCH HAS BEEN *THEORETICAL*. WE THANK YOU FOR PRO-VIDING A MORE *PRACTICAL* INSIGHT.

ALL RIGHT NOW. WE SHALL FOCUS INTO YOU ONE THERMAL UNIT WHICH SHALL BE *INCREASED* EVERY FIFTEEN SECONDS...

...UNTIL YOU *EXPLODE*, OF COURSE.

I'M SO PLEASED OUR BICKERING HERE WILL FINALLY COME TO AN *END*.

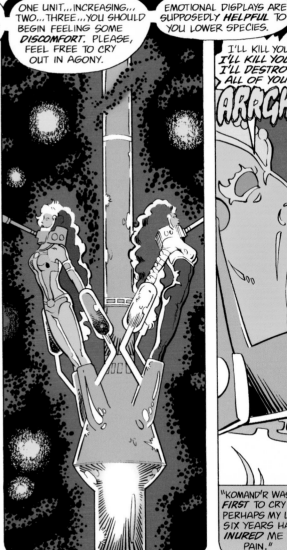

ONE UNIT...INCREASING... TWO...THREE...,YOU SHOULD BEGIN FEELING SOME *DISCOMFORT*. PLEASE, FEEL FREE TO CRY OUT IN AGONY.

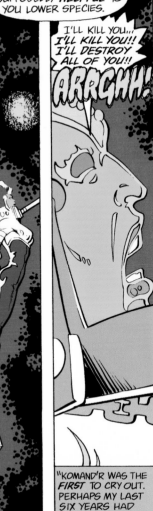

EMOTIONAL DISPLAYS ARE SUPPOSEDLY *HELPFUL* TO YOU LOWER SPECIES.

I'LL KILL YOU... *I'LL KILL YOU!! I'LL DESTROY ALL OF YOU!!*

ARRGHH!

"KOMAND'R WAS THE *FIRST* TO CRY OUT. PERHAPS MY LAST SIX YEARS HAD *INURED* ME TO PAIN."

㉑

I TOLD YOU, FON, THEY CAN ABSORB A FAR *GREATER* AMOUNT OF ENERGY THAN YOU THOUGHT.

I'LL *WIN* OUR BET.

I SUPPOSE *SO*, TRONT.

ALERT! CITADEL ATTACK SQUAD APPROACHING! ALERT! BATTLE STATIONS! ALERT!

EH?

"KOMAND'R AND I WERE STILL TRAPPED IN THEIR *SOLAR ABSORBER*, THE SUN'S RAYS STILL BLASTING INTO OUR SYSTEM.

"BY NOW I WAS IN PAIN, SCREAMING OUT FOR AN *END* TO THIS TORTURE EVEN AS THE CITADEL'S SHIPS POUNDED AT THE PSIONS."

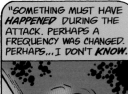

"SOMETHING MUST HAVE *HAPPENED* DURING THE ATTACK. PERHAPS A FREQUENCY WAS CHANGED. PERHAPS...I DON'T *KNOW*.

"BUT, THE MACHINE WHICH HELD ME SUDDENLY *EXPLODED*.

"I WAS *FREE*. AND I HAD SOMEHOW BEEN *CHANGED*."

MY HANDS ARE GLOWING WITH *POWER*.

WHAT *HAPPENED* TO ME?

"I HEARD THE *SHOUTING* THROUGHOUT THE CORRIDORS, AND THEN I GAZED UPWARDS...

"...AND SAW KOMAND'R WAS STILL BEING *HELD*."

22

"I WANTED TO *LEAVE* HER THERE UNTIL SHE *EXPLODED* ... I REALLY WANTED HER TO *DIE*.

"BUT, I COULDN'T *DO* THAT.

"...KOMAND'R WAS STILL MY *SISTER*.

"EVEN IF SHE WAS MY *ENEMY*, EVEN IF I HAD BEEN TAUGHT TO *KILL* MY FOES...

SKREE

"WHATEVER HAPPENED WOULD *HAPPEN*, I FELT.

"SOMEHOW I WAS ABLE TO SENSE THE POWER WITHIN ME... THE FACT THAT I HAD BECOME A LIVING *SOLAR BATTERY*.

"I *CONCENTRATED* FOR A MOMENT, FOCUSED MY POWER, AND KOMAND'R WAS *FREE*.

ARE YOU ALL RIGHT, SISTER? *SPEAK* TO ME.

SPEAK TO YOU? IMBECILE! I'LL *KILL* YOU!

I HAVE THE *SAME* POWER YOU HAVE -- BUT EVEN MORE *INTENSIFIED*!

KORIAND'R, HOW MANY TIMES MUST YOU BE REMINDED TO *SLAY* YOUR ENEMY--

--NOT *PITY* THEM.

23

SHE HAD TAKEN ADVANTAGE OF MY MISPLACED *COMPASSION.*

SHE TAUGHT ME THE *FOLLY* OF COMPASSION.

DURING THE CONFUSION SHE BROUGHT ME TO A CITADEL SHIP WHERE SHE WAS REASSIGNED TO THE CITADEL *HOMEWORLD.*

HER *VICIOUSNESS* IN BATTLE HAD AWARDED HER A HIGHER *RANK...*

...WHICH LEFT US *SEPARATED.*

"I WAS PLACED IN AN *ENERGY-DAMPER* WHICH NULLIFIED MY EXCESS POWER AND I WAS TAKEN ABOARD THE STAR-SLAVESHIP Q'ST'R BOUND FOR THE *PRISON PLANET.*

TROGAAR SAYS YOU WILL *DIE,* GIRL.

A SHAME. I WOULD *ENJOY* SOMETHING LIKE YOU.

OH? YOU STILL *CAN,* GORDANIAN.

...NOBODY NEEDS TO *KNOW.*

COME ON....

OKAY, GIRL, *COME* TO ME.

DOLT!

OUT OF MY *WAY,* SLAVER.

I DON'T NEED *INTERFERENCE* NOW--WHEN I'M SO CLOSE TO *ESCAPING.*

"I SNEAKED ABOARD A *STAR-SLIDER* AND TOOK OFF TO PARTS UNKNOWN."

24

IT TOOK THREE MONTHS TO REACH THE EARTH, AND EVEN THOSE MONTHS WERE FILLED WITH TROUBLES...

BUT, THROUGH IT ALL, I ONLY WANTED MY SISTER BEFORE ME SO THAT I COULD *DESTROY* HER.

HEY, KORY, PLEASE... YOU'RE AMONG *FRIENDS*... YOU DON'T HAVE TO GET ANGRY. YOU CAN *RELAX.*

I *KNOW* THAT, DICK.

BUT SOMETIMES... IT'S SO HARD TO *FORGET.*

HEY, GUYS, THIS IS OUR LAST DAY HERE, SO I THOUGHT WE'D *CELEBRATE.*

CHAMPAGNE? I DON'T REALLY *DRINK,* BUT THIS IS A SPECIAL OCCASION.

I GOT SOME *PERRIER* FOR YOU, RAVEN.

THANK YOU, WALLACE.

AND SOME *COCA COLA* FOR THE WALKING, TALKING SALAD.

YOU *ARE* ONLY 16.

DON'T *REMIND* ME, RUST-POT.

WE SPEND SO MUCH *TIME* TOGETHER, BUT USUALLY WE'RE GOING AFTER THE BAD GUYS. ALWAYS *FIGHTING.*

WELL, WE'VE HAD TIME TO BE WITH EACH OTHER AS REAL PEOPLE, AND YOU KNOW--

--I REALLY *LIKE* ALL OF YOU SO MUCH.

AS *FRIENDS.*

TO FRIENDS... ...AND TO FRIENDSHIP!

LONG MAY IT LAST!

THE END

25

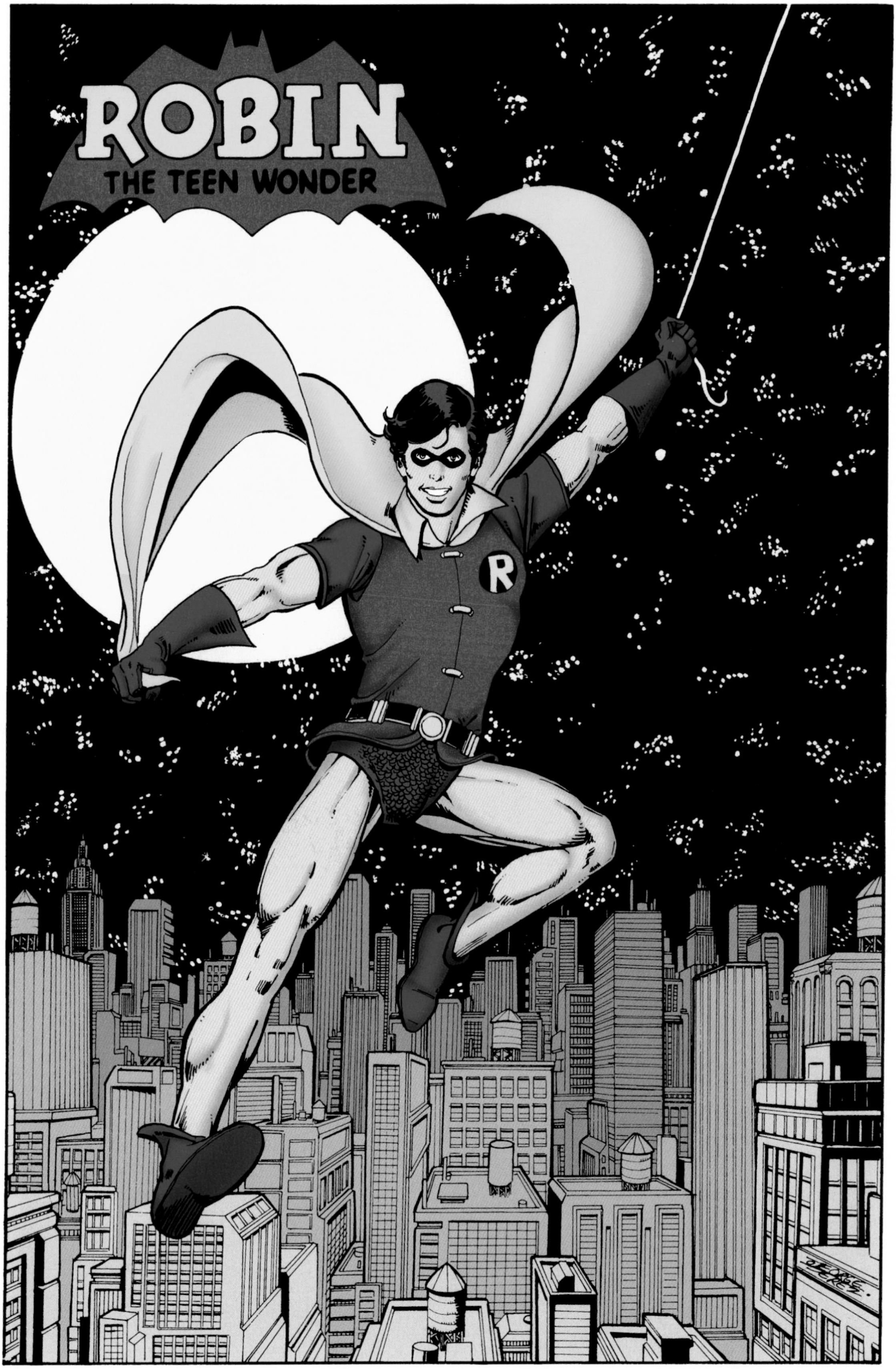
ROBIN
THE TEEN WONDER
™

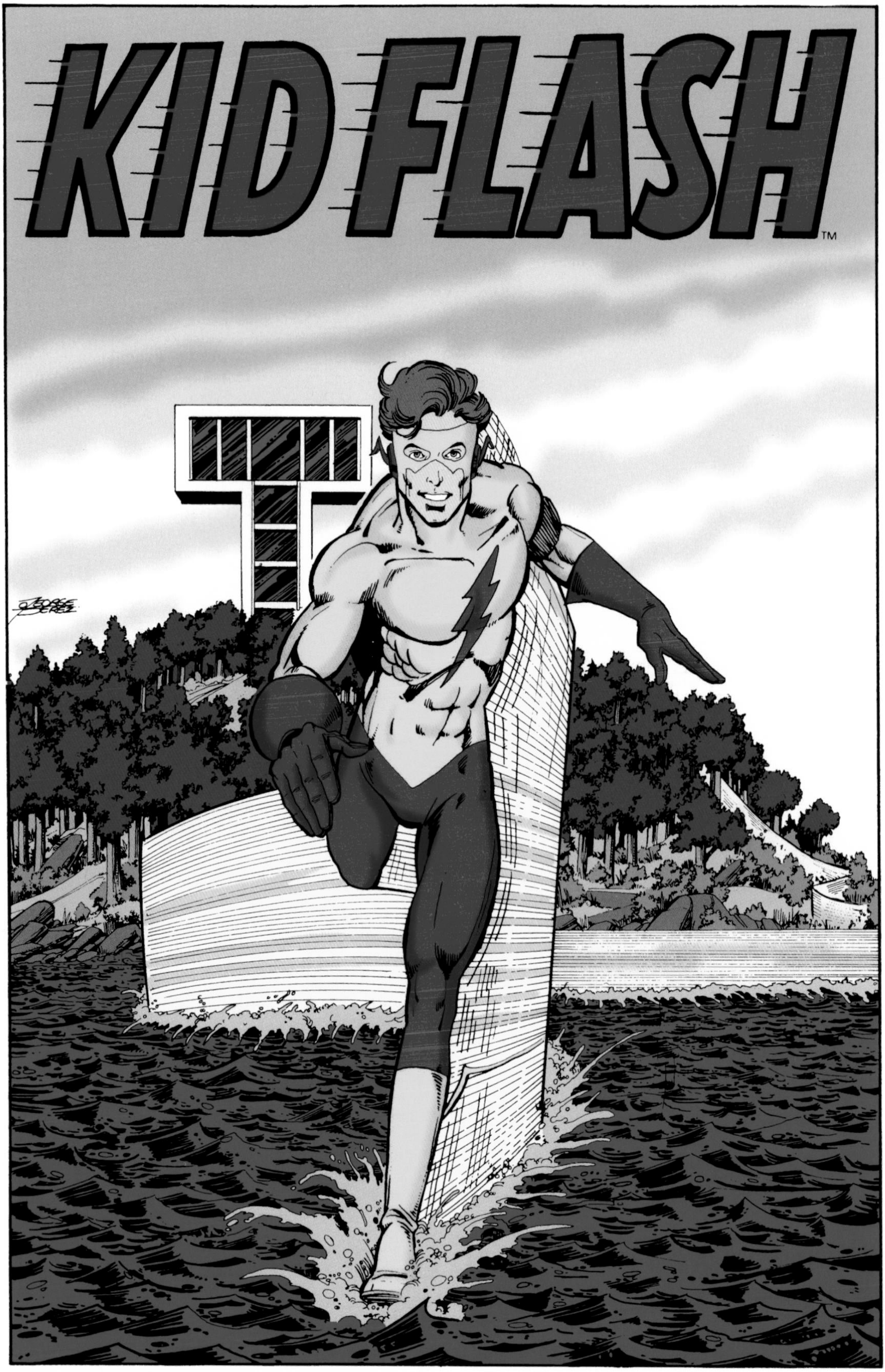
KID FLASH™
GEORGE PÉREZ

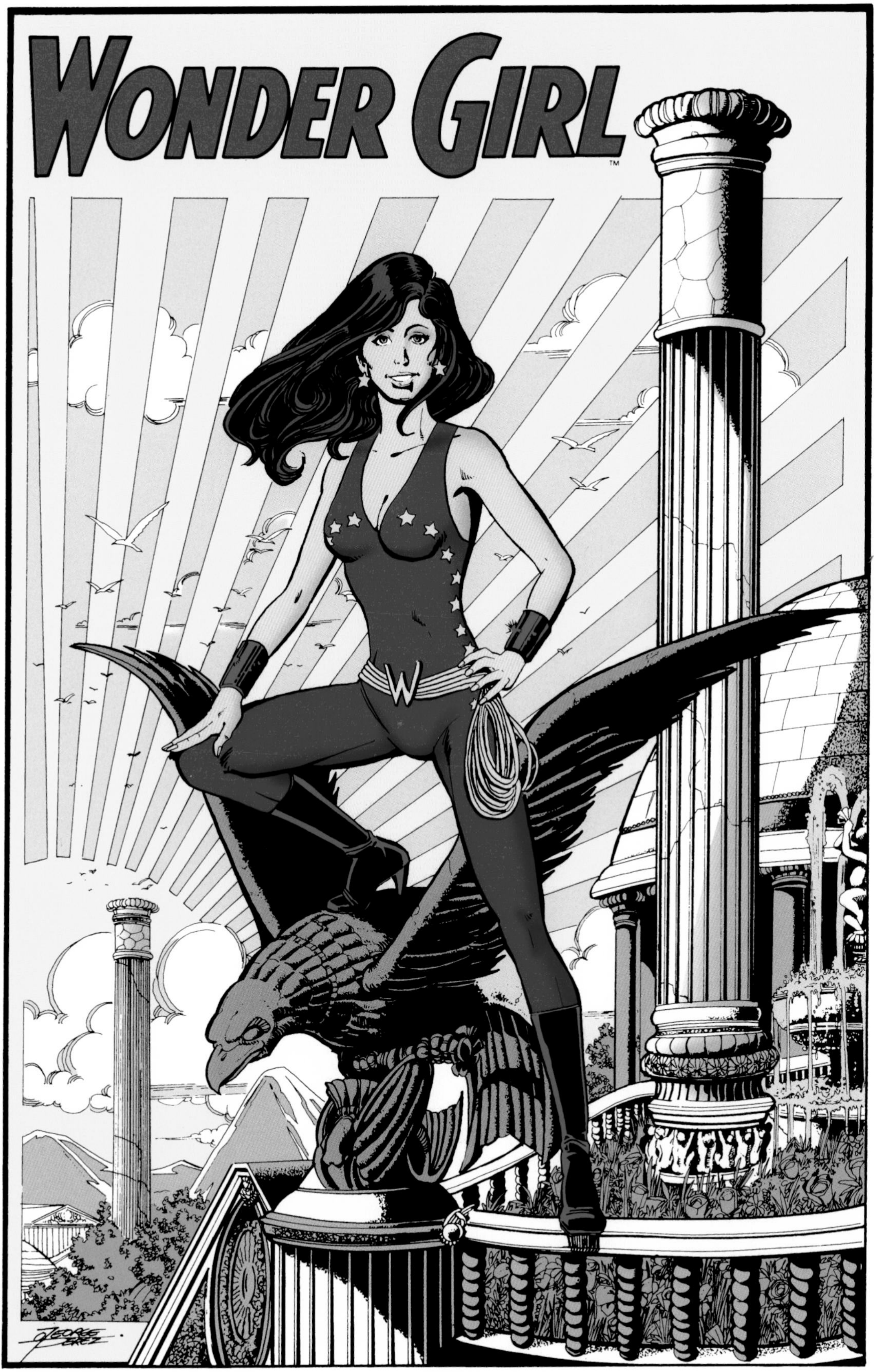
WONDER GIRL™
GEORGE PEREZ

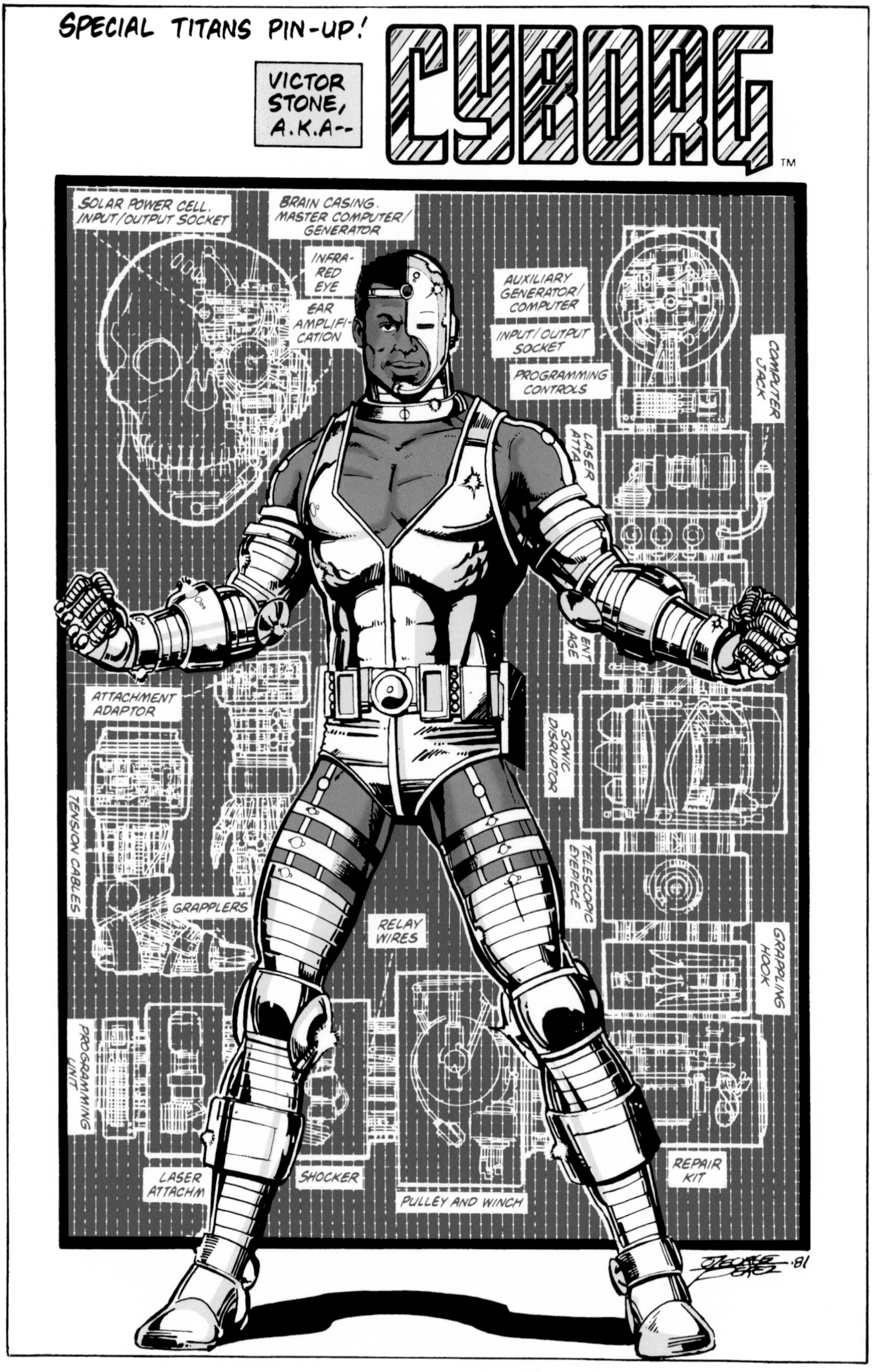
SPECIAL TITANS PIN-UP!
VICTOR STONE, A.K.A--
CYBORG™
SOLAR POWER CELL. INPUT/OUTPUT SOCKET
BRAIN CASING. MASTER COMPUTER/ GENERATOR
INFRA-RED EYE
EAR AMPLIFI-CATION
AUXILIARY GENERATOR/ COMPUTER
INPUT/OUTPUT SOCKET
PROGRAMMING CONTROLS
COMPUTER JACK
LASER ATTA
ENT AGE
SONIC DISRUPTOR
TELESCOPIC EYEPIECE
GRAPPLING HOOK
ATTACHMENT ADAPTOR
TENSION CABLES
GRAPPLERS
RELAY WIRES
PROGRAMMING UNIT
LASER ATTACHM
SHOCKER
PULLEY AND WINCH
REPAIR KIT

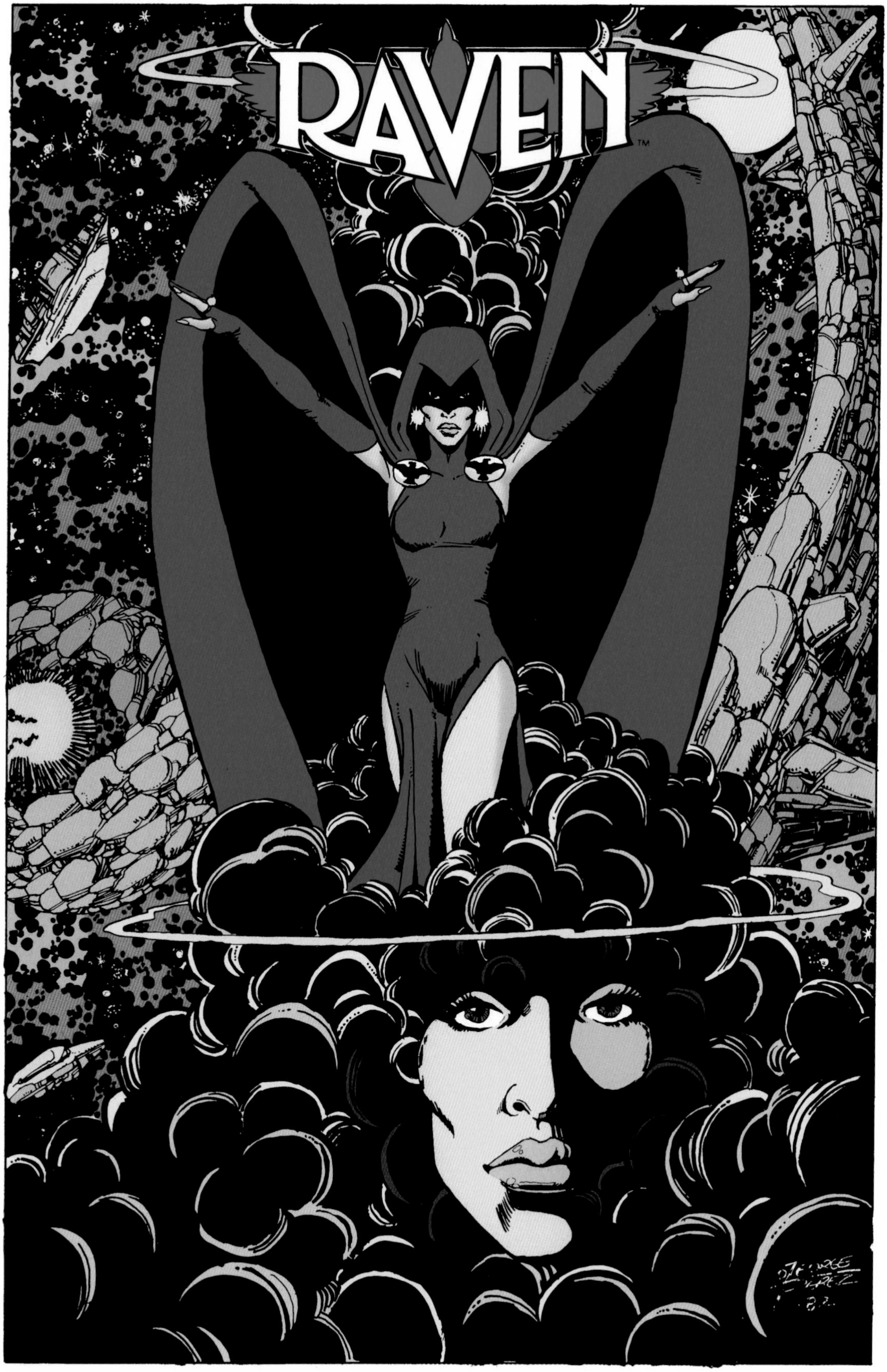
RAVEN™

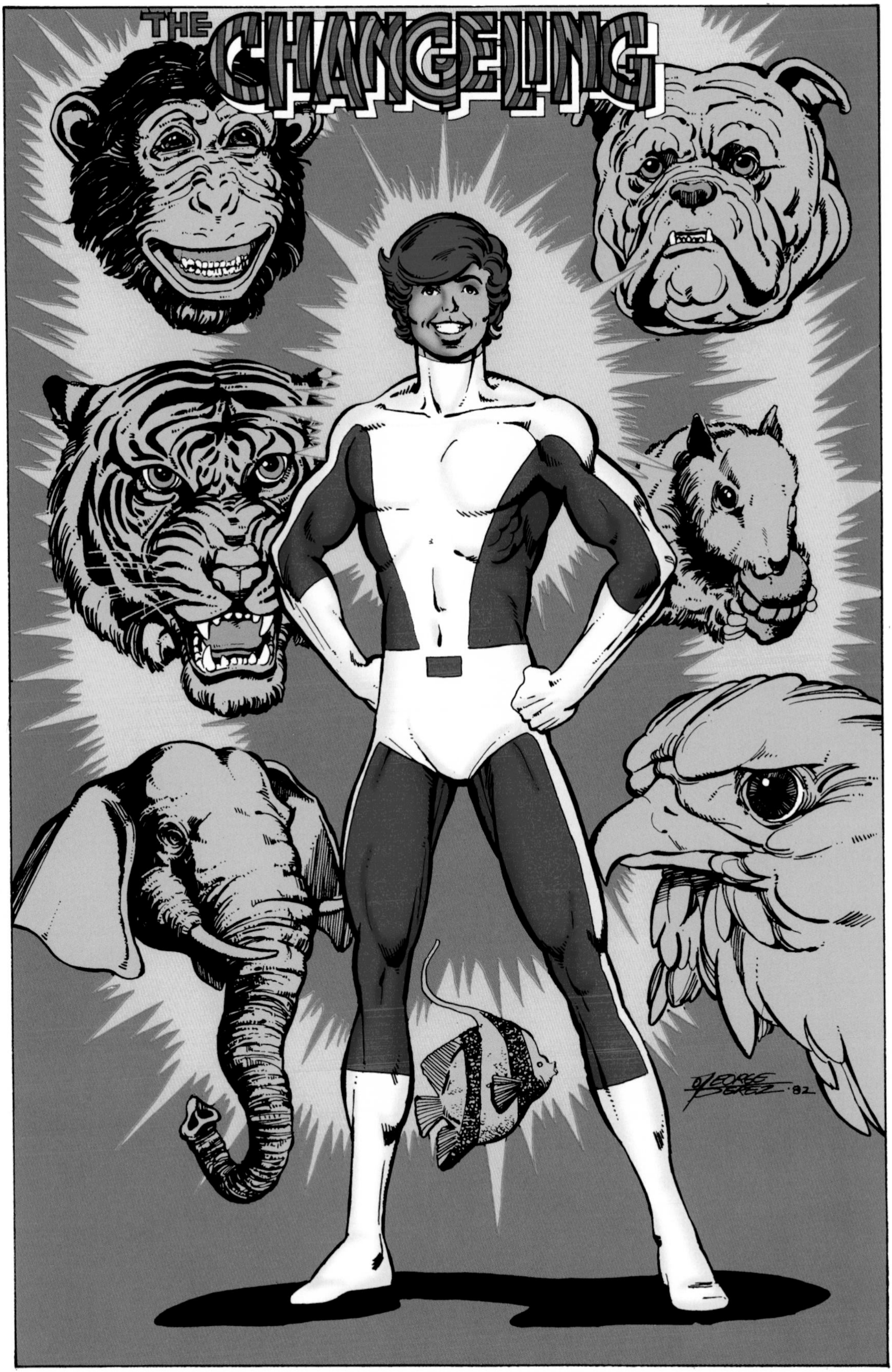
THE CHANGELING
GEORGE PEREZ '82

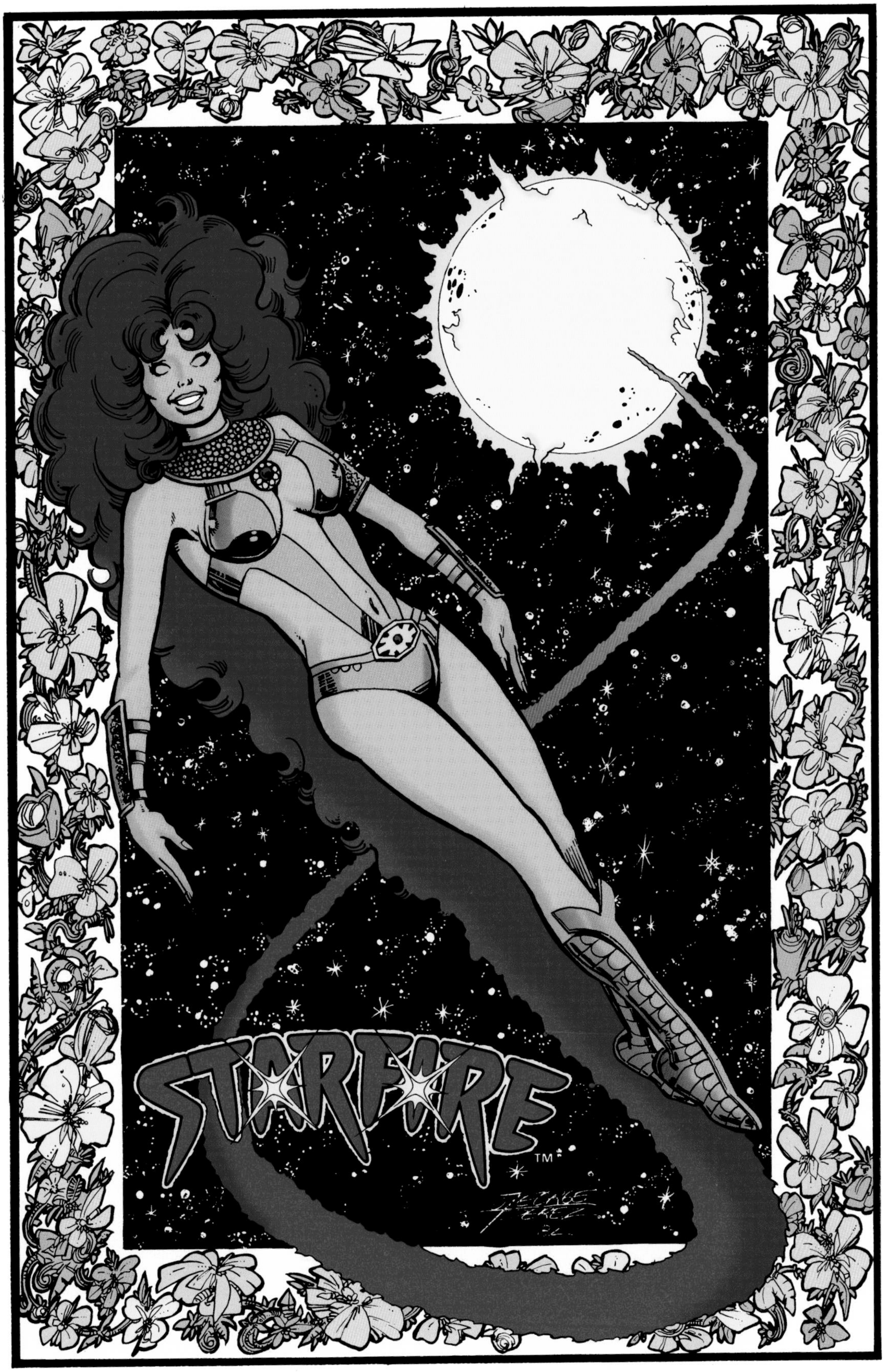
STARFIRE™

MARV WOLFMAN

One of the most prolific and influential writers in modern comics, Marv Wolfman began his career as an artist. Realizing that his talents lay more in writing the stories than in drawing them, Wolfman soon became known for his carefully crafted, character-driven tales.

In a career that spans nearly 30 years, Wolfman has helped shape the heroic careers of DC Comics' Green Lantern, Blackhawk and the original Teen Titans, as well as Marvel Comics' *Fantastic Four*, *Spider-Man*, *Nova* and *Tomb of Dracula*. In addition to co-creating THE NEW TEEN TITANS and the universe-shattering CRISIS ON INFINITE EARTHS with George Pérez, Wolfman was instrumental in the revamp of Superman after CRISIS, the development of THE NEW TEEN TITANS spinoff series VIGILANTE, DEATHSTROKE THE TERMINATOR and TEAM TITANS, and created such characters as *Blade* for Marvel, along with NIGHT FORCE and the retooled DIAL "H" FOR HERO for DC.

In addition to his numerous comic book credits, Wolfman has also written several novels and worked in series television and animation, including the *Superman* cartoon of the late 1980s and the current hit *Teen Titans* show on Cartoon Network.

GEORGE PÉREZ

George Pérez started drawing at the age of five and hasn't stopped since. Born on June 9, 1954, Pérez started his professional comics career as an assistant to Rich Buckler in 1973. After establishing himself as a penciller on Marvel Comics' *Man-Wolf* and *Sons of the Tiger*, he moved on to such Marvel titles as *The Inhumans*, *Fantastic Four*, *Marvel Two-in-One* and *The Avengers*. Pérez first came to DC in 1980, where his highly detailed art style was seen in such titles as JUSTICE LEAGUE OF AMERICA and FIRESTORM THE NUCLEAR MAN.

After co-creating THE NEW TEEN TITANS with Marv Wolfman in 1980, Pérez and Wolfman collaborated again on the landmark maxi-series CRISIS ON INFINITE EARTHS.

In the midst of the revamps of BATMAN and SUPERMAN that came in the wake of CRISIS, Pérez took on the difficult task of revitalizing WONDER WOMAN. As the series' writer and artist, he not only reestablished Wonder Woman as one of DC's preeminent characters, but also brought in some of the best sales the title has ever experienced.

Pérez returned to Marvel for a celebrated three-year run on *The Avengers*, paired with writer Kurt Busiek. He later joined forces with CrossGen Comics, pencilling a number of stories for *CrossGen Chronicles* while launching the series *Solus*. He recently completed work on the long-awaited JLA/AVENGERS crossover miniseries.

BRETT BREEDING

Starting his career as an inker in the 1980s, Brett Breeding's slick style proved popular over a variety of artists at Marvel Comics. Moving to DC, Breeding joined the Superman team, where he worked for many years inking over pencils by such artists as Ron Frenz and Dan Jurgens.

ERNIE COLON

Born in Puerto Rico and raised in the United States, Ernie Colon started his career in the late 1960s working on such series as *Casper* and *Richie Rich* for Harvey Comics. He was also a regular presence in such horror magazines as *Creepy*, *Eerie* and *Vampirella*. After he had worked for them for 20 years, Harvey ceased publishing and Colon turned to freelancing for both DC and Marvel Comics.

JOHN COSTANZA

John Constanza began his career in 1965 as an assistant to comics legend Joe Kubert and shortly afterward began working for DC Comics as both an artist and a letterer.

GENE DAY

Gene Day started his comics career creating and publishing independent and underground comics in Canada. Having inked many books for Marvel Comics, he is best known for his seven-year run on the *Master of Kung Fu* series, first as an inker, then a penciller. Day passed away in September of 1982, shortly after TALES OF THE NEW TEEN TITANS #3 hit the stands.

PABLO MARCOS

One of the best-known comics artists of Peru, Pablo Marcos began his art career in the 1960s, in his native country, drawing caricatures for a political magazine called *Rochabus*. In the 1970s Marcos brought his realistic style of art to America, where he worked for such publishers as DC, Marvel, Warren and Atlas.

BEN ODA

Ben Oda was one of the most prolific letterers in the world of comic books and comic strips. His work has graced literally thousands of pages for every major and minor publisher, dating back to comics' Golden Age. Oda died in 1984.

ADRIENNE ROY

Adrienne Roy began work in DC's famed bullpen before graduating to freelance coloring. She enjoyed long runs on numerous titles including BATMAN, DETECTIVE COMICS and, of course, THE NEW TEEN TITANS.

ROMEO TANGHAL

A veteran comic book inker, Romeo Tanghal's work has been seen in such books as JUSTICE LEAGUE OF AMERICA, WONDER WOMAN, GREEN LANTERN and, of course, THE NEW TEEN TITANS.

LEN WEIN

A mainstay of the comics field, Len Wein has created dozens of characters and held numerous editorial positions at both DC and Marvel Comics. Perhaps best known as the co-creator of DC's SWAMP THING (with artist Bernie Wrightson), Wein was the editorial guiding light for the early years of THE NEW TEEN TITANS. He was also instrumental in the genesis of CRISIS ON INFINITE EARTHS (working again with Wolfman and Pérez) and the original edition of WHO'S WHO IN THE DC UNIVERSE.